THE DIVERSITY FACTOR

Capturing the Competitive Advantage of a Changing Workforce

THE DIVERSITY FACTOR

Capturing the Competitive Advantage of a Changing Workforce

ELSIE Y. CROSS

MARGARET BLACKBURN WHITE

Editors

Boston, Massachusetts   Burr Ridge, Illinois
Dubuque, Iowa   Madison, Wisconsin   New York, New York
San Francisco, California   St. Louis, Missouri

For Oron South

McGraw-Hill

A Division of The McGraw·Hill Companies

Library of Congress Cataloging-In-Publication Data

The diversity factor : capturing the competitive advantage of a
   changing workforce / Elsie Y. Cross. Margaret Blackburn White,
   editors.
      p. cm.
   Includes bibliographical references and index.
   ISBN 0-7863-0858-3
   1. Diversity in the workplace. 2. Organizational change.
3. Corporate culture. I. Cross, Elsie Y. II. White, Margaret
Blackburn.
HF5549.5.M5D567   1996
658.3'041—dc20   96–3208

Printed in the United States of America

9 BKM BKM   0 9 8 7 6 5 4 3

F O R E W O R D

Terrence A. Larsen
Chairman and CEO
CoreStates Financial Corp.

When I assumed the leadership of this organization in 1987, CoreStates was already a thriving financial institution and strong financial performance has remained a password at CoreStates. After a few years of being fairly satisfied with Corestates' condition, I began to recognize that all was not really well. As I walked around our buildings and talked with our employees, I sensed that many people were not happy. Even though our bottom line was excellent, we were commended by Wall Street on our performance, and our shareholders were satisfied, our employees seemed to be just going through the motions. I did not sense in them any excitement or commitment to the organization.

I felt a clear need to change that situation. But first I needed to know why people felt as they did.

We undertook a very detailed employee survey, which on first analysis did not shed much light. On average, people seemed to have moderately positive views of their work experiences.

When we did a different overlay—one that separated out the responses by differing factors such as level, race, and gender—the picture came into sharp focus. We learned that there was a widespread sense of lack of respect across grade levels. We learned that the people of color in this organization were angry and they did not perceive that they had a future here. And we learned that many women shared that perception and that anger. The intensity of the feelings that were expressed surprised me.

As leader of the organization, I firmly believe that all of our people count. It is unacceptable if there are elements of our population who are not provided the opportunity to function at their maximum. As successful as we were, it seemed to me self-evident that if more of our employees felt that they had a fair shake here and the opportunity to contribute their best efforts, we would be a better, safer, and happier community—and we would clearly be even more successful financially.

My commitment to trying to meet that challenge led us to undertake a major culture change effort. That effort, it is now clear, is the biggest thing we have done in my almost 20 years at CoreStates. It's a huge effort. It has cost us many millions of dollars in hard cash and many, many more millions in terms of people hours. We have encountered more obstacles, more dilemmas, and more resistance than I imagined were even remotely possible.

But I have never regretted that decision.

We *began* to have benefits almost immediately. The simplest way of describing that immediate impact is that I began to see hope in people's eyes. Employees who had long ago given up on making a difference in the organization were taking a second look. They responded to the *possibility* that things might be better by coming to work with more energy, more commitment, and more enthusiastic participation. People almost immediately began to take risks and to speak up. Our meeting styles changed; we saw more participation, more discussion, more challenges to doing business as usual.

This initial positive response bought us the time to begin the long, hard, tedious work of educating, changing policies and practices, resisting opposition, and integrating the effort into the ongoing business and management concerns that would take years—and is still ongoing.

As I reflect on our experience over these past few years, I recognize several key elements that have enabled us to sustain our progress. Many readers of this text are at some stage of implementing diversity programs or culture-change programs. I encourage absolute commitment. I also offer what we found to be key elements likely to be important to those efforts.

First, and most important, is commitment and courage—especially the courage to look hard at the facts and not try to rationalize them away. When we studied the facts, we realized that the reason many of our co-workers were unhappy was that we were running this business using processes, procedures, and norms that had been created by one group to suit itself—the group that had been in charge at the points in our history when decisions were being made. The group historically was a narrow slice of our total workforce. It tended to be very male, very white, very highly educated, very traditional, and relatively

older. As we listened to other employees, we began to understand that those processes and norms—which we had assumed
were "one-size-fits-all"—definitely did not fit all of us. And even
more important, they were not necessarily the best ways for any
of us to be doing business.

We had to find the courage to figure out other ways to do
things and the commitment to be sure we stayed on course.

Second is preparing to face opposition. There are tremendous amounts of ingrained biases and stereotypes in society and
in our organization, and these will resurface over and over. The
pressures of business can easily become overwhelming and provide plenty of opportunities for those discriminatory attitudes
and practices to resurface and link themselves to something that
gives them some sense of validity.

We expected that our commitment to change might even
bring about a deterioration in our strong financial position; in
fact, we planned and talked about how we would handle it if it
occurred. Fortunately, that did not happen. But it is important to
be prepared to stand up for the commitment even in the face of
financial challenge. Over the long haul, I am convinced—and our
experience would support this view—that the increased commitment and support of all employees that results from a positive culture change will inevitably enhance the bottom line.

At the same time, however, challenging long-standing bigotry and requiring changes in attitudes and behavior causes
some people to be less productive. Some of those who have
been comfortable in the old culture may see the changes as personally threatening and may begin to act—overtly and covertly—
in opposition. Some may leave. Others may have to be asked
to leave if—after having been provided ample opportunity to
understand the facts and recognize the role we all play in creating and maintaining a negative atmosphere, and being offered
the opportunity to get on board—they will not or cannot make
the adjustment.

We had to anticipate, recognize, and stand firm in the face
of opposition.

Third, and most important, is the need to be absolutely consistent. People who are leading the way must see consistency as
a principle, a value. Leaders must themselves feel strongly about

the effort; they must be morally committed as well as convinced of the solid business value of an inclusive work environment.

You have to be prepared to go all the way. The hope we saw in people's eyes in the early days was a sign of cautious optimism. There was also a healthy dose of skepticism about whether we would get there or not. Even after years of seeing their hopes dashed over and over, not just in this organization but throughout the institutions of our society, most of our employees were willing to give us some benefit of the doubt. Dashing that hope would have been devastating. And it would certainly have resulted in the loss to our organization of many of the leaders who had already signed up for making the changes we had laid out.

It is very, very difficult to convince people that the organization is being consistent and committed to its values. Like any business, we have gone throught major changes during the period we have been working on this culture-change effort: a dozen acquisitions, changes in our industry as a whole, a reengineering program. Each change created tremors in the organization and led to doubt about our commitment to our values. Reengineering, especially, can lead to a "survivor syndrome"; people who feel at risk tend to hunker down, not want to take risks, not want to be visible. A diversity program has to be strong and mature to withstand such a challenge.

We needed to be, and are learning to be, consistent and to communicate that consistency throughout the organization.

Finally, in spite of the difficulty of the challenges we face, I feel this is a great time to be in the leadership of an American organization. While change can create anxiety, it also provides many opportunities. Progress may be slow, but it is progress towards a better future—not just for a small group of us, but for all of us.

PREFACE

As we approach the end of the 20th century, two major forces are having an increasingly powerful impact on organizations: globalism and the global economy, and demographics.

The idea of the world as a global village is already a reality. Telecommunications has made it possible to transact business as quickly between Delhi and New York as between San Francisco and Oakland. The company that does not have multinational components is the exception, not the rule.

At the same time, the populations of the world are migrating restlessly, searching for better lives and more security. In the United States alone, the face of the nation has already inalterably changed. By the middle of the 21st century, this trend will lead to our being quite literally a different nation. Women will continue to enter the workforce in increasing numbers, and those groups now identified as minorities will constitute nearly half of the U.S. population.

White men for the first time in U.S. history will be a distinguishable minority.

The significance of this shift has not been lost on U.S. business and other organizations. The marketplace is already global and diverse. The workforce that is available to reach the market is also global and diverse. James R. Houghton, chairman of Corning Incorporated, put the matter bluntly when he said, "To avail ourselves of the entire pool of talent out there, we cannot rely only on white males. To attract the best talent we must demonstrate that we really believe in and practice diversity in the workplace."[1]

But our policies and practices—the cultures of our organizations—are still cast in the mold of the expectations of white men.

Since the early 1980s, organizational executives have been looking to the future and trying to prepare for change. Two strategies have predominated.

---

1. *Vital Speeches of the Day*, February 15, 1995, pp. 268–272.

The first is essentially a training strategy. Its premise is that providing training that helps individuals understand one another will create a diverse workforce that is cooperative and productive. By giving individuals more skills in interpersonal communication, this theory states, they will learn to be more open and accepting, and the barriers that limit the success of white women and people of color will be torn down.

The second strategy does not discount the importance of interpersonal communication, but it goes beyond it to focus on organizational policies, practices, and culture. In this view, patterns of discrimination are embedded in the culture of every organization. Dealing with individual prejudice alone is not enough to bring about the culture change needed to fully utilize a diverse workforce.

This collection of readings is based on the second perspective. Our writers provide strategies and methods for launching and living with culture change. They also describe some of the obstacles and provide concrete suggestions for how to remove them. In addition, methods for measuring changes in different levels of the organization as well as among individuals in different groups are outlined.

This culture-change strategy requires top executives, including the CEO, to be much more active and committed than does the training approach, which tends to lodge responsibility with the HR function.

A culture-change strategy aimed at creating a more diverse and more productive workforce must tear down the systemic barriers that exist in every organization. It is counterproductive to pretend that all differences are the same. Even though our most cherished ideals include "liberty and justice for all," there has always been a wide gap between this ideal and the reality. There has never been a time in the history of the United States when freedom rang out for people of all races or for women as well as men. The attitudes, policies, and practices that serve to benefit white men and create barriers for the entry and success of others are powerful and deeply entrenched. Changing them requires courage, skill, and fortitude.

These changes that create a more open culture are liberating for everyone—not just for white women and people of color but also for white men. Eliminating the disparities that give white men—as a group—an edge and create barriers for people of color and white women—as a group—gives everyone the opportunity to contribute their best. White men will realize that they have succeeded on their own, not because they are white or male. And white women and people of color will know that they can succeed—or fail—on their own merit.

The focus of this volume is on the future, not the past. Our goal is first to take a hard look at the realities of today and then to create those strategies that will get us to the future—where we are going to spend the rest of our lives.

Elsie Y. Cross
Margaret Blackburn White

C O N T E N T S

PART FOUR

WORKPLACE INITIATIVES

PART FIVE

RESOURCES: A DIVERSITY BOOKSHELF 245

CONTRIBUTORS

Chuck Ball is director of sales and marketing management development at Ortho Biotech.

David R. Barclay, corporate vice president, Workforce Diversity, Hughes Aircraft Company, has been actively involved in equal employment opportunity, affirmative action, and human relations programs for three decades. As corporate vice president and a member of the company's policy board, Barclay serves as the corporate advocate and chief officer for the development of programs for an integrated diverse workforce.

Michael Burkart is an organization development consultant focusing on diversity, quality, and team-based production.

Mark A. Chesler, Ph.D., is professor of sociology and a faculty member in the Program on Conflict Management Alternatives at the University of Michigan. He is also executive director of Community Resources, Ltd., an Ann Arbor-based social justice research and educational organization.

J. T. (Ted) Childs is director of Workforce Diversity Programs, WFS Workforce Solutions at IBM.

Elsie Cross is founder and president of Elsie Y. Cross Associates, Inc., an organization development consulting firm that specializes in helping Fortune 100 companies manage diversity. She is also publisher of *The Diversity Factor*, a quarterly journal providing practical and theoretical information for managers and others responsible for leading increasingly diverse organizations. This volume includes selected articles from the journal.

Mike Emery is senior vice president operations, DuPont, and the retiring co-chair of the Valuing People Committee.

Delyte D. Frost is an organization development consultant specializing in long-term interventions around issues of oppression. She was formerly a member of the faculties of the Antioch New England Graduate School and the American University/NTL masters program.

Jack Gant specializes in training and organizational development in public and private sector organizations.

Gary R. Howard is founder and executive director of the REACH Center for Multicultural and Global Education in Seattle.

Mark Kaplan is a partner in the consulting firm of Kaplan, Lucas and Associates, Philadelphia, Pennsylvania.

Jean Kim is vice president for student affairs and dean of students at the University of Hartford, Hartford, Connecticut. Dr. Kim is also a consultant working with organizations in the areas of managing a multicultural workforce, valuing diversity, cross-cultural communications, and organizational development.

Kate Kirkham is Associate Professor in the Graduate School of Management at Brigham Young University, Provo, Utah.

Sylvia Liu, a veterinarian specializing in pathology, is manager of the Department of Pathology, Toxicology, and Surgery at Ethicon, Inc.

Jay Lucas is a partner in the consulting firm of Kaplan, Lucas and Associates, Philadelphia, Pennsylvania.

Joseph Potts is a contributing editor to *The Diversity Factor*.

Judy Ragona is director of quality systems for ETHICON Endosurgery—a Johnson & Johnson company—in Cincinnati, Ohio.

Bernard Scales is manager of diversity at DuPont.

William D. Schaeffer is vice president of needle technology and process development for ETHICON, Inc., one of the Johnson & Johnson family of companies.

Margaret Blackburn White is editor of *The Diversity Factor.*

Keith Woods is a faculty associate, The Poynter Institute for Media Studies, St. Petersburg, Florida. He was formerly with the *Times-Picayune*, New Orleans.

PART ONE

STRATEGIC ISSUES AND LEADERSHIP

"Managing Diversity" as a management strategy is a relatively new phenomenon. Although some American companies—Johnson & Johnson, Xerox, Corning, to name a few—have been addressing patterns of discrimination for many years, most companies have only recently begun to look at the problems systematically.

Discrimination, however, is anything but new. Organizations that intend to do more than pay lip service to attempts to provide equal opportunities for all employees must first confront the long legacy of racist and sexist attitudes and practices in our country. Trying to "fix the problems" without this basic understanding is much like trying to coax an automobile that has a cracked cylinder head to move ahead by adding more air to the tires. It may roll a little if you keep pushing—but it can't start up and move under its own power.

The essays in Part One begin from the premise that the reader has at least minimal familiarity with the historical context and the current social and political climate. (For suggestions for background reading, see Part Five, Resources: a Diversity Bookshelf.) On that foundation, the writers provide a structural framework for creating a new cultural environment.

In a two-part article, Elsie Cross describes the steps needed to develop a culture-change process: entry, problem identification, education and awareness, and organizing and implementing. She reviews the difficulties involved in trying to change the "mental map" we all carry of the way the world is, and shows how changing that map requires providing new experiences—not just cognitive learning.

Cross goes on to show that education and awareness, though vital, is insufficient when used alone. Awareness of the issues must be put into action by a thorough review of the ways in which racism, sexism, heterosexism, and other forms of discrimination are embodied in the organization's policies and practices. To alter these structures, organizations must develop a critical mass of "diversity champions"—people who understand and believe in the commitment to diversity, and are in positions to create and support action plans which will lead to a new culture.

Kate Kirkham outlines the crucial distinctions between individual bias, group prejudice, and organizational discrimination and oppression. Bad feelings, even based on racial attitudes or sexist denigration, between **individuals** are not the crux of the problem. It is when those bad feelings are part of the attitudes and **behavior** of groups and systems that have the power to turn thought into privilege that we wind up with discriminatory and oppressive "isms."

Mark Chesler addresses an ongoing and difficult topic—how do we get and hold the attention of dominant groups? He suggests that we have to use a combination of the olive branch—appealing to self-interest and good-will—and the two-by-four—providing strong incentives, such as enforcement of nondiscriminatory policies and recognition through the performance appraisal system—to inspire buy-in and prevent sell-out.

David Barclay's study of the relationship between Affirmative Action and Managing Diversity carefully reviews the distinctions between the two approaches, and shows why both are still important. His hard-hitting essay takes to task both members of dominant groups who are looking for excuses to dismantle Affirmative Action for their own ends, and members of minority groups who now purport to have been "stigmatized" by affirmative action. Barclay points out that many white women and people of color have always held qualifications and abilities fully equal to members of dominant groups— and to the lucky few who benefited from Affirmative Action—but were denied opportunities **solely because of their race or gender.**

It is an axiom in diversity programs that nothing can happen unless the top management is committed. In the final article in this section, "Champions of Diversity," a consultant, a champion, and an "ally-advisor" tell how this culture-change process supports leaders in carrying forward the initiative.

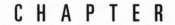

CHAPTER

Getting Started

The End Is in the Beginning

Elsie Y. Cross

The day after Bill Clinton won the presidential election, pundits began emphasizing how important it was for him to clearly state the kind of changes he wanted to make and then organize to make them. They went on to say that four years later, Clinton's success would be contingent on his understanding the relationship between start-up and long-term performance—the end is in the beginning.

The start-up of a managing diversity intervention also contains the seeds of corporate success or failure down the line. Failures in the management of diversity, as well as in quality and renewal efforts, all reflect the same problem: lack of top management understanding of the kind of campaign and commitment needed to bring about organizational change.

VISUALIZING START-UP

Start-up is a process, not an event. It takes place through four overlapping stages: (1) entry, (2) problem identification, (3) education and awareness, and (4) organization and implementation.

During start-up, employees, especially managers and supervisors, must do the following:

- Become aware of their own attitudes and behaviors towards those who are different by race and gender.
- Learn to recognize the behavior of groups of people who discriminate against other groups.
- Become clear about the depth and the breadth of the problem by recognizing the ways in which the organization's policies, practices, and culture perpetuate or systematize patterns of racism, sexism, and other forms of discrimination.
- Understand both the ethical and business reasons for trying to change these established patterns.
- Be willing to provide leadership in the change process and to confront entrenched power centers in the corporation.
- Make a commitment to engage the entire organization in a process of renewal that is often messy.

The start-up phase is most successful when top management and line managers articulate the business reasons for taking on this work and become personally involved in the planning, orientation, and initial workshops. The quality of top management involvement determines long-term results.

Another task of the start-up phase is the development of a research component because ongoing collection and interpretation of data is crucial. The organization must be able to measure the scope of its achievements; it must benchmark progress; it must be able to identify ineffective efforts and subsequently redirect the work; and it must have accurate information about resistance to organizational change.

Choosing a Consultant

Most large corporations engage consulting firms to assist them. Since what takes place in the search process often influences what takes place during start-up and later, it is useful to examine this process.

Word of mouth is still the most effective way to identify consultants. In addition, the press is currently reporting examples of successful interventions and identifying those consultants whose work is most widely known.

A search team should identify a short list of potential consultants and then call or visit companies that have employed their services. The team needs to inquire about competence, and working philosophies and methods, as well as the working style of the consulting group. It is also important for members of the search team to determine whether the style of the consultant would be compatible with the working style of their CEO and top management team.

A further task in benchmarking is to examine the record of quantitative results. What changes have resulted from the consultant's work with other organizations in terms of rates of retention, promotions, recruitment and hiring, reduction in complaints, and so forth? Such quantitative records are beginning to be available. (The next step in benchmarking will be the collection of more qualitative evidence of the changes. However, to date, there are no good techniques for measuring changes in the "atmosphere" of the corporation—attitudes, acceptance, optimism, enthusiasm—the hidden variables that, after all, make the major difference in how we feel about going to work every day.)

After the initial research on consulting firms is complete, four or five firms may be invited to make presentations on what they would do to respond to identified needs. The audience for these presentations can range from 1 to 10 or more people, including the CEO and perhaps one or two board members. These presentations provide a sense of the kinds of strategies that have been developed. Some consultants, for example, will outline a structured programmatic approach, while others offer a collaborative problem identification and planning approach.

It is important to understand the consultants' values and the philosophy about race and gender work that underlies their organizational interventions. Each consultant's particular organizational development approach must be identified to determine whether the approach is compatible with the goals and needs of the client organization.

If task forces or quality teams have been collecting and analyzing data about diversity and have made recommendations to top management, questions to the prospective consultants may be quite specific regarding their ability to accomplish designated tasks. The corporation must be confident that the consultants have the capacity to manage a large-scale, long-term organizational change effort. The consultants' track record must be examined in depth. How long have they been in business? Who are their present and previous clients? What are the credentials of the consulting team?

Each consultant also has her or his goals when invited to meet with a corporation. The consultant must discover the client's true motivations for undertaking the work. Are the motives of the CEO the same as those of the task force and others in the organization? Is there a degree of tolerance of ambiguity and conflict? Both are important elements in a serious approach to managing diversity. If the consultant finds that the organization is looking for an off-the-shelf, prepackaged approach, he or she will know immediately that the organization is not really serious about facing the challenges.

As the client and the consultant interact in this initial session, fundamental dynamics related to race and gender develop, serving as a clear bellwether of what will follow.

If the consultant is ultimately invited to work with the corporation, the information obtained in the initial meetings enables the consulting firm to decide whether the contract will lead to a productive and fruitful working relationship. A key factor in this decision is whether the CEO and the top management team are willing to be full partners in the intervention, starting with participation in the initial education and awareness workshops.

Phase One: Entry

In practice, start-up is underway when a team from the consulting firm sits down with a corporate management team to make specific plans for working together to launch a managing diversity initiative. The agenda will have items such as these:

- Reviewing expected goals and outcomes.

- Identifying the internal corporate structure the consulting team will work with and through.
- Discussing in detail how the internal management and the consulting team/firm will collaborate.
- Identifying the organizational problems around race and gender through data collection and analysis, and the consultant team role in this process.
- Planning for education and awareness workshops (who will attend, how many days, nature of staff, premeetings with consultant staff, etc.).
- Ongoing consultation with senior managers, relevant task forces, and other corporate groups as indicated.
- Establishing expectations for policy and practice review; identifying and challenging structures that discriminate; visualizing a changed culture.

Phase Two: Problem Identification

In the early stages of the intervention, much of the available data about organizational need probably has been collected informally. Once a decision is made to act on the informal data, it is important to gather information more systematically. The company must be able to diagnose the extent to which problems can be seen as barriers, the extent to which racism and sexism are endemic to the organization, and the extent to which executives and other employees are aware that such issues operate in the organization. It is also important to learn what differences there may be in the ways white women and people of color perceive the problems compared with the perceptions of white men.

There are a variety of information-gathering methods to verify or disprove the existence of problems. Some organizations use a questionnaire on a regular basis to assess the state of the corporation on a variety of dimensions—the extent to which people are satisfied, adherence to a credo or vision statement, effectiveness of safety programs, and so on. If such an instrument is being contemplated, it is useful to "tag into the process" and add items that will yield information about race, gender, age, physical ability, and other forms of discrimination. It is important for consultants (or other experts) to be a part of the process of developing the questions, to ensure that the desired information will be forthcoming.

A growing number of organizations find that focus groups are appropriate for gathering data about the issue of diversity. Focus groups may be organized on the basis of race, gender, age, sexual orientation, physical ability, or other characteristics. The focus group technique can be the instrument for gathering the principal data or a method for confirming and supplementing the questionnaire data. It is helpful for consultants of the same race, gender, and other demographics, where available, to meet with the matching focus group. This pairing process improves the likelihood of quickly developing trust and comfort.

In addition to the diagnostic purposes of data gathering, the information from questionnaires and focus groups serves another purpose: confirming to executives and other employees that the information actually comes from their system, not from outside consultants who may be advocates of a particular position. It adds legitimacy to the informal information and credence to the complaints employees have made about discrimination. When these complaints are acknowledged by white men, and when upper managers (who tend to be cut off from the lower levels of the organization) see that human issues that negatively affect high productivity are endemic at all levels of the organization, management is apt to be galvanized into action!

Although most organizations are not yet at a stage in the intervention at which they are calling for precise, statistical measures of the degree to which the intervention will improve the identified problem, it would be useful in the start-up phase to prepare for this eventual need. Thus it is helpful to obtain accurate, statistical measures of the problem prior to the intervention itself. Some of the measurable factors are barriers experienced by white women and people of color, advantages experienced by white men but not extended to all, general employee satisfaction, experience with organizational values, and treatment of employees in general and specifically by race and gender. If the data are collected at the outset, it is important to periodically track progress related to the measures. This kind of evidence can help to build commitment to change, reduce some of the resistance to it, and encourage the organization to go beyond the "quick fix" mentality that blocks the fundamental change necessary to ameliorate racism and sexism.

Once the data are collected, the next challenge is what to do with it. How can the information be translated into problem statements in a way that it can be heard and acted on by top management? Additionally, how can feedback be provided to the organization, especially to those employees involved in the data-collection process?

There are several options:

1. Hold feedback meetings with top executives to present and interpret the data.
2. Prepare a report for top executives, and help internal consultants interpret the data.
3. Hold meetings with employees to provide summaries of problems, trends, and so forth. This is most effectively accomplished in group meetings, where the employees are encouraged to ask for information and otherwise participate in the diagnosis.
4. Start an education and awareness workshop with a presentation of the data and ask executives to "own" or identify the data as their own. This is useful for obtaining buy-in and creating a readiness to begin the work. It is also helpful to invite them to internalize the information and think about the impact the problems have in the organization.
5. Begin a systematic effort for "benchmarking" the progress of the intervention over time. This is useful for measuring the extent to which problems are resolved and new ones appear. It becomes a good indicator of the extent to which the culture is impacted and changed by the process of the intervention.

Phase Three: Education and Awareness

Whatever method is chosen for providing feedback, at some point it is necessary to begin a long-range process of education and awareness throughout the organization. This process is most effectively carried forward through a series of workshops with the following objectives:

- To provide participants with concepts and information about race and gender dynamics in the workplace.
- To provide a forum of learning and discussion among colleagues about issues of diversity.
- To enable participants to understand that differences can be viewed as negative (discrimination and stereotypes) or positive (appreciating the differences employees can bring to the workplace).
- To demonstrate that increasing skills in managing diversity enables managers and others to do the following:
  — Prevent discrimination.
  — Increase accuracy in determining when problems are due to racism or sexism in the organization versus other issues.
  — Better utilize the resources of all individuals.
- To use the data collected in the initial phase, plus the learnings from the workshop, to create action plans for next steps.

Each education and awareness workshop should include about 24 participants representing a racial and gender mix. Careful selection of participants is key to the success of the entire intervention. Initially, they must include top corporate and division executives. However, since virtually no organization has a top management tier that includes wide representation of white women and people of color, it is necessary to invite participants from other segments of the organization to achieve racial and gender balance.

Workshops rely on experiential learning through small-group discussions, simulations, exercises, and skill practice, augmented with short lectures. Participants must have the opportunity to share with others of their own race and gender as well as the challenge of learning in groups of people of other races and the opposite sex.

Subsequently, the workshops are cascaded down through the organization. Since it is not possible to involve all the employees of very large corporations in intensive workshop experiences, it is necessary to design additional educational strategies as the intervention moves downward in the organization. Internal trainers may be trained to provide the workshops; videos and other communication devices may be brought in to assist in the process; or the organization may devise other strategies to guarantee that all employees are offered the education and challenge that the workshops represent.

Experiential learning—learning by doing—is essential in the process of examining racism and sexism and other forms of oppression. With the guidance of the training staff, participants learn from one another how to interact with those who are different from them, especially in terms of race and gender. They also discover how to learn about these issues. In experiential learning, the focus is on the learner as much as on the subject matter. This work legitimizes discussion that was heretofore taboo. It enables people to talk openly about their experiences and feelings about race and gender, racism and sexism, homosexuality and homophobia.

Like any other area of experience, we have to develop competence in addressing these issues. But in contrast to many other experiences, we come to these discussions with a heavy baggage of memory, emotions, and early training. From childhood, we have all been conditioned to see those of different races and of the opposite sex in particular ways, ways which often have been stereotypical or negative. When we grow up, that early conditioning is firmly planted in our memory and imposes its patterns on everyday experience. Without active effort to uncover these attitudes, they are hidden from us in the mists of our developmental processes. If we were taught—either overtly or covertly—that those of another race are inferior, or that those of the opposite sex are unable to accomplish certain tasks, we just continue to see them that way.

The objective in education and awareness workshops is to make people aware of what is stored in their memory and how it affects their thought processes and present perceptions. We must also learn how these early patterns will continue to operate in the future to perpetuate bias and prejudice, unless we work systemically and consciously to understand them and discard them.

The Unchallenged Mental Map

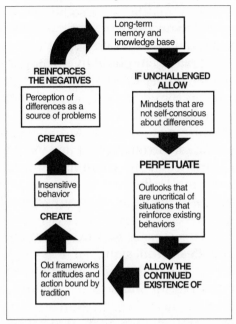

The Dynamic Mental Map

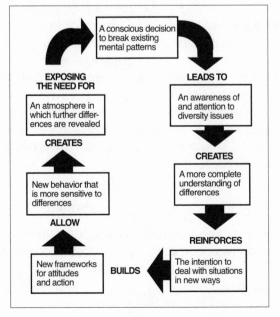

Two specific processes are effective in this effort: awareness and attention. Participants can learn to be aware of what is happening in their minds and feelings, and they can then direct their conscious attention to these thoughts and feelings. In this way, they can break the patterns imposed by memory and learn to perceive other people in a very different way.

The new perception then leads to new behavior and to increasingly broader awareness. The illustration shows this cycle, which is repetitive but expanding. Different exercises and simulations, as well as cognitive instruction and guided practice, provide participants with experience in the power of this cycle and with skills in using their new knowledge.

The new knowledge, gained at an individual level and perceived in a group setting, must be carried forward to an institutional-level understanding as well. At the individual level, early training can lead to attitudes that may be defined as bias or prejudice. But at the organizational level, those attitudes become institutionalized as racism and sexism. Institutional racism and sexism are both the cause and the outcome of organizational policies, practices, and arrangements that result in the unequal distribution of benefits based on race and/or gender. In our culture (and many others as well), the policies, practices, and arrangements reflect the values, norms, beliefs, standards, and expectations of whites, especially white men. Therefore, the power to control resources, reward and punish behaviors, and award privileges becomes a white or white male prerogative and results in the denial of access to power and advancement to people of color and white women. Recognizing the existence of bias, prejudice, racism, and sexism is a complicated and slow-moving process—but it is essential if the organization is really to come to grips with the identified problems.*

Phase Four: Organization and Implementation

After key executives and managers have completed the initial education and awareness workshops, it is useful to design a strategic

---

*For the concepts underlying this discussion of bias, prejudice, racism, and sexism, I am indebted to my colleague, Dr. Kate Kirkham.

planning session of one to three days, facilitated by the outside consulting firm, to tailor a plan for ongoing implementation of managing diversity. This session takes into account the structure of the firm; any particular needs or goals; available resources; data from organizationwide surveys, focus groups, discussion groups, and so on; and what was learned in the education and awareness workshops.

At this point, it is also useful to examine the kinds of ongoing consulting that may be needed by senior management, task forces, and other groups. Executives and managers who are motivated to plan and act in their spheres of influence may want consultants available to support their work and to coach and assist with their plans. Some will want problem-solving or team-building consultation. Often, white women and people of color request special assistance in team building, networking, and transitioning.

The outcome of the strategic planning is a general plan for offering education and awareness workshops throughout the organization, for the involvement of key executives and managers in the diffusion process; for identifying special needs, and for developing the kind of administrative support and resources needed for the long haul. A key element in the planning process is the recognition that organizational structures, systems, and culture play a decisive role in maintaining racism and sexism. Plans will need to include removing organizational barriers and creating structural and cultural changes in order to allow all employees to work to their full capacity.

It will also be important to integrate the managing diversity initiative with other efforts, such as quality, empowerment, leadership, and so forth.

Particular attention must be directed to administrative support because launching an organizational change intervention means that the administrative system has to take on an additional burden above and beyond the capability needed to do business as usual. If the existing system is already stretched to its limits, this does not bode well for the organizational change effort.

As this brief review indicates, a serious effort to change the culture of an organization to enable it to maximize its human capital and become more competitive is a complicated and long-term strategy. Even more than most difficult management initiatives, the management of diversity requires people to attend to deep-seated and often unacknowledged biases and prejudices. Further, it requires the organization to do an honest and careful review of how those biases and prejudices have been incorporated into the entire corporate culture and have become systemic racism, sexism, and other forms of discrimination. If the organization is really committed to the process, the energy and attention it must pay to learn to manage diversity effectively *always* pays off in areas far beyond the identified arenas of concern. Learning to manage diversity competently enhances the overall management skills of the entire enterprise.

CHAPTER

Managing Diversity: A Continuous Process of Change

Elsie Y. Cross

Workforce 2000: Work and Workers for the 21st Century, published by the Hudson Institute in 1987, highlighted a milestone in American history. Recommending reconciliation of the conflicting needs of women, work, and families, along with full integration of all workers into the economy, the report indicated that failure to value a diverse workforce no longer pays—it costs.

Follow-up studies to the Hudson Institute report show three different kinds of corporate response: (1) expressions of concern but no significant action; (2) increased efforts in recruiting, hiring, and training white women and people of color for supervisory positions; and (3) a top-level decision to learn how to manage diversity.

My work is with corporations choosing the third option. My colleagues and I have developed a change process, a managing diversity intervention, designed to provide organizational renewal and the maximum use of human resources through removing individual, group, and organizational barriers that prevent full utilization of all employees. This article provides an overview of the philosophy and methodology of the intervention.

UNDERSTANDING THE PROBLEM

When corporations need energy and creativity from each employee, racism and sexism stand in the way. Specifically, when cultural norms that prescribe a second place to white women and people of color are linked with organizational hierarchy and power, the following systemic problems result:

- Inability to retain white women and people of color, indicated by the "revolving door syndrome."
- Complaints and increases in legal actions.
- Unhealthy tensions between people of differing gender, race, age, abilities, and so on.
- Inability to attract and retain talented people of all kinds.
- Loss of productivity since energy is directed to maintaining the status quo instead of the company's competitive readiness.
- Poor or inadequate communication between employees.

Since white women and people of color now constitute more than 50 percent of the workforce, these problems prevent peak workforce performance.

Clearly, it is in the interest of both the corporation and its employees to create a work environment where diversity is welcomed rather than resented. Just as clearly, most corporations need to learn to manage diversity since the evidence shows that without formal interventions, "business as usual" favors white males. These interventions must focus on executives and managers, who have inherited organizations with attitudes and concepts towards gender and race that are no longer viable. Most of these executives have been socialized in values and norms of white male supremacy and patriarchy—and they usually don't even know it.

The process of managing diversity is a long-term strategic intervention aimed at changing workplace relationships in order to reduce systemic injustice and economic exploitation and create more effective and productive working relationships throughout the organization.

Specifically, managing diversity focuses on the following issues:

- Encouraging managers to confront their behavior and that of their peers, colleagues, and subordinates.
- Altering long-standing power and authority relationships.
- Developing a thorough understanding of how, left alone, the culture perpetuates the old playing field.
- Changing the ways policies and practices are implemented in order to extend to all employees the advantages and opportunities white men have traditionally enjoyed.
- Changing fundamental assumptions embedded in the core values of the organization's culture.

BEGINNINGS

Corporations exploring ways to address the management of diversity must take some preliminary steps. First, they must be clear about what the process is. My view is that the focus of the work is to reduce racism and sexism by providing members of the organization with the knowledge, values, and skills needed to change the culture. The idea is not to promote multiculturalism, nor to advocate "political correctness."

In order to begin the process, the corporation must define the specific problems within that organization. This requires the collection and analysis of data by various means, such as focus groups, interviews, and surveys. To guide this work, corporations often select a management council or board and an experienced consultant. The consultant and the management group work closely to identify the ways racism and sexism affect the operation of this particular culture.

THREE PHASES OF INTERVENTION

While the process of changing organizational culture is not a straightforward linear movement, it tends to move through definable phases. These are (1) individual education and awareness, (2) capacity building, and (3) culture change. Each phase has its own structure, though, in practice, activities in the different phases overlap. Education and awareness workshops, for example, will continue throughout the capacity-building and culture-change phases. Many of the activities are iterative and cyclical.

Phase One: Education and Awareness

Because of the nature of hierarchy and the use of power and authority, the intervention process must begin at the top of the organization. The CEO and his or her staff must "own" the intervention and be the first to invest their time in education and awareness. Otherwise, the intervention has little chance of bringing about systemic change; instead, it may result in a psychology and practice of "fixing the victim."

Since reducing systemic inequities must start at the top, the process begins with a three-day workshop for senior executives. To fully discuss potential problems within the company, there must be diversity of perspective; but because top management teams are almost exclusively made up of white men, it is usually necessary to "import" white women and people of color from other segments of the organization. (Subsequently, as the program proceeds, employees from every level of the organization are invited to participate in these introductory workshops.)

The workshop facilitators must also reflect diversity of race and gender. In our intervention, four people—a woman of color, a man of color, a white woman, and a white man—work with about 24 participants.

During the workshop, top managers must become acutely aware of how differently individuals perceive the same event. For example, a sampling of newspapers across the country during the Clarence Thomas–Anita Hill hearing in the U.S. Senate revealed that men consistently saw harassment as a sexual matter. Women, on the other hand, consistently saw harassment as an abuse of power.

Senior executives need to be aware of these and other differences in perception in order to become competent to make informed decisions about managing diversity as the intervention progresses.

Many people see racism and sexism as primarily centered in the individual. To enhance systemic understanding, the workshop must demonstrate the impact of individual behavior on the organization. This leads to important insights into the "mental models" used to judge instances of sexism and racism and leads to the ability to perform subsequent strategic planning. Unless corporate authorities change their personal mental model of workplace fairness, they may be unable to identify inappropriate behaviors. They may be cast in the role of the U.S. Navy admiral who asked, "What's all the fuss about?" when told of the Tailhook affair.

It is also important to examine the different ways racism and sexism operate in the organization. For example, white women often share a complicity for racism with white men. This may not be intentional or even conscious, but the result is benefits that accrue to one group and not another. Men of color are often as sexist as white males, with the same results. Women of color, while they do not benefit from either racism or sexism, can be personally biased or prejudiced at the individual level.

In a nutshell, the workshops enable management from the top down to come to grips, personally, with the specific problem in their organization. It is important to understand that racism, sexism, and other kinds of discrimination cannot be treated simply as individual issues of awareness. These are organizational and systemic issues as well. The organization must be committed to change, to create a culture that encourages all members' contributions. In the second phase of the intervention, awareness is translated into managerial competence.

Phase Two: Capacity Building

Phase two helps managers and supervisors develop a capacity for managing the new organization by examining policies, practices, and day-to-day systems. As education and awareness take hold, data for this examination emerges from workshop recommendations, from newly formed diversity committees, from formal data-gathering mechanisms, and from follow-up meetings. Then, performance review practices, organizational audits, recruiting and mentoring customs, ranking and rating systems, assignment distributions, and the like are all scrutinized under the lens of diversity.

Phase two is most successful when internal "champions" provide leadership for examining and changing policies and practices. Such champions also confront the inevitable questions of "reverse discrimination" and "preferential treatment for minorities" that arise as the balance of power begins to shift. The implementation of this phase must be closely monitored by top management to be sure that the resources needed to support the change effort are provided. Close and continuous interaction with the consultant team is required throughout all the phases.

A major component of phase two is an organizational culture review. This review may be required at various times throughout the intervention.

Phase Three: Culture Change

Phase three assumes that individual awareness and changing implementation of policies and procedures are necessary—but not sufficient—conditions for eradicating racism and sexism at the systems level of the organization.

This requires ferreting out the "messages"—the behaviors and norms—that are the fundamental indicators of the culture. Once these are clear, members of the organization can define which behaviors and norms are "barriers" to success and which are enablers. This definition will show that most of the behaviors are "enablers" to white men; white women and people of color experience few enablers and many barriers.

Next, corporate leaders must create and support action plans to identify and implement new values. These actions will be specific to each corporation and should help managers develop the skills to articulate and model the new culture. A communications strategy is required to inform the entire organization about the requirements and expected behavior for participating effectively and receiving rewards in this new culture.

The end result of the long process of culture change is that an old frame of reference is gradually replaced by a new, more flexible, and more productive way of viewing reality. The new frame allows the members of the corporate community to relate to one another on the basis of integration rather than assimilation. This, in turn, affects the distribution of power within the organization, the development of standards, and ultimately the identity of the organization. The new organization will be better prepared to meet the challenges of the 21st century.

REFERENCES

William B. Johnson and Arnold H. Packer. *Workforce 2000: Work and Workers for the 21st Century.* Indianapolis: Hudson Institute, June 1987.

Workforce 2000. Competing in a Seller's Market: Is Corporate America Prepared? A Survey Report on Corporate Responses to Demographic and Labor Force Trends. n.p.: Towers Perrin and Hudson Institute, 1990.

CHAPTER

Managing in a Diverse Workforce: From Incident to "ism"

Kate Kirkham

How does a manager know if a difficult exchange between two employees who are different from each other by gender or race is an "isolated incident" or evidence of sexism and racism in the work environment? What can a manager do to accurately identify problems, coach others, or redress systemic inequities? Managers (and other employees as well) who want to contribute to effective work relationships in a diverse workforce must address these questions. Often, a manager's own race or gender affects the answers and actions.

Managers receive a variety of descriptions about problems from their co-workers and employees. Some people suggest that personality differences are the primary factors in any exchange: "That's just the way he/she is." Others imply that a complainant is trying to "make a racial issue" out of an unpleasant incident or that the complainant's "oversensitive" or "strident" behavior results from "baggage" carried into the workplace. There are those employees who will take the manager aside and confidentially suggest that "after all, there is a perfectly logical explanation" for the particular incident. And finally, there may be people who point to racism or sexism as the source of problems.

How can a manager sort through the collection of perceptions and "facts"?

Two assumptions affect the answers to this question. First, the workplace is not "neutral ground"; second, employees who are competent in other arenas are not necessarily competent about race and gender issues.

WORKPLACE DYNAMICS

The reporting relationships, business practices, policies, and even the physical structure of any workplace are based on the cumulative experiences of that organization: the people who have made up the workforce over time, the larger culture they have created, and the total context in which the organization operates.

If all the supervisors in a company have always been men, a woman appointed to a supervisory position faces a situation where her performance is evaluated in a far larger context than her own individual behavior. Such evaluations are simultaneously conscious and unconscious, intended and unintentional. Often, even individuals' traits are evaluated on the shared norms or beliefs of the dominant employee group—beliefs about what constitutes "masculinity" or "femininity," for example, or shared norms about the value of long work days or about assertive or aggressive behavior.

So the workplace is not a totally objective setting. The manager who attempts to figure out the dynamics of differences between employees must understand that the environment itself colors the ways employees relate to each other and to their management. Some managers say that understanding this actually complicates their work life. The white manager who begins to realize the extent that attitudes about race impact behavior—or the male manager who recognizes the complications of sexism in his employee group—may be reluctant to explore further. Yet failure to do so means that many problems will "recycle" without resolution.

GETTING GOOD ADVICE

All of us have people we trust, to whom we look for advice. In the workplace, these relationships have endured the test of problem solving on difficult business issues.

However, the fact that a person has a track record of giving competent advice on business matters does not guarantee that same competence when the focus is on race and gender. For example, a white manager may have often turned to a white colleague for advice on fiscal matters. Trusting that relationship, the manager now raises an issue involving a conflict between a white employee and a black employee. Unfortunately, the colleague may have no expertise in areas of employee diversity.

CONSTRUCTING A FRAMEWORK

In order to contribute to the creation of a workplace that confronts race and gender problems *and* values diversity, a manager must analyze issues at the individual, group, and organizational levels.*

Finding solutions to many workplace problems requires insight into these levels. However, it is crucial to analyze these three levels when the issues concern race and gender. As one of my colleagues has said, "When it comes to race and gender, sometimes people who are ordinarily good thinkers become 'stupid'!" Such poor thinking is evident, for example, when a manager who needs to understand complex problems in the workplace only looks for blatant examples of individual prejudice in employee behavior.

STRUCTURAL LEVELS

At the **individual level,** each person is seen primarily for his or her own unique characteristics—attitudes, assumptions, mannerisms, work style, and personality. This level includes the interpersonal relationships we build one-on-one with others, based on mutuality of interests, similarity of attitudes, and the like.

---

* A fourth level is societal. This discussion, however, focuses only on the first three. My thinking on racism has been influenced by Delyte Frost, John Leeke, Pat Bidol, and Bob Terry, among others. My examination of incidents and "isms" continues to benefit from interaction with colleagues in Elsie Y. Cross Associates, Inc.

The **group level** is the site of our identity as a man or woman and as a member of a racial or cultural group. This level has four important dimensions:

1. Group-level identity can exist whether or not the individual sees it as a primary factor in interactions in the workplace. A senior white manager, for example, may not think of herself as "white"—but others may see her "white" group identity as an important part of their experiences with her in the workplace. So even though, individually, she is known for her sense of humor, she is also one more white manager at the senior level.

2. "Group" does not necessarily mean an actual, numerical group within the workplace. For example, whether or not there are other Asians present, an individual Asian manager can feel and be experienced as a member of an "Asian" group.

3. Individuals also belong to groups on the basis of self-identification. Someone who does not "look" like a person of color to others may identify quite strongly as a "Latino," "First American," or "African-American." Thus the group level includes how people identify themselves as well as how others see them.

4. Group identity impacts work relationships and organizational dynamics not only because of actual behaviors but also because of **perceived possible experiences.** This is tricky business. For example, at the end of the day, a white male manager may not feel that he is a part of the dominant power structure in the organization. In fact, on some days that white manager may feel quite powerless. Yet, in the perception of employees of other racial groups, he is seen as likely to have more access to other white managers, to be less vulnerable to harassment by security guards, or to be less likely to experience negative interactions on the basis of his race. These are all forms of power, or options, that are connected to the **likely experiences** a white person may have.

The basis of these perceptions is the **pattern of repeated experiences** of that group's members in the organization—not on stereotypes. Stereotypes do exist at the group level, but the aspect of **perceived possible experiences** is different from stereotypes attributed to all members of a group because of bias.

The **organizational or institutional level** incorporates the entire culture of the organization, and analysis requires attention to policies, business practices, customs, and norms about behavior. Managers attempting to get a full picture of the issues must look at their roles and responsibilities within this total framework. In addition, each organization—as well as each member of the organization—is influenced by the larger society in which we operate. Employees bring to the workplace the individual expectations, biases, and prejudices developed through the socialization processes of family, school, and community.

NEGATIVE EXPRESSIONS OF STRUCTURAL LEVELS

Each level has both positive and negative implications. At the **individual level,** the negative experience of difference results in **prejudice**. Any two people can be prejudiced towards one another. All relationships have the possibility of some degree of prejudice. I may have negative feelings about people who have different physical abilities. Prejudice is not the prerogative of any one person, nor is it directed at only one group.

At the **group level,** prejudice is translated into the way people behave **in concert with others.** Collective prejudice is expressed in some form of discrimination. Yes, it is individuals who carry out **discrimination.** But discrimination results from more than individual action—it is the patterns, stereotypes, and conditions that are generated by more than one person's behavior. The resulting negative experiences are more potent than one individual can cause. Collective prejudice, or discrimination, determines what neighborhoods people can live in, what schools they may attend, what jobs they are considered eligible to apply for. Discrimination determines who gets to do what in our society. Discrimination assigns value to the color of skin, or to gender, and is the primary reason that some people's "difference" is experienced in a negative or life-threatening way.

The **"isms"** identify this negative experience of difference at the **organizational level.** Racism, sexism, homophobia, and other discriminatory patterns operate through pervasive and pernicious mechanisms that the larger systems control: what is valued, who has authority, how one ought to look, how budgets are allocated, who gets what opportunities in the largest context. The "isms" are the phenomena that underlie the fact that almost all CEOs, managing boards, presidents, and other top management in our corporations are white men. The "isms" require some form of **power** to perpetuate the complexity of beliefs, behaviors, and values that oppress others based on their race or gender.

INTERACTION BETWEEN LEVELS

One way to understand the levels is to think about who we are in relationship to each level. An **individual** can often discern when the person he or she is working with is exhibiting some form of prejudice. Individuals can also collect evidence of **collective prejudice,** or **discrimination:** They can see what's going on around them regarding education or housing in society and, within the organization, can explore to see who gets what positions or training opportunities.

It is harder to see the way the "isms" operate. Obviously, some individuals have direct experience of racism and sexism. But others, particularly the traditional majority group members in the U.S. workforce, have difficulty seeing the "big picture": the workplace patterns based on race, sex, or cultural identity. Therefore, they do not recognize that these patterns create **barriers** that prevent some employees from thriving in the organization. These patterns also **benefit** others, based on membership in the dominant group.

The interaction of the three levels adds to the complexity of the issues a manager must confront. In organizations where individual employees exhibit blatant prejudice, the patterns of the "ism" may be easier to see. Ironically, however, in such organizations, these systemic patterns may receive less attention because the individual bigoted acts require more dramatic attention in the day-to-day relationships.

In organizations where most employees are not personally prejudiced and do not intentionally discriminate, the subtle forms of sexism and racism may be harder to identify. Where the majority of the workforce is well-meaning (or their attitudes well hidden), the search for understanding of the deeply embedded patterns of "isms" may be very frustrating. Some majority group members will regard any discussion of racism and sexism in work practices as a personal attack rather than an attempt to see what is really there.

Racism and sexism (and other "isms") are far more subtle than the overt joke or derogatory comment. The existence of an "ism" means that the norms, values, practices, and way of doing work favor one group at the expense of another. It isn't just that difference exists, *it is the cost of that difference that matters.* An "ism" is always attached to some form of organizational **power** used to enforce the oppression of others.

When new employees join an organization, they receive an orientation to help them "get up to speed" as quickly as possible. This is just as important in diversity work as in every other aspect of corporate life. A new employee needs to know what "isms" are operating in the culture of the organization. Unfortunately, if the organizational analysis has stopped at the individual level, there may be no awareness that work processes may support one group and subordinate another. A manager may decide, "I'm not prejudiced." But if that manager fails to go further into the "isms" of the culture, he or she cannot give new employees an adequate understanding of the environment of the organization. Saying "I'm not prejudiced" is an opening, not a closing, statement on diversity.

DIVERSITY RECYCLING: INTENT VERSUS OUTCOME

Learning to observe the three different levels involved in the dynamics of racism/sexism and diversity is a skill all managers can learn, just as they learn other skills. Further, managers must learn to see that their intent not to be prejudiced or discriminatory may differ from the actual result of their behavior.

For example, a manager may decide that all employees in a certain salary grade are not eligible for educational benefits, based on the amount of funds available in a fiscal year. This decision may have no element of bias or prejudice. However, if all employees in that salary grade are women or people of color, the decision results in an outcome that provides educational benefits dispro-portionately to whites or to men. Therefore, the policy has race or gender **outcomes** that are different from the original **intent.**

Intent and outcome are factors at each level. Personal intent and behavior may or may not match. As a member of a group, I may demonstrate attitudes and behaviors of which I am not aware, and my work practices may result in discrimination and subor-dination that I did not intend. Organizationally, the structures determining policies and practices may actually prevent me from proceeding in a manner consonant with my good intentions.

Therefore, managers must work hard to develop insight into what they intend *and* also develop greater ability to listen to oth-ers who describe the results of the managers' behavior. The work-place is not neutral ground, and my behavior may demonstrate insensitivity, discrimination, or failure to see how I collude with the racism and sexism that operate in a given work unit. I am not required to abandon my intent. But if I am to be successful, I need to make it clear that I am open to dialogue and welcome feed-back when my intent diverges from the outcome expected. The ability to make sure intent lines up with outcome is another skill to be learned, practiced, and internalized. It cannot be relegated to an "interesting experience" in a workshop but must become second nature—just like any other managerial ability.

FROM THEORY TO PRACTICE

Understanding the concept of individual, group, and organiza-tional levels—and recognizing how they play out in a given set-ting—has no value unless managers commit themselves to action. What does the manager do if, for example, there is a difficult exchange between a supervisor and an employee who are dif-ferent from each other by gender or race?

First, the manager should ask a series of questions:

- What do I know about the ability of these individuals to work with each other?
- Are these individuals who are generally not biased? Do they have effective interpersonal skills in most situations?

- If the supervisor is a man, is the problem that the supervisor lacks skills in supervising someone who is different from himself?
- If the supervisor is a woman, does the problem exist because women have not had positions of authority in the organization prior to this? Are her contributions questioned more closely than if she were a man?

In some way, each level may be involved in both the diagnosis of the problem and the action to resolve it. However, the action must be carefully targeted to the level that requires the most attention. It is counterproductive to counsel white women or people of color to "develop more interpersonal effectiveness" when the real problem is the racist or sexist attitudes and behaviors of their supervisors or co-workers.

For example, one black woman was criticized by her supervisor for "always having a chip on her shoulder." She was written up as distant, hostile, not a team player. If the supervisor had been paying attention to the group and organizational levels, the supervisor would have learned that this employee was never included in lunch dates with co-workers and that, organizationally, she knew that no black woman had ever been promoted from her position to the next level. She needed the job and was determined to stick it out. But her determination could not carry her through to responding pleasantly to those who excluded her or to maintaining an optimistic attitude about her chances for success in the face of overwhelming evidence to the contrary.

Managers must consistently be alert to the dynamics at each level. Do men in the organization share a perception that some women co-workers are "too aggressive?" What role do white employees play in the turnover of black employees? Managers need to pay attention to the *behavior* of individuals, the *patterns* of groups, and the *race or gender implications* of any policy and practice.

In general, the more powerful a particular "ism," the more leadership it takes to work against it. At the individual or group level, some problems may be delegated. For example, if the issue is the absence of a certain group in the workplace, the manager can ask others to learn how to recruit more representatively. If the problem is intergroup cooperation, the manager can develop some strategies that create natural arenas where cooperative behavior will develop.

But if the problem is the core beliefs about the abilities of others based on race and gender, and these core beliefs undergird the entire corporate culture, the problem cannot be delegated. The manager cannot delegate his or her role in creating a different workplace climate to human resources or affirmative action personnel.

The manager's own visible commitment to continue learning across all three levels sends a powerful message that individual incidents will be addressed and that systemic "isms" will be challenged.

CHAPTER

Strategies for Multicultural Organizational Development

Mark A. Chesler

As the American workforce changes, organizations look to the field of Organizational Development (OD) for strategies to meet and manage these changes. In this article, I contend that traditional forms of OD are not adequate to this task. A new approach to change, called Multicultural Organizational Development (MCOD), is needed.

WHAT IS ORGANIZATIONAL DEVELOPMENT?

OD is a broad and diverse field and has been the subject of much study.[1] Its principal goals have included increased profitability or efficiency for the organization and the full utilization of human resources. The typical OD strategy assumes the goals of individuals, groups, and the organization itself can be met with minimal conflict. OD views problems as the result of faulty communication, bureaucratic malfunctioning, or improper divisions of power, tasks, or specializations.

Traditionally, OD:

- Is a long-range effort to introduce planned change.

- Is based on a diagnosis that is shared by the members of an organization.
- Involves the entire organization or a significant subsystem.
- Aims for increased organizational effectiveness and self-renewal.
- Uses various strategies to intervene into ongoing activities to facilitate learning and choose alternative ways to proceed.[2]

The major tactics for achieving these goals include the following:

- Training and coaching.
- Goal setting and planning.
- Process consultation.
- Survey feedback (or other data).
- Intergroup problem solving.
- Technostructural intervention.
- Team building.
- Crisis intervention.
- Quality of work-life programs.
- Quality circles.
- Total quality management programs.

Within the broad field of OD, there is a continuum of theory and practice that ranges from a consensus model to a conflict model. For the most part, the principles and tactics listed above are consistent with a consensus model.[3]

Those theorists and practitioners whose views tend to the conflict end of the continuum suggest, however, that understanding and managing organizations requires a political approach. They often see conflict as an inherent aspect of all organizations, starting with the difficulty of creating a harmonious fit between the needs of individuals and the priorities of the organization. A few people—mainly union activists and academics—focus on surfacing and using structural conflict among different organization units or between individuals of different social, racial, or gender categories or between workers and management to clarify and negotiate differences.

In practice, most OD includes elements of both consensus and conflict models.

WHAT IS MULTICULTURAL ORGANIZATIONAL DEVELOPMENT?

The new field, MultiCultural Organizational Development (MCOD), has been developed by theorists and practitioners who see limitations in traditional OD. Influenced by the civil rights and feminist movements, these scholars and practitioners charge that traditional OD has not paid close enough attention to issues of race, gender, class, and other aspects of discrimination and oppression.[4]

According to Jackson and Holvino, "Traditional organizational development efforts have not made the kind of impact on social oppression in the workplace that its founders had hoped."[5] Individual consciousness-raising about prejudice and discrimination has not been effective in creating lasting organizational change nor have training interventions in general led to comprehensive efforts to alter organizational power and culture.[6]

Most innovations in organizations have involved the reduction of the most overt forms of prejudice and discrimination and the recruitment and hiring of people of color and white women. Relatively few research or practice efforts have gone beyond equal opportunity and affirmative action programs. These were important gains, to be sure. But by and large, change efforts have been concentrated at the margins and lower levels of organizations; they have avoided challenges to established power relationships and dominant white and male cultures.

Like OD, MCOD theories occur on a continuum ranging from a consensus to a conflict orientation (see Figure 4–1). Some writers and practitioners focus on diversity and the effort to understand and accommodate differences, while others focus on achieving equality and social justice.[7]

Those who advocate a consensus-oriented approach to MCOD stress the reform of organizational racism and sexism through "understanding differences" and "valuing diversity." While these programs may help organizations make important

Orientations and Assumptions of Different Approaches to
Organizational Change

		Consensus	Conflict
Organizational development		Common values	Disparate values
		Mutual organizational interests	Competing organizational interests
		Harmonious workplace	Contest and struggle in workplace
		Person–organizational fit	
		Trustworthy authority	Exploitative authority
		Coordination via collaboration	Coordination via control
Multicultural organizational development		Imminent racial harmony	Racial hostility
		Treatable gender bias	Deep gender bias
		Problem: prejudice	Problem: organizational and societal oppression
		Issue: appreciating diversity	Issue: reducing dominance/discrimination

gains in educating white managers and in recruiting, supporting, and advancing white women and people of color, they do
not tackle issues of domination and oppression.

On the other hand, those proponents of MCOD who advocate
a social justice agenda generally agree on the following points:

- Racial, gender, class, and other differences have a
  powerful impact on people and organizations. This
  social diversity embodies differences in attitudes,
  behavioral styles, ways of thinking, culture, and
  the like.

- In a society that constantly translates differences into
  ranking systems, some of the characteristic styles of
  diverse groups are seen as better than others. When
  diverse styles encounter one another, white and male
  styles dominate those of people of color and white
  women. People of color and white women (among
  others) have been systematically oppressed in the larger
  society and thus in most organizations as well. In turn,

white males are systematically privileged, empowered, and preferenced.

■ When the oppressed resist their oppression, overt interest-group conflict (racial, gender, and class) naturally ensues. This conflict is not primarily the result of poor communication, inadequate managerial structures, poor coordination of task roles, or poor fit between person and organization. It is primarily the result of systems of oppression and monopolies of racial and gender power in society and the organization.

The social justice approach to multicultural organizational development is often frankly antiracist and antisexist. This approach to multiculturalism does not simply accept or celebrate differences but aims at a reduction in the patterns of racism and sexism that prevail in most U.S. institutions and organizations. One advocate of this approach is Elsie Cross, who makes it clear that her approach to "managing diversity" includes the amelioration of oppression. This necessarily surfaces intergroup conflict.[8]

In my view, traditional organizational development or OD that includes racism and sexism "awareness" programs or even MCOD that proceeds on a consensus basis are not as effective as Multicultural Organizational Development, which takes seriously the challenges of systemic racism and sexism.

EFFECTIVE MCOD

What tactics develop effective MCOD initiatives? While there are various approaches, they all recognize the necessity of challenging the culture and structure of white male oppression. These can involve the following:

■ Informing and enlightening white male managerial cadres through awareness or bias-reduction training.

■ Development and mobilization of leadership among employees/managers of color and white women, and the formation of interest groups, cadres, and caucuses so members of oppressed groups can support one another in their efforts to change the organization.

- Change in human resource and personnel policies and programs to meet diverse populations' needs.
- Creation of new organizational mission statements, symbols, myths, and norms—as well as changes in reward systems to punish or reward managers for behavior on issues of racism and sexism.
- Creation of coalitions across race, gender, and status.
- Negotiated decision-making and interest-based bargaining as ways of using conflict productively.
- Generation of power among people of color, white women, and their allies to influence, threaten, or coerce the change process; and the use of pressure and threat, including whistle-blowing, protests, and external agents.
- Multicultural forms of conflict resolution and dispute settlement that lead to more democratic management structures and procedures.[9]

Power is seldom "shared" or given away without challenge or pressure. When power changes hands, it is generally "taken"; therefore, it is vital to develop new sources of power among formerly oppressed and disempowered organizational members.

While both traditional OD and MCOD use a variety of organizational change tactics, one of the key differences between conflict and consensus models of change involves the relative emphasis on communication and trust, or on power and pressure, as tactics.

Figure 4–2 categorizes some common change tactics by their relative congruence with the consensus (olive branch, or trust and communication) model or the conflict (two-by-four, or power and pressure) model. Careful choices must be made among these various tactics and tactical approaches. Consensus tactics may work well in establishing a cooperative context for change, generating racial understanding, and creating change in a relatively equal power situation. But in situations of great power difference, they may lead to delay, co-optation, tokenism, and agreements to make changes that are not implemented.

On the other hand, conflict—power or pressure—tactics can bring long-repressed issues to the forefront, especially when the divisions between groups are great or differences have become calcified. Conflict tactics can command attention, speed up action,

FIGURE 4–2

Approaches to Organizational Change

	The "Olive Branch" Approach:	The "Two-by-Four" Approach:
Assumptions	Trust and communication— consensus Everyone is in this together Decision-makers can and do want to improve the situation Lower-level members do not have a lot to say or do about it Not too much is wrong Conflict is unnecessary and can be overcome	Power and pressure—conflict Not everyone is in this in the same way or for the same things Power brokers will not improve the situation on their own Lower-level members can and do have a lot to say and do about it A lot is wrong Conflict is natural and can be a force for change
General approach	Cooperative problem solving Appeal to decision-makers with information, with needs or concerns, with grievances/requests, with shared values Educate and persuade managers with reason, with information, with incentives, with support, with new options	Constituency organizing and surfacing conflict Persuade and pressure power brokers, with information, with pressure, with incentives, with demands Threaten managers with disclosure, with embarrassment, with disruption, with lack of support, with a "way out"
Working "with"	Decision makers and staffs Internal informal influentials Consensus	Others of the constituency or interest group Internal cadres External agents/agencies Coalition

and provide the framework for monitoring implementation efforts. Such tactics must, however, be backed by strong leadership and power; otherwise, they may create heat and noise that drowns out dialog, and those elites who experience threat may counterorganize and overwhelm a change effort.

While it is possible to identify the distinctions between consensus and conflict strategies at the extremes of the continuum, in reality the situation is much more complicated; movement back and forth between the poles is common. There is a continuum within MCOD just as there is in OD.

OD DOES NOT EQUAL MCOD!

There are both assumptive and analytic differences between Multi-Cultural Organizational Development and traditional OD. First, MCOD assumes that, on issues of race and gender, power is embedded in the white male hierarchy and white males have a strong self-interest in maintaining that power and privilege. Serious change cannot occur around these issues without serious struggle and conflict. Those who hold the power and benefit from its privileges are not motivated to "share." Typically, power sharing is quickly redefined by managers into "democratic" or "participatory management" and then further redefined out of existence as "employee involvement."

Second, issues of holding and maintaining power and privilege make the concept of working in the interest of the "entire organization" absurd. As a political system, the organization is constantly involved in negotiation among competing interest groups. When consensus-oriented ODers or MCODers say they are working for the good of the entire system, they are usually working for, and for the good of, the managerial cadre—disproportionately white and male—who hire and fire consultants as well as employees.[10] From this position, it's difficult to work for the interests of people of color and white women (see Figure 4–3).

What happens, then, when traditional OD assumptions, analyses, and tactics are employed in an MCOD effort? Can OD be effective in reducing institutional oppression? Can MCOD be done well without challenging the centers of monocultural power and norms?

When OD or a consensus form of MCOD is used in a Multicultural Organization Change effort, the change tactics often seek consensus prematurely rather than surface and explore conflict. These tactics celebrate difference rather than challenge dominance or oppression. They help individuals adjust to monocultural norms and power systems rather than alter the power systems and the culture. They create individual changes while maintaining

FIGURE 4–3

MCOD's Challenges to OD

- White males are unlikely to change without significant appeal (including threat) to their self-interest.
- Power must be taken to be shared.
- Race and gender oppression is the rule; it is a fundamental element in U.S. organizations.
- An organization is composed of units and people who differ from one another and are in (overt or covert) conflict with one another in important ways.
- Organizational norms (and thus reward systems) reflect the dominance of the white male culture and its power.
- People with power who are threatened by struggle will resist change and will counterattack (overtly or covertly).
- The core power for change will come from people of color, women, and other oppressed groups.
- On some occasions, some white males will vigorously support and join the MCOD effort.

organizational structures and cultures of racial and gender power. And they mask real struggle with a patina of enlightened rhetoric and tokenism that maintains or solidifies organizational mono-culturalism.

The current popularity of this approach has led some critics to label diversity programs and MultiCultural Organizational Development as the new "race industry"—an industry more interested in its own maintenance and profit than in combatting oppression and attaining social justice.[11] The consensus approach may well merit such charges.

But is it feasible to adopt an approach that challenges white and male power structures and cultures—an approach that surfaces race and gender conflict and uses that conflict as the basis of the change effort? Can managers and consultants who take this route survive economically and politically?

The evidence is increasing that some leaders in major U.S. organizations are reading accurately the danger of current race and gender oppression. Whether prompted by the anticipated demographic changes in "Workforce 2000," by economic market necessities, by increasing racial and gender conflict in workplaces and living places, or by a commitment to "the right thing," some major players understand the assumptions underlying the MCOD approach. Books on valuing or managing diversity and a diverse workforce are selling like hot cakes, and some writers contend that many corporate managers "are already convinced that the multicultural model is the way of the future."[12] It remains to be seen whether these managers will act on that conviction, making long-term investments and taking the risks necessary to turn the conviction into reality.

On the other hand, there is also substantial evidence that major stakeholders in many U.S. organizations resist this approach and seek to defend their own and others' racial and gender privileges. In these instances, managers, consultants, and academicians who take a social-justice-oriented MCOD approach must fight to survive.

Is it worth it? To protect our own self-interest, should we continue to adopt the more consensus-oriented approach and ignore the realities of the racist and sexist bases of systemic discrimination?

Whose survival is important to us? And survival at what level of economic or moral comfort or security? Oppressed groups in the United States are having an increasingly difficult time surviving—with or without MCOD. Eventually, none of us—or our society—will thrive unless we are able to respond proactively and progressively to continuing racial privilege and oppression.

Traditional Organizational Development theory and practice, and consensus-oriented Multicultural Organizational Development, cannot lead our organizations to the kind of change that is required. We must face the challenges of the real world—which include power struggles, conflict and resistance—with courage and effective, appropriate strategies if we are to develop a socially just, economically viable, and truly multicultural future.

END NOTES

1. See, for example, Burke and Goodstein 1980; French, Bell, and Zawicki 1989; Friedlander and Brown 1974; Sashkin and Burke 1987; Sikes, Drexler, and Gant 1989.

2. Principles are based on the work of Goodstein and Cooke 1984; Pfeiffer and Jones 1978; Sherwood 1983.

3. For discussion of the differences between a consensus model and a conflict model, see Bolman and Deal 1984; Bowen 1977; Burke and Hornstein 1972; Chin and Benne 1969; Crowfoot and Chesler 1974; Crowfoot and Chesler 1982; Espinosa and Zimbalist 1978; Friedlander and Brown 1974; Holvino 1993; Patten 1991; Ross 1971; Thomas 1976; Walton 1965.

4. Such critiques of traditional OD have been offered by Cox 1990; Fine, Johnson, and Ryan 1990; Jennings and Wells 1989. For pioneering studies of race and gender relations in organizations see Alderfer et al. 1980; Alvarez and Lutterman 1979; Fernandez 1981; Kanter 1977; Sargent 1976.

5. 1988, p. 1.

6. Jackson and Holvino 1988; Katz 1988.

7. See Cox 1991; Jackson and Holvino 1988; and Katz 1988.

8. Cross 1991.

9. Jackson and Holvino 1988; Katz 1988.

10. Bowen 1977; Ross 1971.

11. Mohanty 1989–90.

12. See, for example, Jamieson and O'Mara 1991; Johnston and Packer 1987; Loden and Rosener 1991; Thomas 1990; Cox 1991, p. 40.

REFERENCES

Alderfer, C., A. Alderfer, D. Tucker, and L. Tucker. "Diagnosing race relations in management." *Journal of Applied Behavioral Science,* 16, no. 2 (1980), pp. 135–166.

Alvarez, R. and K. Lutterman, eds. *Discrimination in Organizations.* San Francisco: Jossey-Bass, 1979.

Bolman, L. and T. Deal. *Modern Approaches to Understanding and Managing Organizations.* San Francisco: Jossey-Bass, 1984.

Bowen, D. "Value dilemmas in organizational development." *Journal of Applied Behavioral Science* 13 (1977), pp. 543–556.

Burke, W. and L. Goodstein, eds. *Trends and Issues in Organizational Development: Current Theory and Practice.* San Diego: University Associates, 1980.

Burke, W. and H. Hornstein. *The Social Technology of Organizational Development.* La Jolla, CA: University Associates, 1972.

Chin, R. and K. Benne. "General strategies for affecting change in human systems." In W. Bennis, K. Benne, and R. Chin, eds., *The Planning of Change.* New York: Holt, Rinehart and Winston, 1969.

Cox, T. "Problems with research by organizational scholars on issues of race and ethnicity." *Journal of Applied Behavioral Science* 26, no. 1 (1990), pp. 5–24.

————"The multicultural organization." *Academy of Management Executive* 5, no. 2 (1991), pp. 34–47.

Cross, E. "Issues of diversity." In D. Vails-Weber and J. Potts, eds. *Sunrise Seminars*. Washington, D.C.: National Training Laboratories, 1985. Revised, 1991.

Crowfoot, J. and M. Chesler. "Conflict control and organizational reform: Three approaches." In G. Bomers and D. Peterson, eds. *Conflict Management and Industrial Relations*. The Hague, Netherlands: Nijhoff Pub., 1982.

Crowfoot, J. and M. Chesler. "Contemporary perspectives on planned social change." *Journal of Applied Behavioral Science* 10 (1974), pp. 287–303.

Espinosa, J. and A. Zimbalist. *Economic Democracy: Workers' Participation in Chilean Industry, 1970–1973*. New York: Academic Press, 1978.

Fernandez, J. *Racism and Sexism in Corporate Life*. Lexington: Lexington Books, 1981.

Fine, M., F. Johnson and M. Ryan. "Cultural diversity in the workplace." *Public Personnel Management* 19, no. 3 (1990), pp. 305–318.

French, W., C. Bell and R. Zawicki, eds. *Organizational Development*. New York: Irwin, 1989.

Friedlander, F. and D. Brown. "Organizational development." *Annual Review of Psychology* 25 (1974) pp. 313–341.

Goodstein, L. and P. Cooke. "An organizational development (OD) primer." In J. Pfeiffer and J. Jones, eds. *The 1984 Annual: Developing Human Resources*. San Diego: University Associates, 1984.

Holvino, E. "Organizational development from the margins: Reading class, race and gender in OD texts." Unpublished doctoral dissertation. University of Massachusetts at Amherst, 1993.

Jackson, B. and E. Holvino. "Multicultural organizational development." Ann Arbor: Program on Conflict Management Alternatives (Working Paper 11), 1988.

Jamieson, D. and J. O'Mara. *Managing Workforce 2000: Gaining the Diversity Advantage*. San Francisco: Jossey-Bass, 1991.

Jennings, C. and L. Wells. "The Wells–Jennings analysis: A new diagnostic window on race relations in American organizations." In W. Sikes, A. Drexler, and J. Gant, eds., *The Emerging Practice of Organizational Development*. Alexandria and San Diego: NTL-IABS and University Associates, 1989.

Johnston, W. and A. Packer. *Workforce 2000: Work and Workers for the 21st Century*. Indianapolis: The Hudson Institute, 1987.

Kanter, R. *Men and Women of the Corporation*. New York: Basic Books, 1977.

Katz, J. "Facing the challenge of diversity and multiculturalism." Ann Arbor: Program on Conflict Management Alternatives (Working Paper 13), 1988.

Loden, M. and J. Rosener. *Workforce America*. Homewood, IL: Business One Irwin, 1991.

Mohanty, C. "On race and voice: Challenges for liberal education in the 1990s." *Cultural Critique.* Winter (1989–90), pp. 199–208.

Patten, T. "The behavioral science roots of OD." In J. Pfeiffer and J. Jones, eds. *The 1978 Annual Handbook for Group Facilitators.* San Diego: University Associates, 1979.

Pfeiffer, J. and J. Jones. "OD readiness." In J. Pfeiffer and J. Jones, eds. *The 1978 Annual Handbook for Group Facilitators.* San Diego: University Associates, 1978.

Ross, R. "OD for whom?" *Journal of Applied Behavioral Science* 7, no. 5 (1971), pp. 580–585.

Sargent, A., ed. *Beyond Sex Roles.* New York: West Publishing Co., 1976.

Sashkin, M. and W. Burke. "Organizational development in the 1990s." *Journal of Management,* 13 (Summer), pp. 393–417.

Sherwood, J. "An introduction to organizational development." In R. Ritvo and A. Sargent, eds. *The NTL Managers' Handbook.* Alexandria, VA: NTL Institute, 1983.

Sikes, W., A. Drexler, and J. Gant, eds. *The Emerging Practice of Organizational Development.* Alexandria, VA and San Diego: NTL-IABS and University Associates, 1989.

Thomas, K. "Working interests and managerial interests: The need for pluralism in organizational development." Los Angeles: UCLA Graduate School of Management (Working Paper 76-120), 1976.

Thomas, R. "From affirmative action to affirming diversity." *Harvard Business Review* 2 (1990), pp. 107–117.

Walton, R. "Two strategies of social change and their dilemmas." *Journal of Applied Behavioral Science,* 1, no. 2 (1965), pp. 167–179.

CHAPTER

Allies or Enemies?

Affirmative Action and Management Diversity

David R. Barclay

Is "workforce diversity" just another fad that will disappear in several years? Or is it truly an issue the American business community will seriously address? Will affirmative action survive?

Will the increasing conflict between affirmative action and diversity divert attention away from the real problems still confronting this country?

The answers to these questions are not as clear as some may suggest. The real issue is not whether "diversity" or "affirmative action" will survive; it is how we capitalize on the strength of *both* programs. To understand this point, we need to explore the historical background of affirmative action and equal employment opportunity (AA/EEO) and diversity.

THE DEBATE

For decades, this country has been embroiled in controversy over the need for affirmative action programs to ensure equal employment opportunities for people of color and white women. As the debate rages on, opponents have become increasingly vocal.

The national uproar that followed the introduction of the 1990 and 1991 Civil Rights Acts clearly demonstrated how deep-seated this issue is with the American public. President Bush, like many others, continually mischaracterized the legislation as a "quota" bill—even though it contained specific language prohibiting the use of quotas. The president's veto of the 1990 act sent a clear signal that civil rights and race relations were not a high-priority item for his administration. The ultimate passage of the 1991 act has not lessened the resolve of those who still oppose affirmative action. Unfortunately, although the current administration has signaled a different approach through its initial cabinet-level appointments, it has not articulated a vision or specific programs to enhance a civil rights agenda.

In addition, the list of vocal opponents has increased over the last few years. Academicians, industry representatives, and some diversity consultants have joined the ranks of those stating we no longer need affirmative action. Some have described it as a relic serving no useful purpose. Racism and sexism, they contend, have disappeared.

Some of these opponents are themselves members of minority communities:

■ Roosevelt Thomas, a popular diversity consultant, in a *Harvard Business Review* article, "From Affirmative Action to Affirming Diversity," stated, "American businesses are now filled with progressive people—many of them minorities and women themselves—whose prejudices, where they still exist, are much too deeply suppressed to interfere with recruitment."

■ San Jose State University professor Shelby Steele, in *The Content of Our Character* noted, "After 20 years of implementation, affirmative action has shown itself to be more bad than good and blacks now stand to lose more from it than they gain."

■ Economist Thomas Sowell, senior fellow at Hoover Institution, referring to affirmative action, recently said, "We now have a situation where everybody is worse off than if such policies did not exist. Blacks have fewer jobs, whites have more resentment, the company has to settle for its second choice of location, and the society has more internal strife."

THE CASE FOR AFFIRMATIVE ACTION

Is there a need for affirmative action? In spite of the naysayers, my answer is clearly and unequivocally yes!

For many of us who work in both equal employment opportunity and diversity programs, it is impossible to agree with the statements made by Thomas, Sowell, and Steele. In spite of all claims to the contrary, this society still struggles with the "isms": racism, sexism, and all the rest. There is still a reluctance to admit the deep-rooted nature of discrimination, prejudice, racism, and sexism that continue to pervade our society. Until we can admit this reality, developing a solution becomes very difficult.

We cannot bury our heads in the sand and ignore these problems, hoping they will resolve themselves and disappear. One must wonder if our historical patterns of exclusion and differential treatment are so deeply ingrained in the fabric of our society that they will hinder us from capitalizing on the strength of our growing diversity.

Problems of this magnitude cannot and will not be solved by catchy phrases and simplistic dreams and visions. We must do more than just state, "I support equal opportunity." The problems are far too complex. Barriers will not come down with simple pronouncements or a one-time cultural awareness training program that suggests that everything is now OK.

I must ask, "What has changed in our society that leads anyone to believe that racism and sexism have diminished to the point we no longer need affirmative action? What signs are there that we no longer need measurements and accountability?"

I frequently hear the new breed of diversity consultants—even those who have themselves profited from affirmative action—suggesting, "We don't need these numbers—these 'quotas'—any longer." Yet evidence to the contrary is all around us. Hate crime statistics, public opinion/perception polls, glass-ceiling issues, and complaint and litigation activity certainly do not provide any comforting feelings that we are solving our race relations problems.

We only need to look at our history to understand that equal rights have never been provided voluntarily. As unpopular and discouraging as it may be, we must recognize that progress has only been achieved through enforcement mechanisms, including legislation, regulatory requirements, and judicial review. This is true of all segments of our society, including education, employment, housing, public accommodations, voting rights and, to some degree, our criminal justice system.

One attempt to correct the past practices of exclusion was the design and implementation of affirmative action programs. However, affirmative action was never expected to solve *all* our problems. Nor was Title VII of the 1964 Civil Rights Act intended to be a cure-all. Both Title VII and affirmative action were mechanisms aimed at combatting employment discrimination.

But how often have we heard this country's preoccupation with "quotas" and the continuing misrepresentations of being required to "lower standards," provide "preferential treatment," and "hire and promote unqualified personnel?" I would ask, "In what regulation or court order does it state than an employer must lower standards, hire and promote unqualified employees, or use quotas?"

In spite of this continuing backlash, progress *has* been made. During the last 25 years, substantial numbers of minorities and women have entered the workforce and are slowly moving up the corporate ladder. People of color and white women at all levels—not just the highly educated or "fast trackers"—have made these gains.

Affirmative action has focused attention on employment discrimination, has identified "underutilizations" and "no utilizations," and has created a systematic approach for corrective action. It has created a *process* for change. Although affirmative action has not solved all our problems, it *has* worked.

Some people believe they have been stigmatized by this wicked term, *affirmative action*. They may very well have been stigmatized and stereotyped, but it was not because of affirmative action.

Those who are concerned with the "stigma" should not believe that they were the *first* person of color or white woman who was qualified for the position! They were not the *first* to merit such positions—though they may have been the first to receive them. Such reasoning reflects naïveté and a failure to understand that many who came before were well qualified by anyone's standards, but were denied opportunities solely because of their race or gender.

AFFIRMATIVE ACTION AND DIVERSITY

While I stress the historical and current importance of affirmative action, I also recognize the importance of the emerging issue of diversity. But the question is not one of affirmative action *or* diversity. The question is how to integrate the two programs into one coordinated approach and capitalize on the strength of both efforts.

The June 1987, Hudson Institute report, "Workforce 2000," identified many of the changing demographics that would impact the future market. These included the following: (1) the U.S. population and the workforce will grow more slowly than at any time since the 1920's; (2) the average age of the population and the workforce will rise, and the pool of young workers entering the labor market will shrink; (3) more women will enter the workforce; (4) minorities will become a larger percentage of new entrants into the labor force; and (5) the percentage of the population and the workforce represented by immigrants will be the largest since the First World War.

These findings, plus our concern that we would experience shortages of engineers and scientists and require a higher level of skills and education for new jobs, focused the national attention on these changing demographics. Simultaneously, there was a perception that our education system was unable to produce graduates who would be prepared to meet the challenges of the rapidly changing world of work.

Out of these early discussions came the birth of a new industry: valuing and managing diversity. Diversity consultants began to provide "awareness" training, which focused on examining the cultural, racial, and gender factors affecting the work environment. The methodology was similar to the "T-groups" and "sensitivity training" used 25 years ago and was aimed at changing attitudes. But my experience over the years indicates that little change in attitude has in fact occurred.

It is clear that much more than a training program is required to meet our long-range goals. We must aim for changes in *behaviors*, not just attitudes. We must focus on examining and modifying processes, and institutionalizing those changes.

There is also a growing concern that the diversity initiative will lose steam because many of the findings of the Hudson Institute report are being challenged. The current major changes in the *world* economy could not be predicted when the report was issued; it may be that because of these changes, some of the original predictions were overstated.

At the same time that increasing numbers of people of color and white women are entering the workforce, there is an increasing number of white males with higher skills, education, job seniority and experience who are joining the ranks of the unemployed. Large corporate entities are flattening their organizations, resulting in fewer promotional opportunities for everyone. Further, national trends indicate that the lion's share of future employment opportunities will occur in small companies and in start-up ventures. Historically, these employers have been unresponsive to traditional EEO and affirmative action efforts. All of these trends represent potential barriers to diversity efforts and limitations on attempts to break the glass ceiling.

As more attention is directed toward diversity training, there is also the potential of increasing conflict between diversity efforts and EEO/affirmative action. In some companies, the two programs are being separated organizationally, placing them in direct competition for decreasing resources. In a few instances, EEO/affirmative action programs are being deemphasized or even replaced by the voluntary efforts of diversity training. This is a short-sighted and counterproductive approach. The elimination of affirmative action is clearly not the solution to the overall problem. Without the enforcement power of affirmative action and equal employment opportunity legislation, we will quickly lose the gains of the past 25 years.

THE NEW CHALLENGES

Both AA/EEO and diversity initiatives are required to meet the rapid changes we are facing in the last decade of this century. Whatever the limitations may be to the original Hudson Institute estimate, it is nonetheless clear that changing demographics will require different and improved management skills. The new workforce is already radically different from the old—there are more Asians, African-Americans, Hispanics, Native Americans, white women and employees with disabilities. Our population is aging, and older workers are choosing—or being forced—to remain in the workforce longer.

As the workforce changes, there are increasing pressures to accommodate different cultural values and a different work ethic. Employees want more responsibility and authority—and more opportunities to participate in the decision-making process. They are pressing for the chance to apply their individual skills and creativity and to do work that is more comprehensive and holistic.

The new issues are complex and will impact the total workforce. Employers, while confronting financial pressures and the need to downsize, will simultaneously have to focus more attention on child care, employee network groups, alternative work schedules, elder care, work/life concerns, dispute-resolution procedures, career development, and redefining "upward mobility." Employees are demanding a work environment that is fair and responsive to all employees and their concerns.

All of these issues require employers to face the most difficult challenge of all: changing the culture of the organization. Many are asking, "Why should we change? Our company is successful. Change is only disruptive—it creates anxieties and fear among employees."

But change is inevitable. Given the new reality of a more competitive and international marketplace—a more diverse customer base—the historical model of a homogeneous culture of white men, particularly in the management ranks, is no longer valid. The characteristics of the old homogeneous culture included cronyism and the "old-boy network," excluding anyone who was "different." It required assimilation—the expectation that those who were different from the white male norm would try to look and act as much as possible like white men. The old culture relied on subjective selection procedures that generally resulted in hiring and promoting people who were just like those doing the hiring and promoting.

Attempts to retain a homogeneous culture will adversely affect the ability of employers to be competitive. Unless the corporation can nurture diversity at all levels, it won't be able to adapt in a timely manner to market changes. The homogeneous organization finds it difficult to communicate to those who are different. Without the ability to adapt, to communicate, and to understand the changing marketplace, strategic decisions will be made in a vacuum.

A diverse workforce will enhance an employer's creativity and problem-solving ability. It will increase its flexibility to meet new challenges, and it will provide a competitive advantage in meeting business objectives.

FACING THE FUTURE

Where do we go from here? The steps required for implementation of an effective diversity program are not unlike the steps needed to implement an effective affirmative action program. What must be made abundantly clear is that diversity is *not* a replacement for affirmative action; it is an extension. Every diversity program must have objectives, goals, measurement tools, and accountability—the very same essential elements of an affirmative action plan.

Diversity must become a "core value" of the competitive organization, and it should focus management efforts on improving and creating *processes* as well as results. Diversity must become a fundamental management philosophy that is integrated into the company's overall operating plans and strategies.

Diversity initiatives will never be successful, however, unless we can frame the issue to focus on bottom-line results. We must move beyond the rhetoric of the past, which suggested that the primary impetus was "social responsibility," and state clearly and emphatically that the utilization of all segments of our population is a business and economic imperative.

If we are to overcome the historical patterns of prejudice and discrimination that still exist today, we must use every tool available. This is not the time to eliminate programs or processes that have worked! It is not the time to put our hopes only on an effort that has a foundation in volunteerism. We cannot simply wait for "the right thing" to be done. There must be accountability to measure progress in our diversity efforts just as there is accountability to measure progress in achieving production, financial, new business acquisition, and profit goals.

"Valuing and managing diversity" programs must not be subverted to take us back to the days when we pretended that the passage of time would inevitably lead to the end of discrimination. Martin Luther King made the point succinctly: "We must purge ourselves from the tranquilizing drug of gradualism."

To capitalize on the strength of a diverse workforce, we must bring to bear all the resources we have, including affirmative action. The question is still open: "Will this society find the will and the ways to provide opportunities for all of its people?" It is clear that both diversity initiatives and affirmative action programs are essential tools for achieving our goal of creating a society that truly provides equal opportunity.

REFERENCES

Johnston, William B. and Arnold H. Packer. *Workforce 2000: Work and Workers for the 21st Century.* Indianapolis: Hudson Institute, June 1987.

Sowell, Thomas. "Commentary." *Rocky Mountain News.* July 14, 1993.

Steele, Shelby. "Affirmative Action: The High Price of Preference." *Los Angeles Times,* September 30, 1990.

Thomas, R. Roosevelt, Jr. "From Affirmative Action to Affirming Diversity." *Harvard Business Review,* March–April, 1990.

CHAPTER

Champions of Diversity

A Culture Change Process

Delyte D. Frost
William D. Schaeffer
Judy Ragona

As managing-diversity interventions move into a phase of internal capacity building, processes must be developed that allow the learning and the commitments to become institutionalized within the organizational systems and structures. These processes must be carefully tailored to fit the particular culture and the special needs of the individual organization.

In this three-part article, authors Frost, Schaeffer, and Ragona describe a specific process—"champions of diversity"—from the perspective of the consultant and two participants.

THE DESIGN/*DELYTE D. FROST*

champion

n. 1. a valiant fighter 2. a person who fights for another or for a cause; defender; protector; supporter *Webster's New World Dictionary, Third College Edition, 1989.*

As a consultant to corporations on issues of racism, sexism, and other forms of discrimination, I am continually aware of the possibility that a managing diversity process can start out with new awareness and commitment and wane into apathy. Even those cor-porations that make a serious commitment to creating a culture that is inclusive of employees of all races and cultures and both genders find that an initial investment in training seminars is insufficient. Unless the efforts devoted to education and aware-ness are closely followed with processes that create systemic change, the investment will be wasted.

The "champions" process is based on theories of organi-zational change and development and must be tailored to the needs of a particular organization. Organizations that may wish to replicate the process must identify the elements in the cul-ture and climate of that specific institution that will lead to the desired outcome—the development of an educated, committed, and systemically supported group of leaders of the diversity change process.

WHAT MAKES A CHAMPION?

As defined in Webster's, a champion is a valiant fighter, a person who fights for another or for a cause. In some organizations, *champion* is a term that is widely used to mean whoever is accountable for something. So the concept of a "champion of diversity" fits com-fortably within the corporate culture of many organizations.*

There are three key factors that operate in the selection of champions:

- A champion's personal core values must be those that support the organizational commitment to valuing diversity. Most often, those core values will have been clarified and strengthened, or developed, through participation in an initial education and awareness workshop. The champion acts out of these convictions and therefore from a base of personal power.

---

* In this article, I refer to the champion as "he." Since over 95 percent of those who hold top power positions in American corporations are white men, they will most often be the champions whose role is described here. Men of color and women who are in power positions may also carry out the roles and responsibilities of champions; the processes, however, will be somewhat different.

- A champion is someone who is in a position of formal power and authority within the organization.
- A champion is someone who is seen by others in the organization as a person who is a valued member of the *current* culture and thus can be trusted as he moves to create a new culture.

Champions are models, leaders, and implementors of the cultures change process. They are transmitters of the vision of the new organizational culture, and they carry the responsibility for helping the organization make the transition from the old to the new.

Champions are appointed by top management. Sometimes the motivation for making the appointments is that top management has made an investment—in time and money—to the managing diversity process but has come to realize that it does not have adequate leadership to make that investment pay off. Even if the men at the top are not themselves emotionally committed to the values of the work, they may recognize that it is bad business to start a process and not develop the leadership ability to carry it through to success.

It is crucial that the appointed champions be given a formal mandate and be held accountable to it. The people who are accountable for running the company on the business line must be the same people who will be accountable for making the diversity initiative succeed: the people in the organization who provide both formal and informal leadership. *Responsibility, accountability, and leadership are the keys to success in the champion strategy.*

CREATING A CHAMPION SYSTEM

The concept of "champions of diversity" may be strategized in different ways in different organizations. In the process that forms the basis for the present discussion, the system is based on a three-person team. Each champion selects two ally-advisors (AAs), drawn from the three groups of "others" most likely to appear in significant numbers in the corporation: women of color, men of color, and white women.

Choosing Ally-Advisors.

In this three-person team structure, the role of champion is complemented by the role of "allies" and "advisors." The roles reflect the fact that, in corporate culture as well as in most of American society, successful white men experience isolation and deprivation because of lack of exposure to the realities of the lives of women and people of color. They do not know those realities—and, further, they don't know that they don't know!

White women and people of color in the role of allies and advisors enable the white men—the champions—to hear, learn, experience, and be counselled. As allies, the team members provide the champion with support in his effort. As advisors, they give feedback, counsel, and suggestions.

Criteria that champions should consider when selecting ally-advisors include the following:

- Each person selected for the AA role must have had some previous exposure to managing diversity concepts, usually through participation in an initial education and awareness workshop.

- The AAs must be from the champion's own business unit or division, so they can provide first-hand feedback on the impact of the champion's behavior. They might be peers, subordinates, or superiors—but are most likely to be subordinates, often from several ranks down in the organization.

- Each AA must be someone the champion respects both professionally and personally, but *not* someone who often shares his viewpoint. That is, the AA should not be a person the champion chooses because there is already a basic comfort level between them. In combatting oppression, agreement rarely produces growth and change.

- The AA should be someone who will challenge the champion—a person who can be a worthy adversary as well as a staunch supporter.

The champion will benefit from guidance, from a diversity consultant and from his superiors, in the process of choosing the members of the team. It is, after all, very difficult to deliberately choose to set up a structure that is guaranteed to cause one a certain amount of discomfort, especially when the structure itself mandates that one's performance within that milieu is being closely monitored both from above and below. So the tendency is for the champion to choose people he sees as comfortable to be with. He may be tempted to look to people who are not aggressive or challenging or to people he knows can be easily won over or intimidated.

The consultant, or a superior who is tuned in and committed, may therefore need to scout the territory and recommend those people for the AA function who will be effective participants in the process. They should be employees whose job performance and reputation in the organization are solid and whose participation in the process cannot be undermined by weaknesses in other areas.

The persons selected for the AA role will also need support and guidance. It is risky to give honest feedback to one's superiors or even to peers who have direct access to the power structure of the organization. It is important that the two people who will be the ally-advisor component of the team develop a good rapport with one another and learn how to support each other to make strategic suggestions to the champion.

Clarifying Responsibilities

From the very beginning of the process, as the champions and their AAs are being identified, the roles and responsibilities of the teams and the individual members of the teams must be defined.

Roles
The role of a champion is to be as follows:

- The holder of the vision and core values *toward which* the organization is moving.
- A key transmitter of the new culture.
- A model and a manager of the symbolic meaning of activities within the organization.
- A person who empowers self, others, and the organization to act.

The role of the ally-advisor is to provide the following for the champion:

- Support and consultation.

- Challenge and affirmation.
- A broadened perception of reality.

Responsibilities
The responsibilities of the champion, as supported by the AAs, include the following:

- Articulating the organization's core values on racism, sexism, and other forms of discrimination.
- Monitoring the pulse of the division and the organization around diversity issues and defining these issues as phenomena belonging to the organizational *system*, not as individual incidents.
- Moving the managing diversity change process forward by challenging the existing norms—even by "shaking up the system."
- Providing a liaison function to the division head and the board, keeping them informed on ongoing activities, and making recommendations as to changes needed.
- Implementing change strategies in the division, along with the AAs.
- Modeling behavior that reflects awareness of the individual, group, and system levels of managing diversity, and continuing development of the effort at all three levels.
- Acknowledging and engaging resistance, including naming and managing backlash from other white men.
- Challenging other white men in the organization on their assumptions and behavior surrounding race and gender; differentiating himself from the collective of white men who consciously or unconsciously oppress those who are different.
- Using discretionary power positively for the diversity intervention effort and tracking how the outcome of their behavior matches their intent.
- Describing, interpreting, redirecting, and problem-solving issues of race and gender with bosses, peers, and subordinates.

- Troubleshooting and mediating conflict situations involving race and gender.
- Demanding full competence from white women and people of color and recognizing the potential risks of making such demands.
- Affirming work styles that are different from those that are stereotyped as "white" or "male."
- Creating an environment that mentors others in these behaviors and provides rewards for them—thereby developing other champions.
- Helping to develop and maintain the integrity and competence of the champion's group.

Structuring the Process

Once the champions and the AAs have been selected and the roles and responsibilities defined, it is important to involve the participants in an intensive training experience. The workshop must assist the participants in establishing norms, in developing mechanisms for guaranteeing the safety of the AAs, and in providing systematic methods for holding both champions and AAs accountable for their effectiveness.

Additionally, the workshop gives participants an opportunity to learn and practice skills in communicating in these new relationships. White men have to begin to recognize how communication patterns that have served them well in managing in a homogeneous, white-male–dominated structure do not work so well in managing a heterogeneous workforce. AAs have to learn to risk sharing their experiences with the champions, describing their feelings of frustration, helplessness, and rage. Jointly learning that feelings are a legitimate and essential aspect of effective working relationships is a fundamental step in the champions process.

The workshop must also help participants be realistic in their expectations. Not everyone who signs up to participate will succeed. Some men may agree to be champions because it seems to be a new way of currying favor in the organization, but this is not a process in which one can succeed unless there is a real commitment to the values and goals of the effort. Some AAs may find they lack the courage to confront a champion, or they may become too fearful of possible consequences to be able to maintain honesty and openness in their interactions.

Each organization will need to design ongoing mechanisms for ensuring the ongoing success of the process. Typically, the champions and the AAs will meet as separate groups, as well as in the three-person teams. These group meetings provide challenge, support, and monitoring of the effort.

REPLICATION

Not every corporation will be able to create a successful process for developing champions of diversity, nor is such a formal process always necessary. In a few cases, the leadership for the effort is so strong that champions emerge naturally. Leadership is, however, an art. Many organizations lack true leadership from the top. Leadership from a vision that includes all races and cultures, men and women, takes a particular gritty mix of heart and stamina. A champions process provides fertile ground and cultivation for the growth of true leadership in a diverse organization.

The design of programs and processes for developing champions to lead a diverse workforce must be company-specific. You can't work to change the culture of an organization by providing off-the-shelf training programs. The consultant and the organization must collaborate in the design and planning process to be sure that the training and organizational development intervention are what is needed in this organization, at this time, and for this organization's future.

If an organization perceives that one of the things it needs to move forward effectively is the development of leaders for diversity, the champions–AA process is one of the most powerful and effective I have experienced. It supports white men in *being* white men; it gives them a way to translate a sense of shame or guilt into positive action. A champions process offers a unique opportunity for white men to empower themselves in a nurturing way. On the other hand, it provides an arena in which these emerging leaders are constantly on view. One of the traps white men fall into is their ability to disappear into the overall white-male-dominated culture if things get tough. Having been formally appointed as a champion of diversity, and having had key co-workers assigned as allies and advisors as well as witnesses to their efforts takes away that possibility. Knowing the allies and advisors as real individuals—as well as representatives of their groups—makes it impossible for the champion to retreat to stereotyped views or biased practices. It prevents them from objectifying those particular people—and therefore makes it more difficult for them to objectify others of different races and the opposite sex.

True leaders have the capacity to connect emotionally to what a group of followers needs. They can then take that connection and form it into a vision that has value and worth—something that other people want to strive for, articulate, and live by. Connecting to those who are different from ourselves by gender, race, color, sexual orientation, and culture, and providing leadership is the challenge facing us today.

THE CHAMPION/*WILLIAM D. SCHAEFFER*

ETHICON, Inc., operates in seven locations around the United States and Puerto Rico, with international affiliates in Germany, Scotland, and France. As the United States struggles to reform its health care system and contain its costs, our company has come to realize we have to compete and thrive in a totally new environment. We recognize we have a lot to learn from other countries and cultures, especially in terms of being more flexible and understanding the demands of a marketplace that is quickly becoming very different from our traditional customer base.

We are fortunate that we began to position ourselves for these changes before they were upon us. Several years ago, for different reasons, we initiated a process called "managing diversity." Our need to understand the issues around diversity in our own organization not only is helping us realize the value—and unleash the power—of all our associates, it is also helping us meet the challenges of a very competitive global economy.

Managing diversity is not a process that leads to overnight success. Our work began in early 1989 in our sales organization.

We were experiencing a high turnover rate, resulting in lost sales, poor customer service, and excessive training costs. Thanks to the probing of our executive vice president of marketing and sales, Robert Croce, we learned that the highest turnover was among white women and people of color.[1]

We recognized this as a management issue, and, for a year or two, we concentrated on sending as many managers as possible to managing diversity education and awareness workshops. As the number of participants grew, we realized we had to capitalize on our learning and take positive action to carry the process forward.

Our diversity consultant suggested we develop a group of senior managers as "champions of diversity." The idea of champions—people who "carry the flag" and make things happen— is a familiar one in the Johnson & Johnson culture, so the extension of the process to the diversity effort was natural. I'm not exactly sure how the candidates were selected and approached; in my case, my boss, Dr. Pat O'Neill, vice president of research and development, asked if I would be interested. He explained the basic concept, and, since I was already committed to the diversity process, I was glad to volunteer.

Initially, all the champions were white men, which reflected the demographics of the organization's senior managers. All the champions must have participated in a managing diversity awareness workshop. Not having that preparation would be like trying to play a professional team sport without any training. First of all, you have to understand who you are and what you represent. More importantly, you must take personal responsibility for your behavior and be committed to learning the impact of your actions.

Probably the most important element was that each champion had to be a leader, someone who was trustworthy and who evoked trust in his decisions and personal interactions. He also had to walk the talk, lead the process, and support individuals, groups, and the organization as we tried to change the culture.

PREPARATION

Once champions had been identified, each of us identified two "ally-advisors (AAs)" to work with us. The AAs had to be either white women or people of color in our respective organizations. And they were to be people who were respected by their peers and who would challenge us by pushing back and telling us when we were wrong! They could not be people who would agree with whatever we wanted to say or hear. In some cases, they directly reported to a champion, but most of the AAs came from lower levels in the organization. So the champions were apt to be their boss's boss. The two people I asked to serve as my ally-advisors, Rose Coleman and Judy Ragona, met the criteria perfectly, and I was honored that they accepted my invitation.

When the group of champions and AAs had been selected, we worked with our consultants in an intensive three-day off-site session. Today we call this the "diversity leadership" workshop. We thought we had learned a lot in the awareness workshops, but we soon realized we had only scratched the surface of some very deep-rooted problems.

The purpose of the leadership workshop was to help the champions and AAs understand each other, both as individuals and as groups, and begin to develop honest and trusting relationships. Immediately, the session forced the champions to deal with the impact of our behaviors on white women and people of color. We learned that white men at the top of the organization viewed the company culture in one light, while the people of color and white women had a very different perspective. This workshop prepared us to communicate and *value* our differences for the development and well-being of everyone.

This may sound simple, but it was extremely difficult. The AAs had to give us brutally honest feedback about our behaviors, both as individuals and as leaders. They presented specific examples—individually and as a group—of the kind of things we were doing or allowing to happen that made life difficult for them and created an organization where the leadership is still dominated by white men.

We had to learn that our beliefs about equal treatment and opportunity for women and people of color were not correct. And we had to understand what actions it would take to change things.

This process generates an incredible amount of fear, both for the champions and, especially, for the AAs. For the champions, the fear is of losing power, accepting responsibility for your own actions and those of your fellow white males, and recognizing that your beliefs and values are biased. The AAs are in a very vulnerable position; they must give tough feedback to managers who have control over their jobs and, to a great extent, their professional careers. In addition there is the fear of retribution, of their feelings not being valued, and—most of all—of nothing changing.

To begin to establish the initial levels of trust for the process to work—and to break down some of the barriers—we made a number of personal commitments. These began with the champions, when we invited each AA to join us. We had to be able to say, "I *want* you to be my ally and advisor, and I *am asking* for honest feedback." As we progressed through the process, we began to define a set of expected behaviors—"cultural vows," as it were. At the end of the leadership workshop, as champions and as AAs, we made these into formal pledges. Together we wrote exactly what we expected of one another, what we didn't want to see, and the responsibilities we shared.

Another important commitment was that the champions— as a group—had to publicly commit to the process. In practice, that meant that if one of us reneged on our pledge, the other champions would call him on it.

BEING CHAMPIONS

Following the champions workshop, with the help of our consultant, we developed specific strategies to put our commitments into practice. First, we arranged regular meetings with our ally-advisors—about two hours each week. The arrangements varied; some teams went to lunch together, and some just met informally during the work day. We soon learned it was important to make a hard-and-fast commitment to hold regular meetings. Otherwise, when the going got tough, it was too easy to find excuses for not getting together.

In addition, "special interest" groups of white women and people of color started to form and meet regularly. We encouraged this, because we had a cultural hurdle to overcome. There had been a silent yet strong feeling that regular meetings of ethnic or racial groups—or of women—would be threatening. However, we *wanted* people with similar interests or perspectives to come together and network, to discuss issues that affect them both positively and negatively, and—most importantly—to recommend changes to eliminate the barriers blocking their productivity, growth, and opportunities for advancement.

The champions and the AAs also met together regularly as separate groups. In the case of the champions, we reserved the lunch hour every Tuesday for discussions of diversity issues and our leadership of the process. We didn't talk generalities, we shared experiences—the good and the bad. We wrestled with difficult situations as we considered feedback and input from our AAs and tried to find the best solutions. Throughout the entire process, and especially during these meetings, we maintained absolute confidentiality. Often, we invited participation from people directly involved in the issues but who were outside the group.

For example, at one meeting, one of the champions informed us that a person of color was about to be promoted in his area. He expressed deep concern about the strong potential for white male backlash. With so much emphasis on managing diversity, we all realized the promotion would probably be chalked up to affirmative action, discrediting the individual's accomplishments and competencies. So we dove into this head on!

We strategized and planned how to manage this situation to achieve the right outcome: preventing rumors, ensuring the organization would know the decision was based on merit, and diffusing the impact of naysayers. We made sure all the champions and as many of the ally-advisors as possible knew the position requirements in terms of skills and experience, as well as the incumbent's achievements and competencies. We also made sure all announcements emphasized the individual's credentials and made it clear this person was the best candidate for the position. When people challenged the appointment, we were well prepared to respond appropriately and to positively support the individual and the promotion.

Then there was the time when Kathy Shipman, director, Endo Project Management, met with us to recommend that the champions start a mentoring program. Representing one of the "special interest" groups, she presented this proposal, complete with definitions of purpose, structure, and desired outcomes. We agreed it was a good idea. There were already a couple of mentoring efforts underway, so we spent several weeks trying to understand the specific needs and expectations of this proposal and deciding whether the process should be formal or informal.

Suddenly we realized we were procrastinating. We were being asked for commitment and action. That afternoon, we announced we were willing to be mentors and invited those who were interested to contact us individually. We kept the process informal; as a result, it has expanded to many areas of the company and continues today. I started working with four people and have seen all of us grow personally and professionally.

Most of the champions—and the champion group—worked hard to keep our pledge to the AAs, who made major commitments of time and energy to support the process. We had our failings, and in one or two situations the white men who had agreed to accept leadership responsibility didn't follow through. In these cases, we made sure their AAs were invited to participate on other teams; and we reassured them of the group's continuing support.

As champions, we had many difficult face-to-face discussions with our AAs and with other champions—hearing things we didn't want to hear, struggling to change oppressive behaviors, learning the impact of our actions, and offering support to one another. Often we would take three steps forward but two steps back. Progress was slow, but determination was high.

MOVING ON

Even as the champions process was developing, awareness workshops continued. The commitment to diversity was starting to spread throughout the company. In addition to the "special interest" groups, diversity alumni groups were meeting regularly to share experiences and discuss the issues. There were many different types of responses to all this activity.

People at all levels who had not been invited to participate in the workshops began to feel excluded. They recognized that this process had management board commitment and high visibility from the top to the bottom of the organization. Through state-of-the-business communications and company newsletters, everyone knew that managing diversity was directed at eliminating racial and gender biases, valuing people's differences, and leveling the playing field for everybody.

In particular, white male managers who had not been asked to attend began to feel threatened. They were used to having access to, or being involved in, major company programs—yet here was something seemingly targeting everyone else.

There were several reasons why many of the white men had not yet attended an advanced diversity workshop, including the champions session. Perhaps they were not managers; the process focuses on those who directly supervise people and are responsible for instituting change. Maybe they had not been through initial diversity awareness training due to limitations on the size of the groups and the requirements for balance of gender and race in each session. There may also have been scheduling conflicts or individual time constraints that prevented their participation. Despite these realities, some white men and others throughout the organization were beginning to feel discriminated against. Both the champions and the AAs worked with many of these individuals to explain the process, confront the issues, and alleviate some of the fear.

Months later, there was a second champions workshop. It included our plant managers and their AAs from all our manufacturing facilities around the country. Judy Ragona and I were invited to participate again, to introduce a new ally-advisor to our team (Rose Coleman had left the company). While the content and structure of the second workshop was similar to that of the first, I found the experience just as challenging and enriching. The fact that people from the plants were participating in this workshop added new issues and perspectives. I found that each workshop helped me understand the problems more clearly and to feel the impact of my actions more directly. Even though I was exhausted at the end of the session, I came away recharged and more committed than ever.

At the same time, new champions were emerging throughout the company as well. Even associates who had not been part of the formal process were stepping out and assuming leadership roles, especially in our plants. The greatest revelation for me was when these champions took charge and reached out to answer the cries for understanding.

Over a period of several months, the diversity alumni, including people from the "special interest" groups, the ally-advisors, and the champions, conducted a series of four-hour and one-day diversity orientation sessions for most of the organization. They wanted to help everyone understand the diversity initiative, to clarify the objectives of the effort, and to eliminate the anxieties associated with the unknown. In some ways, this was the true beginning of the effort.

We eventually reached a point where many people felt we needed to move from awareness to action. We had spent several years at the individual and group level working to value each others' differences and changing our behaviors to eliminate personal biases. Now we faced the real challenge: changing our organizational behavior, our policies and systems—our company's culture.

In early 1992, our human resource organization and our consultant heard the calls for action, and recommended a formal change to the process. Diversity action teams were established in each functional division and in each plant. Many of the AAs and the new emerging champions provided the core leadership for these teams. Their primary purpose was—and still is—to identify any procedures, policies, or practices that adversely affect white women or people of color. These teams have direct access to the management board and are charged to recommend changes that systematically level the playing field and ensure equal opportunity for personal growth and advancement.

By design, the champions are not members of the action teams. Instead, we continue to work at the foundation. An 80-year-old company does not change overnight—old habits are tough to break. Working together, we are able to send a very clear message: "Diversity leadership is everyone's responsibility... and opportunity!"

At this point, we stopped differentiating between champions (white males) and ally-advisors, and the champions process officially became Diversity Leadership—a management skills workshop.

I don't want to create an overly optimistic vision of what we accomplished. There are many people who feel we did not progress quickly enough. There is still some resistance. And a few white men are still waiting for diversity to go away, and for life at ETHICON to return to business-as-before.

The champions process is not the end-all. In fact, it is just one of many steps in the long and arduous process of changing our attitudes and behaviors. The champions process is, however, powerful. It breaks management out of our intellectual world and forces us to face the realities of the organization. For ETHICON, the process was critical in helping us really understand the challenges of diversity and enabling us to own the process and lead the way for change.

Above all, the champions process made us realize that the leadership at the top of the organization must believe in diversity as a core value. As a group, we had to commit the time and the money to enable the process to move forward and for all of us to achieve its goals. As individuals, we had to break through the barriers that divide us by race, gender, age and level and commit ourselves to valuing and developing trusting relationships with all people.

END NOTE

1. See Robert Croce, "Keeping Good People on Board," in *The Diversity Factor* 1, no. 2 (Winter, 1993), pp. 29–31.

THE ALLY-ADVISOR/*JUDY RAGONA*

When I participated as an "ally-advisor" (AA) in the Champions Culture Change program, I was manager of regulatory compliance for ETHICON in Somerville, NJ, and had been with the company for about 23 years. I have a background in medical technology and had worked in experimental surgery for 14 years before moving into the quality organization.

I was very pleased when Bill Schaeffer asked me to be a member of his "champions" team. I had been an enthusiastic participant in the managing diversity program for some time and had participated in one of the very first education and awareness workshops, as well as several specialty workshops for women.

I have a passion for this work because I experienced discrimination very early in my career because I am a woman. I have also experienced the impacts of sexist attitudes and behaviors in my personal life. The diversity initiatives provided a way of raising awareness in the organization by helping people understand how difficult it is to compete when the playing field is not level. I thought we could have some impact on leveling that field, as well.

I'm not sure why Bill asked me, specifically, to be on his team. Perhaps it was because we had an established pattern of good communication, we had worked well together on several projects, and we were candid with each other. He probably felt I would be able to give him honest feedback.

I did not feel anxious about agreeing to do this, for two reasons. First, I did not report to him directly at that time; second, the fact that I had been with the organization for more than 20 years, and had been successful in my career, gave me a certain sense of security.

ALLIES AND ADVISORS

I entered into the process of being an AA with some fairly clear expectations. I knew the men chosen as champions were high enough in the organization—and enjoyed sufficient respect from the leadership—that they could have a major impact on the business. Having the opportunity to share with them, one-on-one and honestly, what it was like to live and work in this organizational culture as a white woman or a person of color was a once-in-a-lifetime experience. Their awareness would affect their future decisions—and that would, in turn, affect the culture.

We always met as a team—Bill, the other AA, and myself. We met for lunch with a formal agenda that we went through systematically, just as in a business meeting. But the subjects were hardly business-as-usual.

We learned it was crucial to set a specific time for our meetings and to keep that time as a high priority in our schedules. In the first few months, we were canceling meetings much too often. Finally, we got on the phone together and realized that if this was going to work, we had to make our dates and stick with them.

Looking back, I can see that part of what was happening was resistance to what was going on. We were just getting to

know each other in this new context, and some of this interaction was very new to Bill and difficult for him to handle. I
suspect that some of those early cancellations were the result
of his just not being able to deal with what was happening
right then. Some of the other teams fell apart because they
allowed other commitments to take priority over the champions process—or they allowed themselves to use other commitments as an excuse.

It took a lot of courage for Bill to stick it out. Some of what
we were sharing with him wasn't pleasant, and some of it meant
he had to take a hard look at his own actions and behavior. That's
a tough assignment.

Here's an example. In one of our early meetings, the other
AA and I were sharing our concerns about our treatment in the
ETHICON culture. Bill tried to defend the organization and his
own behavior. He had no idea of the impact he was having on
us or how his customary style of communication affected other
people. We had to tell him, up-front and honestly, "This is how
we feel when you talk to us like this; these are the ways your speech
and your behavior affect us. We don't like it, and it keeps us from
being heard and seen and accepted."

It took a while, but he heard us. Not that he changed right
away. In fact, it was a struggle; he'd say the same kinds of things
in the same way, and we'd call him on it; and then it would happen again and again. Eventually, all we'd have to do was make
a gesture—raise a hand or something like that—and he'd hear himself, and stop.

I learned something important from this. Before, I really
thought that white men were acting deliberately, with forethought
and knowledge, when they behaved in bigoted or disrespectful
ways. After working through this process with Bill, I learned
that people in power often are unaware of the impact of their
words or actions—it's ignorance, or at least inexperience. Now
Bill's not a stupid person—he's very intelligent. But it was a
struggle—even with the best will in the world, the best of intentions, and a real commitment to learn and to change.

This was an important learning experience for me; I began
to understand how we all got into the situation we're in and
how difficult it is going to be to change it. I also learned that

attitudes and patterns *can* be changed, but people have to genuinely want to change, and we all have to work hard at learning and changing.

PUTTING IT INTO PRACTICE

I don't want to suggest that our work together was just about learning how to communicate across race, gender, class, and functional differences. That was a prerequisite, though, for moving on to learning how to have open communication about other issues. We talked about a lot of things: systems, procedures, policies. We talked about the performance evaluation process. We spent a lot of time on how career development was managed in our organization and how people of color and white women often ended up being "no-see-ums" regarding career development. We talked about hiring practices and reviewed promotion practices.

Most of the time, we discussed these things generically; but, from time to time, one of us would bring up a specific incident, either as an example of why the system wasn't working properly or because it was a hot issue that needed to be resolved.

Whenever we brought out specific issues, they were always resolved one way or another. And a significant number of the policy and procedural issues we worked on were implemented as well.

The example I remember most vividly was the career development process. Once Bill realized what the problems were, he hired a consultant to help us put together a process with specific guidelines and suggestions, so we could all take responsibility for our own career advancement. The process was for all employees, not just white women and people of color; and it had a major impact on leveling the playing field.

Another instance was when a black man and a black woman left the organization at about the same time. Our team followed up to find out if their departures had anything to do with diversity or discrimination. In one case it did, but not in the other. We carried out a number of similar investigations. The information we gathered helped the organization better understand the problems black people have in the ETHICON culture.

KEEPING IT REAL

I don't think the champions process can work unless it has a structured format. One requirement must be that all the participants—champions as well as the AAs—must have participated in an initial education and awareness workshop. You can't go into this process cold; a champions team will not work if the team members are just beginning to look at their own attitudes and behaviors and at the systemic presence of racism, sexism, and other forms of discrimination in the organization.

Second, all the participants must be aware of the specific expectations of the champions process. There must be specific ground rules, and there must be consequences if participants don't adhere to these rules. Our champions workshop was pretty much like boot camp. The norms were laid out, they were clear, and we all agreed to them. The norms specifically provided for the safety of the AAs and created separate support groups for both champions and AAs.

These groups had a double function. They provided a network of support for people in the process, but they also provided a way of making people accountable for their behaviors. The groups met regularly. In our AA group, we talked very openly about how we were getting along with our champions. Some people reported serious problems; some of the champions were giving lip service to the process but had no real commitment. Some were not making themselves accessible: They would frequently cancel meetings or have disorganized agendas or maybe no agenda at all.

We also shared what we knew about what was happening in the champions' meetings—and what we did in our group was shared, with them. Everybody knew that what was said was going to be shared, and that kept the process both open *and* honest. The consultant met with both groups from time to time and monitored the flow of information.

KEYS TO SUCCESS

Properly designed, the champions process can be a powerful force for redirecting a corporation's culture toward more openness, inclusiveness, and creativity. There are several elements that are crucial to a successful design.

First, the organization must be prepared to take this step. It must be committed to creating a more open culture. It must have already made the kind of commitment of resources that prepares people to undertake this challenging process; you can't nickel and dime a diversity program. A "quick fix" approach just teases people with false expectations and creates serious negative reactions.

Second, participants must be chosen carefully. Champions must want to be in the process; you can't use the process to change or convert people. In every organization, there are some natural champions—people that everybody already knows, respects, and recognizes as real leaders. These people should not only be asked to serve as champions, they should also help identify other potential champions in the organization.

Finally, you have to be realistic in your expectations. There's no magic in the champions process or any other diversity program. Patterns of discrimination are so deeply embedded in our organizations that we're going to be struggling with them for a long time. Some things will work, or will work for a while; and there will be times of backsliding or reaction or disinterest. Then, with luck, a new initiative will get off the ground.

You have to be in it because you believe it's important—for you individually and for your organization—and you have to be willing to deal with failure as well as success. Championing this process comes from your heart; you must touch your core values and work from that level. It's tough, but it's rewarding. And it's the only way to make change happen.

TWO

BARRIERS

While it is true that each organization is unique, it is also true that there are numerous similarities in the issues of discrimination and lack of equity that each faces. This section reviews some of the most common obstacles.

A major concern in all U.S. organizations that are attempting to become more open to and accepting of white women and people of color is the reaction of white men. While the "angry white man" is largely a product of the media, it is undeniable that white men face a special set of challenges. Chuck Ball and Gary Howard draw on their own experiences of coming to terms with what it has meant in their lives to be white men and describe how they have found new ways of living and working that capitalize both on their personal strengths and on the opportunities for new alliances that are offered in a more heterogenous context.

Jean Kim provides valuable insights into the confusing dynamics of a person of color who comes from another country into the structural racism of U.S. society. Coming from Korea as a young girl, she was unprepared for the discrimination she encountered here. In this moving article, she describes the long and painful journey required to come to terms with this experience.

A similar long and painful journey faces the gay, lesbian, or bisexual employee in an American organization—or in American society in general. Is it better to "live the lie," or to risk all in the gamble of "coming out?" Mark Kaplan and Jay Lucas share their own experiences and provide practical advice for groups that want to change the climate in their organizations.

CHAPTER

A White Man's Journey

Chuck Ball

For the past four years, I have been a manager in a company committed to creating a culture that welcomes people of both genders and all races. We are involved in a serious, ongoing "culture change" effort that requires close scrutiny of all aspects of the ways we interact. As I have participated in this effort, I have come to understand that collectively, white men confront a unique dilemma. We must be able to admit that, as a group, we have a history of discriminating against other groups and benefitting from that discrimination. And we must find ways to use that knowledge to help create a different kind of environment.

I have observed that those of us who accept the necessity of changing our attitudes and behaviors seem to pass through various stages of growth. In this article, I describe how I came to this understanding, what the stages are, and where the work is leading us.

BEGINNINGS

I grew up in the South, in tobacco country. I never knew any African-Americans as peers. Like every other white family I knew, we had black people working for us. We pretended they were "part of the family," but it certainly wasn't true.

When I was 14 years old, my first job was picking cucumbers. I was the crew leader, and the crew members were all adult black men. At 15, I followed family tradition and went to Georgia to the tobacco markets, where I became crew chief again. I didn't know beans, but I was the boss of a group of experienced black men. And they responded to me! My little brother wouldn't listen to me, but a grown black man didn't have a choice.

It was years before I really thought about what this meant. I was the boss's son, or I was the boss, and I didn't know anything about the business at all. I got the job because I was white. I was unaware of how these black men felt about that or about me. I was oblivious to the ridiculous nature of the situation.

My father, who was in the tobacco business, traveled all over the world, so my family had a peek into other cultures. Egyptians, Asians, Japanese, Germans, and others were guests in our house. We took this in stride, but our friends always thought it was kind of strange. But relating to people of color from other places was very different from relating to black people at home.

In high school, I went on a road trip with the football team. We had one black player, a running back, and the coach asked me if I would room with him. I didn't see any problem. Years later, I discovered the coaches actually went to my father first to ask if it was okay. There was no sensitivity for the black player alone with a bunch of whites, only for the white player who would have to room with him. I'm sure the coach didn't ask the black guy's father for permission for *him* to room with *me*!

I was in college during the Vietnam era. The best thing that ever happened to me from playing football was that it left me unable to pass an army physical. I felt a huge sense of relief but also some guilt. So I left school and joined the Merchant Service (they didn't require as extensive a physical), and I ended up in Southeast Asia after all!

That was the real beginning of my education. I worked on Norwegian, Portuguese, and Spanish ships. I saw every kind of racism and exploitation. I remember being off Singapore, on a ship that carried liquid latex. Once the latex was pumped out, the residue had to be removed. Normally we (the crew) would put on oxygen masks and go down with steam guns and get it off. It would take about 10 of us two days to do it. But it was cheaper to hire 50 or 75 Indonesian women to come on board and work around the clock to peel the latex off by hand—with no oxygen, of course. They had no food, either, except for a tiny bowl of rice. Rice, two cigarettes, and a few pennies a day—that's about all they got. These were young women, chronologically, but they looked old. I saw things like this everywhere I went.

I came back from that experience transformed from a mediocre, disinterested student into somebody who challenged the professors all the time. I was a real pain. It took me a long time to learn that you can't be in people's face all the time, confronting them with what they don't know or the inadequacy of their attitudes. They just shut down. You have to learn how to meet people where they are. This is a lesson that anyone who tries to do diversity work has to learn.

GOING TO WORK

My early jobs continued to educate me in what it means to be white. For a while, I worked in a cotton mill in Virginia. I had a lousy job pushing 55-gallon drums of dye from the basement to the dye house, five stories up. I went from that job to something better pretty fast, partly because people thought I was a returning veteran and partly because I was white. All the supervisors were white; all the workers were black.

I was asked to play on the mill's basketball team. It turned out I was the only white guy on the squad, so traveling with the team was interesting, to say the least. I could walk into any hotel and eat at any restaurant, but my teammates couldn't—and this was 1971. Back at the factory, I still wanted to be teammates—to have lunch together and sit around and shoot the breeze. But it was clear that was not OK. Blacks sat in one corner of the warehouse, and whites sat on the other side of the loading dock. We were all eating bag lunches, but separately.

I finished college and wanted to turn my Merchant Service experiences into the great American novel. When I accepted that this wasn't going to happen, I contacted a friend of my father's who was a personnel director for a large textile manufacturer. He hired me, and I went in as a manufacturing trainee, then a supervisor. It was the same scenario: the supervisors were white, the workers were mostly black.

On one assignment, I supervised 45 women, black and white. What an experience for a single guy! Some of the women wanted to be my mother, others wanted dates, and I kept getting lectures about not mixing with the people who worked for me. My supervisor said, "Son, keep your pecker in your pants and out of the payroll." That was ironic because two months later he was fired for not following his own advice. It was very unusual that a man would be fired for that; the practice was so common.

Eventually, I got bored. The company wouldn't move me; so I quit, went back to North Carolina, and got a job as a personnel manager for a small manufacturing company. Of course I was a personnel manager in name only because I had no clue to what that job required. Once again, I was hired because I was white, I was male, I was young, and I fit the company image.

What struck me in that plant, which manufactured fiberglass boats, was that there was a wall down the middle. One half of the building was air-conditioned and the other half wasn't. The side with no air conditioning was where employees worked with raw fiberglass, which has to be at a high temperature to harden. The other side was where all the parts were assembled to make the boat.

The workers on the air-conditioned side were all white; those who worked with the raw fiberglass on the other side were all black. The explanation was, "Well, blue-eyed white folks can't work with those chemicals because the fiberglass gets under their skin and eats them up." I don't know how they figured that didn't happen to blacks, too. I used to play basketball with some of the African-Americans. There was one guy whose job was to grind the parts down before they went over to the air-conditioned side. He had so much fiberglass embedded in his skin that you could actually smell it when we played basketball, because he'd sweat it out. Who knows what it was doing to him? He worked with a little dust mask, and that was it.

The discrimination in the boat company really hit me the first day I walked in. Racism permeated the whole atmosphere: It was very clear and very open. The supervisors told me point-blank,

"You have to hire a white person for this," or "This job is only for blacks." And of course, all the "whites-only" jobs were in the air-conditioned section, and the "blacks-only" jobs were on the other side. This was around 1975, so this kind of discrimination was illegal, but the EEOC wasn't doing anything about it. I never remember being inspected or receiving comments from any federal agency about our hiring practices. This was a company of about 400 people, so you couldn't say the "under 100 employees" exemption applied.

There was no recourse. Employment was pretty high at the time, so people tended to come in, get fed up, and get a job across the street. But they'd find the same situation there. The jobs open to blacks all offered minimum wages, either in agriculture or manufacturing.

After about a year in that job, I left the business world for a while and worked in a group home. My next business positions were in life insurance, then pharmaceuticals.

I got into pharmaceuticals by accident. A life insurance customer told me about a job he was leaving and suggested I take a look at it. Once again, I knew nothing about the field, but I looked and acted like their idea of a salesperson.

When I came into the pharmaceutical world, it was a white man's business. I vividly remember my first sales meeting. We were all white men, and we were classic salesmen. The manager brought a stripper into the meeting for entertainment. There was alcohol, and there were lots of racist and sexist jokes.

I was a sales rep for about five years in North Carolina, then I was promoted to division manager in Birmingham, Alabama. I hired the first woman in the division, and she had her MBA. Before I hired her, I asked my regional manager what to look for—what were the employment criteria? But there weren't any. Actually, he had them, but he wouldn't have stated what they were. They amounted to hiring another white man, somebody like him or me. When he saw that I was interviewing women, he said, "Be careful!" And when I decided to hire a woman, he really wanted to check her out. At the time, shoulder pads and loose-fitting fashions were in style for women, and he said, "I can't stand women who wear those clothes; I can't tell what they look like!" But I knew this woman had tremendous potential and told him,

"You'll be working for her some day." He laughed—but it's come true. She's gone right up the ladder.

Having even one woman on board in my division made a tremendous difference. The meetings changed immediately. Before, I'd had a terrible time trying to keep the guys on track. They just wanted to tell jokes and break up with uncontrolled good-old-boy laughter. When she came in, they started acting like Southern gentlemen, putting her on the Southern belle pedestal. But they also started paying attention and getting on with business.

In 1984, I transferred from Birmingham to Washington, DC. The first thing I noticed when the people in my division got together was that there were no blacks. Here we were in a largely African-American city, and we didn't have one black sales rep. I asked the regional manager about it, but he didn't understand the problem.

So I thought I'd try to find a way to recruit a black salesperson, although I hadn't a clue how to do it. I went to a job fair at Howard University. I was the only white recruiter there, and all I had was a little table with my calling cards. The big companies had black couples in fancy booths with elaborate displays and information. I thought I would be doing the black community a big favor,

---

Discrimination Hits Home

Another of my windows into gender issues is the experience of my wife, Lesley. Lesley is an outstanding athlete who grew up in the 1950s and 60s, when girls received no coaching and had to use equipment that was no longer considered adequate for boys' sports. Her family never understood her ability or potential. But I am convinced that given a chance, she would have been a "world class" athlete. Throughout her career as an athletic director, coach, and referee, she has struggled against gender discrimination. The impact of her work far surpasses my own, yet she has not even begun to reap economic rewards commensurate with her talents.

waltzing in and saying, "Hey, come work for us." But it turned out not to be easy at all.

When I talked to other white managers and asked if they made an effort to recruit in the black community they'd just say, "Oh, they don't answer ads; there aren't any qualified people there anyway; they can't speak well; they don't understand this technical language."

It was clear to me that those were just excuses. Then I got an idea. I was out with a sales rep near Howard, and we were calling on a black physician. I thought he was very receptive, so I asked if I could come back and see him again. He was puzzled. I said, "Look, I have an opening for a sales rep, and I figured that you as a physician would know better than anyone else what kind of person you'd want to call on you. Maybe you even know someone." Of course, he could read between the lines and understood immediately what I was asking, but he didn't say anything. I gave him an application and an envelope addressed to me and told him, "If you know someone, give it to him or her."

So I started making contacts and developing networks. I contacted black physicians and received referrals to other people in the black community. I would call and introduce myself, invite them to lunch, and explain what I was trying to do. One time I was talking to a man who was a recreation supervisor and a lay preacher. He got so excited that he said he'd announce it in church on Sunday. I said, "Wait a minute, we've got criteria here!" I could imagine 300 phone calls from his congregation.

I shared my approach to recruiting black professionals with my regional manager and other white managers, but they really weren't interested.

Eventually, I hired a black woman in Washington. I think if I asked her now, she'd say it wasn't such a wonderful experience. She was the only black woman in the division and in the training school. There was no support, no one for her to relate to. When I was promoted, my successor had no interest in seeing her succeed. She eventually left the company.

When I was promoted to manager of training, I brought two women into the department, including the MBA from Birmingham. We had a really great team. We took that department from "executive day care"—a place to put white guys who had retired on the job—to a place where everybody wanted to be. We had a good time, too. But then there was management restructuring along with a merger, and everything we did went right down the tubes.

PUTTING IT ALL TOGETHER

All those different experiences over the years gave me some insights and led me to try to do a few things in a different way. But it wasn't until I came to Biotech in 1989 that I started making sense of what I had learned. At Biotech, we have been working on creating a corporate culture that is really inclusive—not "politically correct" or just trying to dodge EEO lawsuits. Some of the leaders of this organization believe we will be more effective and more productive if we get rid of discrimination, and they have committed substantial resources to this effort.

As I reflect on my own experience and what I have seen happen to other white men who get serious about this work, I see that we go through some fairly predictable stages.

First, we have to recognize that we have been lying to ourselves and each other about our experiences and what we know. I remember a workshop where we drew pictures of our memories of our first racial experience. I started drawing our housekeeper in North Carolina—and I suddenly realized that my rosy picture of her as "part of the family" was baloney. She worked for us. She was African-American and we were white. We fit into one stratum in American society, and she fit into another. There was no way there was any equality between us.

After that, I started seeing, hearing, and feeling racism and sexism everywhere. I became self-righteous. I began to call people on these issues all the time. I completely lost my sense of humor.

Naturally, other people—particularly white men—reacted negatively to the new me. I probably isolated myself by being too outspoken, by not choosing my battles carefully, and by not trying to understand where the other guy was coming from. But I really rejected the white male culture; I almost began to identify with blacks and black culture.

One day, after an intense workshop session in which black people shared their fear, I had a very strange experience. I was riding my bicycle behind the hotel on a dirt path. There was no one around. Suddenly I had an overwhelming sense of fear—a terror that I'd never before experienced. I'd wandered all over the world, down dangerous streets in San Francisco and along a road in Singapore where the death rate was phenomenally high— yet I'd never been afraid. But all of a sudden, I had this bone-chilling anxiety and I couldn't get out of that place fast enough. It was as though I had actually *experienced* the fear of my black colleagues from the stories they were telling. That experience made me withdraw from whites even more.

At some point, the isolation and loneliness turned to anger. This is a dangerous stage, because militancy only pushes people further away. If it had not been for the help of an African-American woman who was a member of the consultant team, I might not have gotten past that anger; then I would have become ineffective in this work.

The next phase is aligning. I recognized that I needed support—I needed allies. The consultants who were working with us could help, but they were here for awhile and then went away. Yet I needed to deal with these problems every day at Biotech. Finally I found another white man who was also beginning to see what I was seeing. We started a relationship that developed, cautiously, into a real, honest friendship. He welcomed what I had to say and wanted to hear it. I pushed on him a lot, he would push back, and I'd push on him some more. He didn't get angry. Through this friendship, I realized that the few of us who are working on diversity issues have to try harder to support each other. We can only be effective if we join forces with other white men.

WHAT'S NEXT?

There are days when I just don't want to do this stuff. And I certainly recognize that I have that privilege. I don't *have* to deal with diversity issues. I can always assimilate, blend in, become just one of the guys again. Sometimes I wonder why I don't go somewhere else; I could join another corporation and be a director in some department where they're so far behind what we're doing here that it would be 20 years before anybody even *says* the word "diversity." But I know that if I did that, about two days after I got there I'd be saying, "Hey, do we have a budget? Can we do something about all this discrimination around here?"

Our president made a wonderful speech to our sales managers in January. He said he believed one major reason for the phenomenal achievements we had in 1992 was our culture-change process. I think he really believes that. What's the connection? It's hard to evaluate empirically, but I think it's there. And I know he believes it's there.

It's tremendously hard to keep the momentum going. We've gone through peaks and valleys. We've raised some awareness, we've worked on some skills. We've developed some good ideas and some energy. But right now I think we're in a slump. The primary resistance is in middle management—white middle management. After all, these changes could affect jobs at this level a lot more than at the level of vice president or board member.

We certainly don't have 100 percent buy-in at any level. We have islands of commitment. I think in some places the islands are coming together to make little continents. But it's so slow.

But there are signs of hope. On Martin Luther King Day, I discussed racial issues with a diverse group of high school students. They responded with insight and passion, and I realized the struggle is about their future. That's why this work is important, not because of sales or competitive advantage or global competition. We have to keep at it for our young people—those kids with the glowing ember of hope in their eyes. Hope, I believe, is the "renewable stage" in this work.

CHAPTER

The Limits of 'Cultural Enlightenment'

Jean Kim

Multiculturalism is very popular these days. I wouldn't call it a fad, but it's definitely the "in" thing. Many practitioners are approaching it from the perspective of "cultural enlightenment," assuming that if we understand each other's culture better, we'll get along with each other better and create a harmonious, multicultural environment.

Cultural understanding does play an important role in some situations. People need to have accurate information so that they can understand the reactions and realities of people who are different from them. For example, European-Americans who are going to work in Korea need to understand the Korean language, the food, the customs, the holidays, and so forth so that they can interact effectively with Koreans. However, learning about another culture in order to live or work in another country is quite different from creating a multicultural society in this country.

Cultural enlightenment alone is an insufficient base for creating a truly multicultural environment that values people *because* of the differences they bring, rather than *in spite* of them. This is because cultural understanding alone does nothing to change the equation of power. Who's in charge? How is power used? Who are the losers in the social/political power game? In addition to cultural understanding, people need to understand how racism, sexism, heterosexism, ageism, and all the other "isms" are maintained in our society and what role each person plays in protecting the status quo. Unless we are willing to look at these hard and uncomfortable issues, multicultural programs become yet another detour on our road to establishing equitable organizations.

COMING TO AMERICA

I began to experience racial prejudice and oppression when I came to Springfield, Massachusetts, from Seoul, Korea, at the age of 12. I was sent for by my mother, who is Korean, and my stepfather, an American who had served in the U.S. Army in Korea. I spent my first weeks here crying and praying and fantasizing about going back to Korea. I didn't speak any English, I had no friends, and the only person I could communicate with was my mother.

By the end of that year, I had learned to speak English. I could read. I had made some friends. But I also realized that being Korean in this country meant that I was "less than" European-Americans. I suffered the ridicule and racist taunting that anyone who is not European-American in this culture receives. African-Americans are taunted primarily around their skin color; for Asians, it's centered more on physical features, such as the shape of the eyes or nose. For some reason it seems that many Asian-Americans, including me, are near-sighted—and that became another target of ridicule. I was so sensitive about it that I wouldn't wear glasses, so most of those years went by in a blur.

Since I knew I was here to stay, my survival depended on my becoming fully assimilated and acting more American than Americans. In this attempt to be acceptable, I denied who I was. I gradually lost the ability to speak my own language. I went through a major life-detour from the time I arrived here until I was about 23.

In graduate school, I began to figure out what all this meant. With the help of a strong support network and knowledge of how racism and sexism operate, I was able to develop a positive identity as an Asian-American and regain my self-confidence.

As part of my comprehensive exam for the counseling psychology degree, I wrote an autobiographical analysis of my experience dealing with racism, explaining what it had done to me, and the psychological price I paid. That led me to explore what other Asian-Americans may experience: living with a negative self-concept, denying their racial identity, and eventually regaining positive self-esteem. For my doctoral dissertation, I researched how Japanese-American women perceive their struggle to achieve positive identities in America.

THE MANY FACES OF RACISM

All of that research and hours of conversations with other Asian-Americans—mostly women but some men as well—helped to reaffirm my own racial identity and gave me insights into the subtleties of racism and oppression that affect Asian-Americans. All Asian-Americans share the experience of racial discrimination, regardless of our diverse ethnic and generational backgrounds. The ties that bind us together are those of pain and suffering.

However, the ways we respond to racism seem to vary. For one thing, the experiences of Asians who are born in America or who came here as children are very different from the experiences of Asians who came to this country as adults. It is easier for folks like me, who experienced racism during their formative years, to internalize the racist messages. We get steeped in the American ideas of the superiority of one race over another, and of men over women.

Asians who come to America after they have established themselves in their home country have better defenses against these racist messages. They are less apt to *internalize* the racist attitudes and to go through a painful period of denial, as I did. They tend to be more assertive, more vocal, and more successful in business. Of course, this applies more often to Asian men than to Asian women. Asian-American women, like other women of color, experience the double bind: first racism, and then sexism.

We also should not overlook the fact that those who come here from Asia, whether as children or adults, bring with them antiblack racist attitudes from their exposure in their own countries to American culture in movies, television, the print media, and so forth. The fact that Asian-Americans experience discrimination and racism does not automatically enlighten them to the oppression experiences of other minorities. Asian-Americans need to come to terms with their own prejudices and ignorance about other racial groups.

In the corporate world, the lessons of racism and sexism produce stereotyped expectations. Common stereotypes of Asian-Americans include the idea that we are inarticulate, submissive, quiet, nonassertive, hardworking, technical but not very creative, and lacking leadership or management potential. Asian-Americans are *not* stereotyped as lazy or stupid—a view too often held of African-Americans or Latinos. These stereotypes help explain why Asian-Americans have had greater access to professional opportunities in corporate America than have African-Americans or Latinos. Another reason there is easier access to professional work for Asian-Americans is that as a group we have the highest level of education of any racial group in this country.

Stereotypes have many negative consequences. For example, when I am assertive, my actions are often perceived as being aggressive because many people have stereotypical expectations of the Asian-American female as being quiet and submissive. So when I behave outside their expectations, my actions are amplified in their minds. There are also new labels. An Asian-American woman who doesn't fit the "passive" stereotype is subject to a new stereotype: she may be called a "Dragon Queen" or some other derogatory term.

DIVIDE AND CONQUER

In spite of all the stereotypes about us, and the reality of our experiences in this country, some Asian-Americans believe there is no racism in the United States. Because many Asian-Americans have been successful academically, professionally, or in business, there is a tendency for some to feel that if other people of color are less successful, it's their own fault. Sometimes it is difficult for Asian-Americans even to think of themselves as "people of color" since that means identifying with people who are looked down on in mainstream American culture.

For Asians who have come here as adults, it is under-
standable that they do not want to be identified with those who
are the objects of scorn in this culture. For those who came as
children or were born in this country, this reluctance to identify
with other people of color derives mainly from their internal-
ization of the racism they have experienced and the subsequent
denial of their own racial identity. When people are in the midst
of denial and are internalizing oppression, they spend most of
their energy trying to avoid acknowledging their feelings about
racist slurs that come their way. So there is little energy left to
defend or sympathize with other people who may be in the
same boat. The fear is that the more you associate with others
in the despised groups, the more pain you will bring on yourself. It is only when people begin to emerge from the denial
phase and begin to understand how racism works that they can
identify with others in the same situation. Asian-Americans must
come to terms with their own feelings about being discriminated against, and their own racial prejudices, before they can
see that they have much in common with other "people of color"
in this society.

Of course, there are also some good historical reasons for
the way various groups of Asian-Americans have adapted. Japan-
ese-Americans who went through the experience of internment
in World War II later opted to be as invisible and as American as
possible. They are more likely to distance themselves from other
Asian ethnic groups. Another historical factor is that Asian-Americans are used as pawns in the power games of racism. We are
often held up as model minorities to keep other minorities in line.
One outcome of this has been to place Asian-Americans at odds
with other people of color who question the legitimacy of our
minority status.

DIVERSITY AND THE ASIAN-AMERICAN

Corporations that are serious about addressing these complicated
issues of race, gender, ethnicity, and national origin have to be
willing to work slowly and carefully with these issues. As a consultant to organizations, my preference is to begin by working
with racially homogeneous groups. It is important to deal with

intraracial group issues before we can productively explore interracial group issues and then organizational issues.

For example, in one corporation, I am helping a group of
Asian-Americans look at the differences among them in terms of
ethnicity, generation, gender, and socioeconomic class. This group
includes Americans of Korean, Japanese, Filipino, Southeast Asian,
and Asian-Indian backgrounds. The cultural differences from one
group to another are as great as those found among European-
Americans. Filipinos, for example, have a very different cultural
background and relationship to the United States than do the
Vietnamese, Cambodians, and other Southeast Asians.

We are also exploring the norms governing male–female
relationships in each Asian group. There is no question that
Asian culture in general is very sexist—more sexist than U.S.
culture—but the manifestation of this is slightly different from
culture to culture.

Our work also tries to understand racial identity and racism
awareness. We plan to examine how these racial learnings impact
the ability to interact with other racial groups, such as African-
Americans and European-Americans. Simultaneously, we will be
developing strategies to change organizational policies and practices that negatively impact Asian-Americans in the corporation
as well as other people of color.

THE AMERICAN PARADOX

The interesting thing about America is that equality is part of the
credo, even though the reality is far from it. At some level though,
we really do believe that equality is our national goal. The most
racist or sexist Americans may still say they believe in equality,
albeit conditionally. It is part of our heritage; without it, there's
no possibility of a moral imperative.

On the other hand, very few American corporations tackle
multiculturalism or diversity for moral reasons. Often they get
involved because they see the business reasons for trying to make
diversity work, but these values of fairness and equality are somewhere underneath their efforts.

In Asian countries that ideal of equality among races and
genders does not exist. And that fact probably contributes to the

unwillingness of the first-generation Asian-American immigrants to see racism and sexism as problems.

An American corporation that is committed to the values of fairness and equality, and that wants to maximize its diverse workforce, must make it clear that people will not succeed if they act out their racist or sexist attitudes—whatever their cultural background. If you tell an Asian-American man that the right thing to do in his organization is to treat women as equals, he's going to try as hard as he can to do that. He may not believe that women are equal to men, but he may have a strong respect for a visible authority. One cultural value will outweigh another.

My perception is that African-Americans and white women have a much stronger sense of entitlement than Asian-Americans. Like Americans in general, they have bought into the American ideal of equality. Once they bring the realities of racism and sexism into conscious thought—as opposed to just being angry or depressed without knowing why—they tend to be more demanding and say, "We deserve an equal deal, and we deserve to get it without being hassled." Asian-Americans as a group need to be reassured that it's acceptable to demand their rights.

Approaching the development of a diverse workforce based on these concepts of cultural enlightenment and awareness of oppression requires a lot of time, a lot of training and a lot of money. Too often, a corporation will prefer the cultural-enlightenment-only route, because it is a short-term effort and less conflict-oriented. But it won't do the job. Getting the job done requires training, reinforcing the training with follow-up activities, creating networks, changing policies and practices—in short, a total organizational change/development process. It demands more time, but in the long run it is more cost-effective to take the slow route. The "quick fix" version of cultural-enlightenment-only may start out with a bang; but unless the support is there for the ongoing, structural changes, the investment may prove to be money down the drain.

CHAPTER

Heterosexism as a Workforce Diversity Issue

Mark Kaplan and Jay Lucas

At the Senate hearings on the issue of gays in the military, Senator Sam Nunn offered the following compromise: "We won't ask any questions, and you don't give any answers." In other words, we won't ask if you are gay or lesbian, and we don't want you to tell us, either. This "compromise" would require gays and lesbians to stay in the closet or risk losing their jobs.

For gays and lesbians, this has been the tacit agreement that has long governed their relationships with their employers. This agreement is finally beginning to crumble. The issue of sexual orientation is edging out of the closet and onto America's agenda.

A total of eight states encompass sexual orientation in their laws against discrimination. Further, according to a 1991 *Fortune* magazine study, major American corporations such as AT&T, Digital, Lotus, and MCA are including sexual orientation in meaningful and significant ways in their workforce diversity programs. These corporations are beginning to support the existence of gay and lesbian employee networks, and a few even offer benefits to the same-sex domestic partners of their employees.

Most heterosexual people know very few openly gay and lesbian individuals. The image of gays and lesbians is stereotyped.

Those who fit the stereotype are assumed to be gay or lesbian, and those who don't are assumed to be heterosexual. Most people are simply unaware that there are many gay and lesbian people around them on a daily basis, both outside and inside the workplace. Many probably agree with the Sam Nunn compromise and assume that the invisibility of gay and lesbian people is evidence that this arrangement is working just fine.

Our personal experiences and our experiences working in corporate America lead us to the conclusion that the compromise is not working at all well. No one benefits when people are forced to live a lie—neither the individuals who must hide their true identity nor the corporation that forces this deception on them.

HETEROSEXISM AND OTHER "ISMS"

Racism and sexism have been acknowledged as negative facts of life for a long time now in our society. Heterosexism and homophobia, however, have much more recently begun to emerge as serious social issues.

There are important similarities, but also important differences, between discrimination based on race, gender, and sexual orientation. Like all other forms of prejudice and discrimination, heterosexism creates attitudes, policies, and practices that lead to limiting the full participation of individuals and groups of individuals in our workforce and our society at large. Gays and lesbians who wish to be honest and open about their sexual orientation face the same kinds of jeopardy—to employment, to career advancement, to acceptance, and even to personal safety—that people of color and white women experience.

However, men and women of color, and white women, are generally visible and identifiable. Because race and gender are usually obvious physical characteristics, women and people of color are *forced* to confront the impact of personal identity in the workplace. They face predictable and consistent types of barriers—barriers that have been, historically and currently, raised to limit the progress of those who share race or gender characteristics. Gays and lesbians who are people of color face the barriers of race and gender, of course. But they, and gay white men who are open about their orientation, also face a different set of challenges.

Unlike most people of color and white women, gays and lesbians are not automatically identifiable. A gay man or lesbian woman usually has the option of choosing whether to stay in the closet or to be open about his or her sexual orientation. Because the majority of gays and lesbians tend to hide their sexual orientation at work, there is often little evidence of discrimination based on sexual orientation. Many nongay people believe that gays and lesbians are not oppressed in organizational settings. And few nongay people understand why gays and lesbians would feel compelled to disclose their sexual orientation and why the closet is an oppressive place to be.

This article explores why that disclosure is important, how and why sexual orientation is a workplace issue, the ways homophobia and heterosexism impact workplace performance, and some ways that organizations can address these issues.

WHY GAY, LESBIAN AND BISEXUAL PEOPLE STAY CLOSETED

The essence of the Nunn compromise is that heterosexuals are not prepared to deal with the reality of homosexuality. Apparently, those who buy into the compromise accept the view that most Americans are homophobic—that is, that they have an unreasoning and unreasonable fear of homosexuals and homosexuality.

This fear plays itself out in the corporate world and in other aspects of society as heterosexism. In our work as consultants to organizations on these issues, we hear many stories of blatant harassment and discrimination, as well as accounts of the pervasive practice of telling antigay jokes. Lesbian and gay leaders of employee networks regularly receive harassing phone calls and notes. One openly gay employee in a Fortune 50 company received death threats so regularly that company security officers advised him not to stay at work past 5:00 PM.

Even co-workers who do not display or condone such practices are often uncomfortable in the presence of openly gay or lesbian people. Most managers prefer to avoid the issue altogether. Therefore, the burden lies with the gay or lesbian person, for whom coming out of the closet would be viewed as taking a militant stance. The message from the heterosexual world is, "What we don't know won't hurt us."

NEGATIVE IMPACTS

At the *individual level*, the necessity of keeping one's sexual orientation hidden creates a high degree of stress. The gay man, lesbian, or bisexual employee lives on the edge—never knowing whether disclosure of her or his sexual identity may lead to harassment, discrimination, mere discomfort, or possibly even support. His or her future is subject to the biases of various individuals within the workplace; thus gays or lesbians must continually "test the winds" and must always be on guard.

At the *group level*, the issue is how well the homosexual person is allowed to fit into the group. A person who must hide some of the most important aspects of her or his personal life must maintain some distance from other members of the group or team. On the other hand, the gay, lesbian, or bisexual person who chooses to share his or her sexual orientation must depend on other team members to be supportive. This is risky for everyone, gay and straight alike, because heterosexuals who choose to confront homophobia and heterosexism in the work setting may also be ostracized.

The group level is critical because it is at this level that job assignments and promotions are often determined. The ability of employees to form comfortable and productive working relationships within the group often powerfully affects their career prospects.

It is, however, at the *system level* that discrimination against homosexuals in the workplace is most thorough and most evident. Most organizations assume all employees are heterosexual, whether they are married or single. The policies and practices of the organization are based on that premise. Due to this assumption, gay and lesbian people receive mixed messages:

- "We need your full commitment and energy in our competitive environment. Please bring all you've got to offer to this organization *(but please leave out the information about your personal life!)*"
- "We value and respect the fact that employees have a life outside of work. We want to include the important people in your life in our office parties and picnics; we encourage you to socialize with each other outside of work and to place pictures of the

significant people in your life on your desk *(but not if those significant people are same-sex partners!)"*

- "Effective teamwork is important here; we recognize that it is built on good relationships and mutual trust *(but please keep* **your** *personal life out of the workplace)."*

- "We value diversity and recognize that each individual should have the opportunity to be in a supportive environment *(but that diversity does not include homosexuality)."*

- "Work and family issues are at the forefront of our human resources strategy; therefore, we provide medical benefits, parental leave, bereavement leave, and so forth *(but only for heterosexual families)."*

COPING STRATEGIES

While there are no hard statistics on how many gays and lesbians live in our society, the *Fortune* article points out that recent surveys support Alfred Kinsey's 1948 studies, which suggested the figure is about 10 percent. The article also advises that we forget the stereotypes as to where they work: More are employed in science and engineering than in social services; 40 percent more in finance and insurance than in entertainment and the arts; and 10 times as many in computers as in fashion.

So the fact that there are gay and lesbian people in all our corporations—whether closeted or not—is inescapable. And since being open about one's sexual orientation has not been a career option until very recently, it is also clear that some 10 percent of employees have had to find ways of coping with their situation.

In our work in major corporations, as well as from our personal experiences, we have collected numerous examples of the ways gay and lesbian people cope. One man told us he was resigned to spending his life in the closet. Even though he had excellent skills and had been recognized as having high potential for career success, he felt he had no other choice. A lesbian in a midsized company found the dilemma so stressful that she was pondering leaving the organization and starting her own business—just as she was being considered for a position in senior management. A third person told us with great sadness of having to continue to go to work and pretend everything was okay—when in fact his life partner was dying.

Recent research we have conducted with James Wood indicates there is a continuum of strategies that people use to cope with the dilemma:

■ **Choice One—"The Closet."** A *hiding* strategy. The metaphor of the closet is apt. A closet is a dark, stuffy, stifling, cramped, and windowless space. Closeted employees operate in a climate of secrecy that is continually stuffy and stifling. They feel *forced* to pretend to have a heterosexual lifestyle: to bring other-sex dates to company social events, to lie about their weekend activities, to disclose nothing about the joys and sorrows of their lives with their partners, to keep their family photos off the desk. Staying in the closet requires lying for self-protection. This pressure causes psychological stress and drains energy that could be used more productively.

People who choose this option tend to organize their lives within the boundaries of two circles—their life in the world of work and their life outside of work. The two circles barely overlap. The constant fear that one will impinge on the other keeps the individual in a state of uneasiness and tension.

■ **Choice Two—"Avoidance."** Unlike those who are trying to "act straight," people who take the avoidance route tend to cultivate an aloof demeanor at work and steer clear of any personal discussion that might lead to questions of sexual orientation. Avoiders may become vague and distant, isolating themselves from close relationships with co-workers—including mentors or team members—because becoming too closely involved might mean discovery. They tend to stay away from those settings where informal conversation and sharing naturally occur, in order to reduce the possibility of discovery.

■ **Choice Three—"Coming out."** Coming out can be risky. The gay, lesbian, or bisexual employee who is faced with this choice always knows of incidents where choosing to reveal a homosexual orientation has cost a friend or acquaintance a job, a promotion, a career. Gay or lesbian employees know that choosing to disclose their sexual orientation may destroy whatever recognition they have earned through hard work, competence, loyalty to the firm, or support of fellow employees. If they choose to simply present the facts of their lives—by placing photos of loved ones on the desk or by talking freely about vacation plans or hobbies or about their relationship with a life partner—they put their future in jeopardy. Thus, it is an act of courage to come out.

Despite the risks, however, coming out can be very rewarding. Many gays and lesbians who come out at work report feeling "freed up" from the burden of editing out so much information about themselves in the workplace. They report experiencing less stress, an increase in support from co-workers, and improved relationships. Our own research with approximately 400 gay or lesbian employees showed that the top two reasons for coming out at work are "to feel more honest" and "to stop misleading co-workers." For many, the rewards outweigh the risks.

However, the risks are ever-present. Thus, it is little wonder that most gay and lesbian employees choose to remain invisible. The choice of invisibility, however, adds to the problem. The fact that so few lesbians and gays identify their sexual orientation promotes the myth that they are few in number. So the heterosexual world proceeds on false premises.

RECOGNIZING MYTHS

For the sake of individual gays and lesbians—and for the organization as a whole—it is important to attack the myths that undergird homophobia and heterosexism. As in any other form of discrimination, the "problem" is with the majority community, not with those who are the targets of discrimination. The challenge is to destroy the myths, to provide opportunities for education about this form of "difference," and to create structures by which the policies and practices that embody the discriminatory attitudes can be dismantled.

There are a number of widely held myths:

■ **Sexual orientation is a behavior based on choice. Therefore, gay and lesbian people should live with the consequences of their choices.**

While the debate about what causes sexual orientation continues, three things are clear. First, no one—lesbian, gay, bisexual, or heterosexual—chooses a sexual orientation. Second, in a workplace setting, everyone—straight or gay—should be expected to maintain an appropriate workplace demeanor. Third, this myth is irrelevant because the real issue is what kinds of attitudes and relationships among employees are most productive for the organization as a whole. Discriminatory attitudes and treatments—whether towards women or people of color or gays and lesbians or older workers or the disabled—are not good for the organization.

■ **Gay and lesbian people should keep their sexual orientation to themselves.**

Buried in this assumption is another assumption: that heterosexuals do not make their sexual orientation obvious. But for the heterosexual community, sexual orientation is an acceptable and even expected part of social interaction. It is demonstrated in discussions about weekend activities, in pictures of family members on the desk, in patterns of socialization with co-workers and life partners, in the distribution of company benefits, and in many other ways. To fail to disclose their sexual and familial relationships would be strange, stressful, and limiting to heterosexuals. It is just as strange, stressful, and limiting for gays and lesbians not to be able to share these important parts of their lives.

■ **If the organization becomes proactive and visible with regard to issues of sexual orientation, we are endorsing this lifestyle. This goes beyond our commitment to diversity.**

Organizations do not need to endorse any set of beliefs. Every individual has a right to his or her belief system. However, individuals do not have the right to translate those beliefs into discriminatory behaviors. No one should be able to translate beliefs into discrimination against people of different sexual orientation any more than one should be able to discriminate against others because of race, gender, or age.

TAKING ACTION

The integration of sexual orientation issues into diversity interventions often proves to be a major challenge. To keep sexual orientation on the table, and to move ahead, requires that the corporation utilize the full repertoire of diversity management processes—and a few more techniques as well.

As in any other arena, the first task is to identify the problem. What do employees know (and what are they willing to say) about the incidence of harassment or discrimination around sexual orientation? What information can be gathered from individual interviews or focus groups of gays and lesbians concerning their comfort level in the organization? What are other employers doing about non-discriminatory policy development, awareness training, and changes in benefits?

Second, discussion of homophobia and heterosexism needs to be carefully integrated into diversity education and awareness workshops. Consultants and trainers must be sensitive to their own biases and prejudices and cognizant of the ways prejudice is built into the systemic practices and policies of the organization. As with other diversity issues, it is crucial that the workshop provide an atmosphere in which both heterosexuals and homosexuals feel comfortable and safe in sharing information and feelings.

Finally, even more than in work on racism, sexism, ageism, and other kinds of "difference," work on homophobia and heterosexism may meet with resistance. The key to handling resistance is to counter it with information on the numbers of gays and lesbians in the organization, on nondiscriminatory policy and state and local laws, and on the bottom-line value of eliminating the bias against and barriers to success of gay and lesbian employees.

But providing information alone cannot overcome resistance. Organizations seriously committed to opening access to all employees—*including gays and lesbians*—must be prepared to deal with emotional responses and a high degree of discomfort. As in approaching other kinds of resistance, it is important to search for common grounds of understanding and feeling.

BENEFITS

Organizations that choose a proactive stance in creating a supportive environment for all employees—including gays, lesbians, and bisexuals—stand to realize substantial benefits. If the percentage of Americans who are gays and lesbians is in reality about 10 percent, those organizations that actively recruit in this community will have access to a presently untapped resource. Further, if the organization can create an environment in which gays, lesbians, and bisexuals are supported, they will gain an additional competitive edge in retention.

Another advantage may be avoidance of litigation. In a case reported in *Business Week*, Shell Oil in Seattle lost a decision involving a charge of discrimination on the basis of sexual orientation. That court said that Shell fired a gay employee, Fred Collins, solely because he is a homosexual, and awarded damages of $5.3 million. At the time of this writing, the case was on appeal.

Including sexual orientation as an important part of a workforce diversity intervention sends a clear signal to all employees that the company is serious about diversity. It reinforces the message that everyone needs to have the opportunity to be successful if the company is going to thrive. Organizations must challenge the assumption of invisibility. They must work to develop strategies and practices that will allow gay, lesbian, and bisexual employees to contribute fully to the corporation.

REFERENCES

"Gay in Corporate America." *Fortune*, December 16, 1991, pp. 28–34.

Jay Lucas. "Integrating Sexual Orientation in Diversity Interventions." *Managing Diversity* 2, no. 8 (May, 1993), pp. 2–5.

"The Shell Oil Case." *Business Week*, August 26, 1991.

James D. Wood with Jay Lucas. *The Corporate Closet: The Professional Lives of Gay Men in America*." NY: Macmillan, 1993.

CHAPTER

White Americans in a Multicultural Society: Rethinking Our Role

Gary R. Howard

Sometime during the first half of the 21st century, a profound transition will take place in the United States: White Americans will lose their status as the numerical majority. In a nation where the term "minority" has traditionally meant people of color, this new reality will require a significant rearranging of our psychic maps, particularly for white Americans.

How does a historically dominant ethnic group adjust to a more modest and balanced role? How do white Americans learn to be positive participants in a richly pluralistic nation? These questions have always been a part of the multicultural agenda; now they are coming more clearly into focus. Most of our work in race relations and workforce diversity in the United States has emphasized the particular cultural experiences and perspectives of black, Asian, Hispanic, and American Indian groups. These, after all, are the people who have been marginalized by the weight of European-American dominance. With the shifting tide of population in the United States, however, there is now a need to take a closer look at the unique and changing role of white Americans.

Part of this need is generated by the growing evidence that the transition out of their dominant position may not be a comfortable one. As our population becomes more diverse, we have seen an alarming increase in acts of overt racism, and the number and size of hate groups in the United States is actually on the rise.

Of equal or perhaps greater concern has been the prolific outpouring of anti-multicultural sentiment from some of the *most* educated and accomplished members of white academic circles, who tread frighteningly close to providing an ivory tower rationale for the hate group activity of their less erudite counterparts on the streets. In addition, many white politicians fan the flames of racial fear and hatred to lure various constituencies into their camps. Too many segments of our white American population remain committed to their position of dominance, willing to defend it and legitimize it even in the face of overwhelming evidence that our world is rapidly changing.

Taken as a whole, these realities strongly suggest that a peaceful transition to a new kind of America, where no ethnic or cultural group is in a dominant position, will require considerable educational change and deep psychological shift for many white Americans. Attempting to effect these changes is part of the challenge that leads us to a central question: What must take place in the minds and hearts of white Americans to convince us that now is the time to begin the journey from dominance to diversity?

It is critical that we white Americans come to terms with our reality and our role. What does it mean for white people to be responsible and aware in a nation where we have been the dominant cultural and political force? What can be our unique contribution, and what are the issues we need to face? How do we help create a nation where all cultures are honored with dignity and the right to thrive and express their full potential? I explore these questions here from the perspective of a white American.

AMERICAN IMMIGRANTS

European Americans share at least one commonality: We all came from somewhere else. In my own family, we loosely trace our roots to England, Holland, France, and perhaps Scotland. However, with five generations separating us from our various "homelands," we have derived little meaning from these tenuous connections to ancestral cultures. This is true for many white Americans, who are often repulsed by the appellation "European American." They simply prefer to be called American and forget the past.

On the other hand, many white Americans have maintained direct and strong ties with their European roots. In the Seattle area, there is an Ethnic Heritage Council comprised of 103 distinct cultural groups, most of them European. These people continue to refer to themselves as Irish American, Croatian American, Italian American, or Russian American—terminology that acknowledges the two sides of their identity.

European Americans are a diverse people. We vary broadly across cultures of origin, and we continue to be diverse in religion, politics, economic status, and lifestyle. We also vary greatly in the degree to which we value the melting pot notion. Many of us are ignorant of our ethnic history precisely because our ancestors worked so hard to dismantle their European identity in favor of what they perceived to be the American ideal.

The farther our immigrant ancestors' cultural identities diverged from the white Anglo Saxon Protestant image of the "real" American, the greater was the pressure for assimilation. Jews, Catholics, Eastern Europeans, Southern Europeans, and minority religious sects all felt the intense heat of the melting pot. From the moment they arrived on American soil, they received a strong message: Forget the home language, make sure your children don't learn to speak it, and change your name to sound more American.

In dealing with the history and culture of European Americans, it is important to acknowledge the pain, suffering, and loss often associated with their immigrant experiences. For many, it was a difficult struggle to carve out a niche in the American political and economic landscape while preserving some sense of their own ethnic identity. Some white American workers resist the diversity movement today precisely because they feel their own history of suffering from prejudice and discrimination has not been adequately addressed.

FAMILY REALITIES

Like many white Americans, I trace my roots in this country back to the land, the Minnesota farm my mother's great-grandparents began working in the 1880s. My uncles and aunts still farm this land, and I spent many summers with them. On this land and with these people, I have known my roots—my cultural heritage—much more deeply than in any connection with things European.

I have a close friend and colleague whose traditional Ojibwa tribal lands once encompassed the area now occupied by my family's farm. This farm, which is the core experience of my cultural rootedness in America, is a symbol of defeat, loss, and domination for her people. How do I live with this knowledge that my family's survival and eventual success have been built upon the removal and near extermination of an entire race of people? In this reality is embodied much of the irony of the white American experience.

Some of my relatives hold narrow and prejudicial attitudes about cultural differences. The racist jokes they tell at family gatherings and the ethnic slurs that are part of their daily chatter have been an integral part of my cultural conditioning. It was not until my college years, when I was immersed in a rich multicultural living situation, that these barriers began to break down for me. Most of my relatives have not had that opportunity. They do not understand my work in diversity and multicultural education. The racist jokes diminish in my presence, but the attitudes remain. Yet, I love these people. They are my link with tradition and the past, even though many of their beliefs are diametrically opposed to my own.

My family is not atypical. For most white Americans, racism and prejudice are not theoretical constructs; they are members of the family.

When we open ourselves to the historical perspectives and cultural experiences of other races in America, much of what we discover is incompatible with our image of a free and democratic nation. Our collective security and position of economic and political dominance have been fueled, in large measure, by exploitation of other people. The cultural genocide perpetrated against American Indians, the enslavement of African peoples, the exploitation and discrimination against Mexicans and Asians as sources of cheap labor—on such acts of inhumanity rests much of the success of the European enterprise in America.

THE LUXURY OF IGNORANCE

In the face of our past and present, many white Americans simply choose to remain unaware, a luxury uniquely available to members of any dominant group. If you are black, Indian, Hispanic, or Asian in the United States, daily survival depends on knowledge of white America. You need to know the realities that confront you in the workplace, in dealing with government agencies, in relation to official authorities like the police. To be successful in mainstream institutions, people of color in the United States need to be bicultural, able to function in two worlds, able to play the game according to the rules established by the dominant culture. For most white Americans, on the other hand, there is only one game, and they have traditionally been on the winning team.

The privilege that comes with being a member of the dominant group, however, is invisible to most white Americans. Social research has repeatedly demonstrated that if an African-American friend and I walk into the same bank on the same day and apply for a loan with the same officer, I will be more likely to receive my money—and with less hassle, less scrutiny, and less delay.

Likewise, if I am turned down for a house purchase, I don't have to wonder whether it was because of the color of my skin. And if I am offered a new job or promotion, I don't worry that my fellow workers may feel I'm there not because of my qualifications but merely to fill an affirmative action quota.

Such privileged treatment is so much a part of the fabric of our daily existence that it functions outside the conscious awareness of most white Americans. From the luxury of ignorance are born the Simi Valley neighborhoods of our nation, which remain painfully out of touch with the actual experiences and sensibilities of multicultural America.

EMOTIONS THAT KILL

At some level, however, we are aware of our past and the fact that our prejudicial attitudes are out of synch with our belief in equality and justice. This is the basis for the cognitive dissonance we experience. When we are asked to participate in programs confronting these attitudes, we resist. We wrap our uncertainties in protective layers of denial, hostility, fear, and guilt.

Denial

The most prevalent strategy that white Americans employ to deal with the grim realities of our history is denial. "The past didn't happen. All the talk about workplace diversity and different cultural perspectives is merely ethnic cheerleading. My people made it, and so can yours. It's an even playing field and everybody has the same opportunities, so let's get on with the game and quit complaining. We've heard enough of your 'victim's history'."

Hostility

Another response is hostility. The Aryan Nations organizing in Idaho, the murder of a black man by skinheads in Portland, Oregon, the killing of a Jewish talk show host by neo-Nazis in Denver, cross burnings and Klan marches in Dubuque, and the increase of racist slurs and incidents on college campuses all point to a revival of hate crimes and overt racism in the United States. We can conjecture why this is occurring now: the economic downturn, fear of job competition, the rollback on civil rights initiatives by recent administrations, or increasing diversity that is seen as a threat by some whites. Whatever the reason, hostility about racial and cultural differences has always been a part of American life and was only once again brought into bold relief by the first Rodney King decision and its violent aftermath in Los Angeles.

Fear

Underlying both the denial and the hostility is a deep fear of diversity. This is obvious in the violence and activism of white supremacist groups. Because of their own personal and economic insecurity, they seek to destroy that which is not like them.

The same fear is dressed in more sophisticated fashion by many of those who continually resist attempts to bring multicultural awareness and equity to the workplace. The uncertainties of the current business climate, from the shop floor to the board room, exacerbate underlying feelings of resentment of the new workers. People who have faced competition only from others "like them" now must compete with people they neither understand nor respect. So they attempt to characterize diversity work as "political correctness" and claim "favoritism" and "reverse racism" when a new worker receives a promotion or a position.

They try to defend a cultural turf that was never really theirs. The United States was never a white European Christian nation, and this fact is becoming more evident in our places of work every day.

Denial, hostility, and fear are literally emotions that kill. Our country—indeed, the world—has suffered endless violence and bloodshed over issues of racial, cultural, and religious differences. And the killing is not only physical but emotional and psychological as well. These negative responses to diversity threaten to destroy the precious foundation of our national unity, which is a commitment to equality, freedom, and justice for all people.

Ironically, these negative responses to diversity are destructive not only for those who are the targets of hate but also for the perpetrators. Racism is ultimately a self-destructive and counter-evolutionary strategy. The positive adaptation to change requires a rich pool of diversity and potential in the population. In denying access to the full range of human variety and possibility, racism drains the essential vitality from everyone, victimizing our businesses, our communities, and our entire society.

Guilt

Another emotion that kills is guilt, a major hurdle for well-intentioned white Americans. As we become aware of the heavy weight of oppression and racism that continues to pull our nation apart, it is natural for many of us to feel a collective sense of complicity, shame, or guilt. On the rational level, we can say we didn't contribute to the pain; we weren't there. Yet, on the emotional level, there is a sense that we *were* involved, somehow. Through our membership in the dominant culture, we remain connected to that painful history, continuing to reap the benefits of past oppression.

There can be a positive side to guilt, of course. It can be a spur to action, a motivation to contribute, a kick in the collective conscience. But ultimately, guilt, too, drains the life blood of our people. If we are finally to become one nation of many cultures, we need to find a path out of the debilitating cycle of blame and guilt that has occupied so much of our national attention.

RESPONSES THAT HEAL

It is possible to move on. We have the opportunity to overcome the dissonance that characterizes our national consciousness and create a new kind of national unity. It is still possible to redefine the meaning of "America" by helping people learn how to bridge the chasms of ethnic, racial, and gender differences and create new ways of honoring ourselves and one another. Moving on in this way for white Americans requires honesty, humility, respect, and co-responsibility.

Honesty

Facing reality is the beginning of liberation. As white Americans, we can face with honesty the fact that we benefit from racism. We must support historical research providing a more inclusive and multidimensional view of our nation's past—even when that view confronts us with the woeful immoralities of our forebears. American business needs to be visible in its support of the work of scholars and educators who are searching for the literature, the experiences, the contributions, and the historical perspectives that have been ignored in our Eurocentric schooling. The children of today who are to be our workforce of the future must be prepared to recognize the worth and validity of one another's traditions.

Humility

The future belongs to those who are able to work with and walk beside people of many different perspectives, cultures, and lifestyles. A healthy dose of humility can help white Americans overcome the Eurocentric limitations of our past. Part of the unfortunate legacy of our European dominance is the lingering assumption that this perspective is better than others. But where diversity is a bottom-line issue, corporate leaders are recognizing that this single-perspective thinking prevents employees from dealing effectively with change.

Respect

One of the greatest contributions white Americans can make to cultural understanding is simply to learn the power of respect. In the Spanish language, the term *respeto* has a connotation going far beyond mere tolerance or even acceptance. *Respeto* acknowledges the full humanness of other people, their right to be who they are, and their right to be well treated. When white Americans learn to approach people of different cultures with this kind of deep respect, it enables us to see ourselves more clearly as well. Understanding the strengths and weaknesses of others, we have a measure of our own—and we can build on our mutual strengths to create more productive, stronger organizations as well as a safer and saner society.

Co-responsibility

The race issue for white Americans is ultimately a question of action: What are we going to do? It is not a black problem or an Indian problem or an Asian problem or an Hispanic problem— or even a white problem.

The reality of cultural diversity in the United States is an inclusive human issue, a struggle and an opportunity we are all in together. No one group alone can solve the problems we face. We have become embroiled in these issues together over the 500 years of our history, and if we are to survive and thrive as a nation we will have to solve them together.

THE SEARCH FOR AUTHENTIC IDENTITY

When white people become aware of the realities of our history, it sometimes becomes difficult for us to feel good about ourselves. Where do we turn to find positive images?

In the 1960s and 1970s, while blacks, American Indians, Hispanics, and Asians were experiencing an explosion of racial and cultural awareness and energy, what were white youth doing? There was a revolution happening with them as well—a revolution of rejection. While the civil rights movement, the antiwar movement, and the women's liberation movement were bringing to public attention the fundamental flaws of white, male-dominant culture, the youth of white America were searching for an alternative identity.

White America was at war with itself. The children of affluence and privilege, the very ones who had benefited most from membership in the dominant culture, were attacking the foundation of their own privilege. In creating a counterculture of rebellion and hope, they borrowed heavily from black, Indian, Hispanic, and Asian traditions. Their clothing, ornamentation, hairstyles, spiritual explorations, jargon, values, and music became an eclectic composite culture—a symbolic identification with the oppressed. In their rejection of the dominant culture, they sought to become like those whom the dominant culture had historically rejected.

When the truth of our collective history is brought home to us, we turn to other traditions for a new place to be.

But there is another alternative for a legitimate white identity. It is not necessary for us to look for culture in other peoples' traditions because we can find a rich source of identity in our own. This became clear to me when, during a study tour in 1990–91, I was immersed in experiences with Navajo, Hopi, Maori, Aboriginal, Balinese, and Nepalese people. I gained much from exposure to these cultures, but the most powerful personal experiences came in the place I least expected them—my own ancestral Europe.

In a prehistoric cave in the Basque country of northern Spain, I discovered 21 hand prints created by ancient Europeans that were in the exact style of prints in the caves of the Anasazi and the Australian Aboriginal peoples. In this experience, I recognized that I had not only found a connection to my own people's ancient culture but a connection to the universality of all human experience as well.

In touring ancient sacred sites in England and Scotland, this sense of rootedness and connection was deepened. The culture of my Celtic ancestors had been overwhelmed by the twofold aggression of the Roman Christian church and the Roman imperial army; thus, much of their history is lost to us today. Stone circles, such as Stonehenge, testify to the power of that cultural history and its sacred connection to both earth and sky.

My experience in Europe taught me that white Americans do not need to look to other cultures for our own sense of identity. The history of oppression and expansionism perpetrated by European nations is only part of our past—a reality, but not our only heritage as white Americans. We have a rich and diverse history just waiting to be discovered. And when we push back far enough in our cultural history we come to a place of common connection, where people of all races are brothers and sisters on the same planet.

In this recognition, both of our uniqueness as European Americans and our universality as human beings, we can begin to make an authentic contribution to the healing of our nation.

WHO ARE MY PEOPLE?

It is time for a redefinition of white America. As our percentage of the population declines, our commitment to the future must change. It is neither possible nor desirable to continue to be in positions of dominance. We need not continue to identify only with that strand of our history that is a legacy of oppression. White Americans can be full participants in the building of a multicultural nation.

In the America of the 21st century, white Americans will still have a major role to play in the leadership of our businesses. Rather than continuing to be isolated in our role of dominance, we now have an exciting opportunity to join with Americans of all cultures in creating a nation that actually embodies its own ideals. At the deepest level, we are all one people—and this could be our vision.

Adapted by the author from his article, "Whites in Multicultural Education: Re-
thinking Our Role," which appeared in *The Phi Delta Kappan* (September, 1993).
With permission of *The Phi Delta Kappan*.

PART THREE

SKILLS FOR
MANAGING DIVERSITY

None of us is really prepared for the long-term commitments of time, money, and energy that are required to change the culture of an organization. While it is a cliché, it is nonetheless true that the fish has no awareness of the water it swims in—nor do we easily become conscious of the patterns of interaction that make up the fabric of our social and professional lives.

Learning about those patterns requires a different methodology than learning about financial structures or marketing strategies or purchasing new products. To understand how to talk to people across racial, gender, ability, and other differences, we must *practice* new ways of communicating. Reading about communication or watching videos showing how other people are solving communication problems doesn't help us understand where our particular blind spots are or to more clearly see how we can improve our effectiveness.

"Learning from Experience" is an introduction to the concepts of experiential learning and their application to the field of diversity management. Jack Gant carefully outlines the six stages of a managing diversity intervention and describes the central role that experiential learning must play.

Becoming aware of one's blind spots can be unsettling. In "Diversity Shock," Sylvia Liu describes her first exposure to diversity concepts in an education and awareness workshop. A veterinarian who grew up in China, Liu discovered that she held negative attitudes towards African-American coworkers. She also realized that many white Americans hold similarly negative attitudes toward people of her race and gender.

Another challenge in developing diversity programs is knowing exactly where the problems reside in a given organization. Joseph Potts describes how to use a diversity assessment survey to pinpoint specific issues and provides a technique for comparing the data from one organization with information on the same issues collected in similar organizations. Thus armed, leadership can develop strategic plans for a culture-change program aimed at the self-identified concerns of the particular organization.

The progress of culture change is never steady. The final two essays in this section provide specific and practical suggestions for dealing with particularly difficult issues. Mark Chesler addresses the mind-boggling complexity of the dynamics of race in America by drawing on his own personal experience—as a white man in a white-male–dominated organization. Chesler's down-to-earth ideas are useful for individuals as well as for organizations that want to change negative patterns.

Finally, Michael Burkart presents a unique notion: White men have special skills and competencies that can be capitalized on in a diversity program. While some "managing diversity" programs take a "blaming" approach—attacking individual white men for the *structural* realities of the way power is balanced in our society—Burkart sensibly shows that, as individuals, white men have not chosen to be members of the dominant group—white men—any more than women or people of color have chosen to be members of groups that have been assigned subordinate roles. Once the distinction between the fact of group membership is separated from the ability of the individual to make particular choices of behavior patterns and attitudes, it is easy to take the next step—enabling white men to draw on their knowledge of power and power structures to *change* the organization for the better.

CHAPTER

Learning from Experience:

A Cycle of Growth and Empowerment

Jack Gant

As corporations, businesses, and public sector organizations in the United States are facing the challenges of a more diverse workforce, a variety of approaches is emerging. Some organizations provide conferences, seminars, or workshops; others have embarked on large-scale efforts to change the culture of the corporation.

This discussion of an intervention model describes a large-scale culture-change effort and is presented primarily to assist managers and consultants/trainers who are responsible for the success of such efforts. My focus is on race and gender because these are so pervasive in our society. I do not intend, however, to minimize the importance of class, social status, ethnicity, anti-semitism, homophobia, or other arenas of discrimination. It is my experience that the concerns and strategies that relate to issues of race and gender apply to other forms of discrimination as well.

My comments are drawn from my work as a facilitator in culture-change interventions in the corporate world and my experience in multiracial workshops and desegregation efforts, especially in education. I have observed that successful, large-scale intervention efforts proceed through six definable and predictable stages and that each stage produces particular emotional responses in both participants and facilitators.

The six stages of the intervention cycle, as I see them, are as follows:

1. Confrontation.
2. Dialogue.
3. Experiential learning.
4. Challenge, support, and coaching.
5. Action-taking.
6. Organization and culture change.

Progress through the stages is not continuous; in practice, there are many regressions. Also, the cycle may have to be repeated as different issues are addressed. For example, the initial problem might arise from sexist attitudes and practices.

Intervention Stages and Emotional Responses

Stages	Victim	Oppressor	Facilitator/ Manager
Confrontation	Accused Frustrated Helpless Reverse discrimination	Accused	Frustrated Helpless
Dialogue	Angry Guilty Sympathetic	Angry(no self- blame) Guilty Sympathetic	Depressed Discouraged Anger (at oppressor)
Experiential learning	Empathic Frustrated	Empathic Frustrated	Exhilarated Angry Frustrated
Challenge and coaching; support	Positive anxiety	Positive anxiety	Positive anxiety
Action-taking	Joy/Empowerment Anger/Frustration	Joy	Joy/Empowerment
Organization and culture change	Advocacy Self-worth	Advocacy Self-worth	Advocacy

Somewhere along the way, it may become clear that racism or homophobia or ageism is also a major factor in limiting the effective development of all employees. So the intervention may have to begin again, at the confrontation stage, and move through the various phases to work on the newly defined issue.

Before discussing the stages in detail, it is important to address the qualifications and makeup of the consultant team, and the composition of the groups that receive the training.

QUALIFICATIONS OF THE CONSULTING TEAM

The makeup of the team of consultants, or facilitators, for the managing diversity intervention is of utmost importance. When participants must work only with consultants who are different from them in race or in gender, they carry into the process the baggage of previous experiences with difference. On the other hand, when consultants share racial and/or gender identities with participants, a dynamic develops that fosters more openness and trust. Further, the presence of a consultant who is traditionally a member of a "victim" class challenges members of the "oppressor" group to learn new behaviors. For example, a black woman in the power role of consultant raises interesting and sometimes difficult issues in the process of interaction with a high-level, white, male executive who has never related to either black people or women as equals. This dynamic, when monitored and guided by an expert leader, can model a whole new set of behaviors for the entire group. One effective arrangement for consulting teams is to work in groups of four: a man and woman of color and a white woman and man.

Understanding deep-rooted attitudes and feelings about race and gender requires work at the emotional as well as the cognitive level. Therefore, the consultants/facilitators must have excellent skills in managing group dynamics and creating a safe though challenging atmosphere in which the work can go forward successfully. In addition, the competent facilitator of diversity management work must have a strong commitment to understanding her or his own emotional and intellectual reactions to racism, sexism, and other forms of discrimination and must have had considerable experience in helping others deal with these sensitive issues.

WORKSHOP PARTICIPANTS

The people who participate in the workshops must also be carefully selected to achieve a good balance by gender and race. When working at the top levels of the organization, it is nearly always necessary to "import" people of color and white women, since white men predominate at those levels. As the work is "cascaded" downwards, it is important to maintain adequate representation of both sexes and all racial groups.

FINDING A LANGUAGE

The question of appropriate language must be addressed at the very beginning. The reality is that some groups of people in our society receive more benefits and experience less discrimination than others. This pattern is not accidental, nor is it simply "the way things are." The fact that some kinds of people are more advantaged and some are more disadvantaged is an outcome of deliberate actions taken over a distinct period of history— actions that were incorporated into our legal, governmental, social, and economic structures. These actions and their results in public policy "oppress" and victimize some people; those who benefit from them are, consequently, part of groups that do the oppressing— therefore, "oppressors."

These are not words that any of us like. No one wants to be seen as a victim any more than others want to be seen as oppressors. But the words reflect the facts.

It is crucial, however, that we make a clear distinction between being a member of a group—"oppressors," "oppressed," "victims"—and being, individually, an oppressor or a victim. It's kind of a good news/bad news situation: The good news is that if I don't go around oppressing people I don't have to regard myself as an oppressor. The bad news is that if the group I belong to acts in such a way as to oppress other people, I can't escape being part of the problem. This is a difficult concept to deal with; we have to learn by experience both what this means and how to cope with it.

CONFRONTATION

The confrontation stage is the initial awareness-raising stage. Raising awareness requires that issues of diversity in the organization be identified and examined at the individual, group, organizational, and societal levels. It also requires that ideas, feelings, behaviors, and core values be examined at each of these levels. The intensity of the responses to confrontation differs according to individual or group awareness of diversity issues.

The usual sequence of learning begins with doubt and denial, moves through guilt and shame and maybe anger, and (ideally) ends up in understanding and action. Initially, many people in the organization will complain of "feeling accused" when confronted with ideas such as these:

- Racism and sexism are oppression.
- "Oppressors" are white men and men of color, where sexism is concerned.
- "Oppressors" are white men and white women, where racism is concerned.
- "Victims" are those who are discriminated against: white women and men and women of color, generally; but also white men, who are often the "victims" of hierarchical discrimination in organizations.
- The term *people of color* is preferable to "minority group."
- The terms *diversity* and *integration* are more appropriate than *assimilation*.
- Diversity is to be valued and celebrated.
- Racism and sexism are learned attitudes and behaviors and can be changed in organizations.
- American organizations need to use all of their human talents to remain competitive.
- Support of the ideal of diversity is central to American democracy.

The power of each particular concept relates directly to its "newness" to the hearer or to its emotional content. The more powerful the concept, the more intense the response of feeling accused. People may feel exceedingly uneasy with terms like *oppressors* or *people of color.* Some white participants, particularly white men, may feel they are being unfairly singled out by many of the terms, especially the term *oppressor* and sometimes the term *person of color.*

An organization in the very beginning stages of addressing its problems in the management of diversity may respond to such reactions by proposing a new policy advocating the use of gender-free language or implementing a strong policy against sexual harassment. Those who are feeling accused may react in very negative ways to these efforts. They may withdraw, become silent, exhibit defensive behavior, or even claim that they have become victims of reverse discrimination.

These reactions form a pattern of denial, an unwillingness (or even, at first, an inability) to admit the reality of what is being explored. The initial task of the work is to help people recognize— and to acknowledge that they recognize—the actual ongoing existence of prejudice and racism (or sexism or other "isms"). Once that recognition is there, it is important to move beyond blame, beyond guilt, beyond confrontation, to the second stage: dialogue.

DIALOGUE

To move beyond confrontation to dialogue requires strategies that allow members of all groups and races and both genders to be together in a setting that provides an atmosphere of safety and allows trust to build. This is the function of the initial education and awareness workshops.

The very first task of an education and awareness workshop is for the group to agree upon its own norms for the work. It is imperative for people to feel both *safe* and *challenged*. Throughout the balance of the time together, the group itself—not the facilitators—must monitor the norms and make sure that the atmosphere of safety and challenge is protected.

The tasks of learning how to participate in dialogue and interaction with people of the opposite sex, other races, or other "differences" groups are often easier to master when the activity is a simulation rather than direct involvement in discussions of real life issues. It is essential, however, that in the discussion following the simulation, the participants speak from their own group identities—that is, as white men, black women, gay people, or whatever. The dialogue must culminate in interaction about real issues, real problems, real experiences in real life.

Simulations arouse powerful responses. Depending on the intensity of the interaction and dialogue, members may demonstrate a "fight" or "flight" reaction. Some people long to run away; others become angry and vigorously confront the facilitators or other participants they experience as hostile or unfair. And some participants will express sympathy, sadness, or guilt.

Each of these reactions is to be expected; they represent particular kinds of past experience and background.

The *sympathizers* are often the following:

- "Victims" who collude with "oppressors." For example, a white woman may support a white man, even when the issue is clearly sexism or sexual harassment. This kind of collusion may derive from a desire to gain membership in the dominant group, to gain favor with the majority, or from a sincere desire to help the oppressor change his or her attitudes or behavior.
- "Oppressors" who identify with the plight of the "victims" but do not know how to help or are unwilling to try to change the situation.
- "Oppressors" who may be completely unaware of their own roles and who try to insulate themselves from blame by expressing concern for the "victims."

In each of these cases, though for different reasons, oppressors and victims have some genuine feeling for each other. Each recognizes that the other has some value; yet, in the workplace, they take no action to change the level or nature of the oppression.

The *angry* responders may be identified as follows:

- "Victims" for whom this particular experience, or the memory of a previous experience, is unpleasant or even painful. The anger in this case is often directed inwardly or at other "victims" who are perceived as being in collusion with "oppressors."

- "Oppressors" who identify with the victims and express anger at the evidences of discrimination that have surfaced. These participants are usually already sensitive to the issues and may be anxious or impatient about the slow rate of change. Many are also angry with themselves and other members of their group for their past lack of awareness and oppressive behavior.

- "Oppressors" who feel they are being "dumped on" by the facilitators or other participants. They reject being seen as a representative member of a group. They resent what they experience as blame for transgressions of other whites or other men—transgressions for which they do not feel at all responsible. Those "oppressors" who are not able to overcome these emotional blocks may report after the workshop is over that the effort is mostly "white-bashing" or "male-bashing." Anger, both inner-directed and outer-directed, emanates from past experience. Confronting the reality of racism and sexism creates an uncomfortable situation in which it is easy for people to strike out indiscriminately and generate even more anger. Some participants cannot handle this level of emotion and may retreat from participation even if they don't actually leave the room. Therefore, it is crucial that skilled facilitators enable the participants to experience and own their anger, and at the same time create an atmosphere that limits the intensity of interaction to a level that the group can tolerate and learn from.

People whose response is *guilt* may be difficult to identify by their overt actions. While some may be open about this reaction, others may be defensive. Some may be identified as follows:

- "Victims" who feel guilt because they have "played the game" of the oppressor. While their motivations for collusion have often been a positive desire to succeed in the workplace or in social settings, they nonetheless may feel ashamed of the behavior.

- "Oppressors" who identify with the plight of the victims and feel a sense of guilt because they nonetheless enjoy their position of entitlement. They may openly acknowledge their awareness of the conditions of discrimination, but they will rationalize why these conditions exist. They do not confront other oppressors. Their identification with victims usually ends at expressions of sympathy and understanding.
- "Oppressors" who openly acknowledge that they benefit from discriminatory attitudes and practices and express their shame and disgust at this history.

Guilt is a subtle phenomenon. It can be immobilizing or energizing. The group's commitment to specific norms and the agreed-upon goal to maintain a climate of safety and challenge make the difference between a negative or positive outcome.

Emotional reactions to issues of racism, sexism, or other forms of discrimination should be viewed as evidence of progress rather than as stagnation or hopelessness. During the dialogue stage, all three types of responses may be present at the same time. Those experiencing sympathy, anger, or guilt may engage in dialogue with each other over the same issue. The facilitator's role is to recognize the disparate emotional responses and help participants confront both the issues and the emotions.

But it is counterproductive to allow these initial reactions to set the tone for subsequent efforts. It is important to avoid an atmosphere of guilt, blame, and judgment. The facilitator must enable the group to acknowledge that racism, sexism, and other forms of discrimination exist and hurt many people in our society—then move beyond that recognition to the next phases of the intervention.

EXPERIENTIAL LEARNING INTERVENTION

Once the participants in the education and awareness workshops have confronted the issues and there has been some interaction and exploration of reactions, it is necessary to find new ways of thinking and acting. Experiential learning interventions are critical in this process.

The basic premise of experiential learning is that we do not come to our attitudes about difference cognitively. While it is true that "we have to be carefully taught" to hate or fear, this instruction is not presented in a formal way. We learn about differences by watching our parents, reading the newspaper, seeing how our teachers treat different children in class, and through a myriad other experiences that reinforce the idea that some people are better than others. Whether those who participate in managing diversity efforts are in the "better than" or "less than" group, they have received the same message. The fact that the message is not true does not mean that it does not *feel* true. Since the feeling is at odds with logic, we cannot approach it only by logical, didactic means. We must find ways to get to the deep-seated feelings themselves.

Experiential learning relies on a whole range of activities that allow the participants to bring their feelings into the realm of consciousness, examine them, and then decide whether to retain the beliefs, attitudes, and behaviors that derive from those feelings. In addition to the use of simulations referred to earlier, the experiential learning-based workshop uses role-plays, structured experiences, various kinds of interactive exercises such as "fish bowls," journal writing and reflection, audio-visual aids, and the like.

Activities are chosen to meet the needs of each group in the context of the organizational climate. It is important to recognize that during simulations and especially in the discussions that follow, participants are talking about real-life, real-world issues. Racism and sexism, racist and sexist incidents, harassment and discrimination—these are not abstract concepts but part of our daily life, at work and in the larger world.

To begin to sort out these learnings, participants must examine how they learned the behaviors that are characteristic of "victims" or "oppressors." Further, they must learn how much of this learned behavior is rooted in their culture and how powerful that culture is in shaping individual, group, and organization behavior. It then becomes clear that changing behavior at one level requires change in all three, for they are inextricably linked.

Experiential interventions also help members of the group to understand their anger, shed their guilt, empathize with their forebears (whether "oppressors" or "victims"), and realize without blaming that the subtle messages we received early on are still with us. Participants can then begin to see that they have a choice as to how they will behave in the future. They may choose to persist in the roles programmed for them by their family traditions, media, the culture, or the organization. Or they may develop their own personal beliefs and behaviors about the value of diversity.

Those who are able to move successfully through the education and awareness workshop experience emerge with a feeling of *true empathy,* for oppressor and victim alike; coupled with a feeling of *frustration* because they do not yet know how to be different. Through this experiential learning process, participants begin to ask, How can we overcome the racist and sexist (and other forms of discriminatory behavior) patterns, taught by the culture and the society?

Interventions designed to help individuals answer this question may be aimed either at the group or at the individual. The activities may lead participants to reflect on past experiences, or they may encourage examination of present issues in the organization. They may serve as a call to action, to examine the here-and-now behavior of a work group. Participants at this point are encouraged to provide feedback to each other in the spirit of consciousness-raising and support.

As the process moves forward to address "real-time" issues and problems, some participants who had previously remained withdrawn and passive may become angry or guilty. Others, on the other hand, will be eager to move on to positive action. Because of the differences in the backgrounds, emotions, and reactions of the participants, it is often necessary for the various stages of the process to be addressed simultaneously. That is, one participant may still be dealing with the need for confrontation or for developing skills in dialogue, while others have resolved these issues successfully (at least temporarily) and are ready to apply their new learning to specific situations in the work setting.

Another phenomenon that arises is that the problem focus may shift as the work progresses. For example, early needs assessment in the organization may have indicated that the primary issue was racism. The experiential activities of the education and awareness workshops thus are designed to address racial difference. If successful, these activities may lead to group maturity and affection, as the members learn to speak honestly with one another about their different experiences as members of diverse racial groups.

Inevitably, though, questions will arise about sexism and other forms of discrimination in the workplace as well. The gender issue, however, is a *new* challenge for the group. Now the men, who may have been supportive of women around racial issues, may revert to the confrontation stage. As the women attempt to share their feelings and address the men's behavior around gender issues (the dialogue stage), the men may withdraw or express guilt, anger, or sympathy—almost as though they hadn't worked through the same emotional reactions in the previous work on racism.

The facilitator's challenge here is to keep up positive, forward movement, and avoid getting stuck (perhaps for a second time) at the dialogue stage. The more regression to the open dialogue stage, the slower the pace of the work. The previous experience, however, will equip participants to deal with the challenge of new issues more efficiently and enable them to move on to the next stage.

CHALLENGE, SUPPORT, AND COACHING

Confrontation, dialogue, and experiential learning all have the goal of raising the awareness of issues of racism, sexism, and other forms of discrimination in the workplace and in society. In the education and awareness workshops, participants learn through simulations and through sharing of real experiences how the "isms" permeate our lives in corporations and in the larger world.

Developing awareness is not, however, a guarantee that anything will change in individual lives or in the corporate culture. Organizations that invest in one-shot lectures, panels, or conferences or even commit themselves to putting the majority of the workforce "through" education and awareness workshops but are not prepared to continue with the tedious, time-consuming, and often frustrating work of translating awareness into action are apt to find they have wasted valuable time and money.

Awareness must result in action. The first step in the action process is the development of systems that reinforce the benefits

of the education and awareness workshops and create new structures of liaison and relationships throughout the organization.

Members of the organization who are concerned about diversity issues must be helped to examine options that are available
to them. "Oppressors" and "victims" must learn how to become
effective members of working teams, drawing on the learnings
of the education and awareness workshop experience to practice
new patterns of behavior. These new team members will feel awk-
ward and tentative at first, and will make mistakes—just as all
of us do as we try out and perfect new skills. The new teams
must learn how to share, how to give and receive feedback effectively, how to communicate across race and gender barriers, how
to confront as well as how to support one another. And they must
learn how to use their power to begin to create the new culture
they are beginning to envision.

Interaction in the challenge, support, and coaching stage
occurs at all three levels: the individual, the group, and the organization. Progress is most evident when all three levels are integrated—when the individual functions as part of a new kind of
group, and the individual and the group recognize their roles
within the total organization. A team-based, cooperative learning
model is most effective at this stage as individuals and groups
form networks and coalitions that are different from the traditional
groupings within the organization. The group members must help
each other learn from each other's experiences.

The emotional response to this stage is the same for participants and for facilitators: a feeling of positive anxiety. There is
some hope, a sense of urgency, a fear of failure at the thought of
attempting to use the new knowledge and test their power. The
"challenge, support, and coaching" stage is the moment before
the big game, the time when all the players wonder, Will it work?
Can we win?

The only way to find out is to take the field, to try—to *take
action.*

ACTION-TAKING STAGE

Initial action is taken by individuals. Each person must recognize
that he or she has discretionary power and can do *something*

to change things, even if the action is seemingly insignificant. Each step is important: The man who refuses to laugh at a sexist joke or confronts those he once joined in this behavior by making the uncomfortable statement, "I no longer like sexist jokes." The woman who gathers her courage to insist that she be recognized in meetings or that her ideas be recognized as hers, not her boss's or a male co-worker's. The person of color who decides that security may not be as important as challenging the organization for the increment or the promotion that is clearly due her. The white person who challenges his or her supervisor to provide adequate feedback to a person of color who is not being helped or expected to meet the organization's performance standards.

If the action-taking is successful, the result is a feeling of joy and empowerment. Risk-takers recognize that they can take control of their own lives, and extricate themselves from the culture-bound expectations of their group—and still maintain, or even enhance, the positive values inherent in membership in that group.

The action-taking is more likely to be successful if the participants get practice and coaching in the awareness and education workshop. Participants act out skits of real-life incidents that occur in the workplace. These skits give participants the opportunity to experience their real-life identity and learn how discretionary power may be used to differentiate oneself from the oppressive behaviors of a particular group identity (such as racism, sexism, or other forms of discrimination).

Observing the skits provides participants with practice in identifying subtle acts of oppression and in generating actions that might be taken to create a more positive and diverse team atmosphere. The goal of this learning process is to help oppressors, victims, and the organization function more effectively. As participants develop new skills in identifying and confronting subtle acts of discrimination, they feel empowered and joyful, and have an increased sense of commitment to the process.

It is critical that support be built into post-workshop activities so that the celebration of successful action-taking may be shared with co-workers who are also growing in their practice of including others, in acknowledging others, in empowering others, and in advocacy.

As action-taking continues, the fear of hurting others' feelings, of alienation, of being ostracized by group members, of losing friends, of not being liked, of not being perfect, disappears. These negative feelings are gradually replaced with positive ones: the sense of being helpful, of functioning as a good team member, of being powerful *with* others, not *over* them, of being interdependent and loyal to a higher purpose of service to the organization and its clients.

At this stage, participants begin to realize that this new way of "becoming" can move out into the broader community of peers, friends, family—the entire cultural arena—and can gradually replace the negative behaviors that were taught in childhood. Once fear is replaced with action, and a critical mass is present in the organization, the sixth stage of culture change has begun and can be openly addressed.

ORGANIZATION AND CULTURE CHANGE

The progress of an organization through the initial five stages brings together a critical mass of empowered participants who are committed to the creation of a culture in which diversity is promoted as a positive value, and the utilization of the talents of all members of the organization is maximized. If this critical mass includes the top management of the organization, and if these leaders are prepared to define the organization's values around diversity and to lay out a clear agenda for change, the prospects for the creation of a new culture within the organization are bright.

If this leadership is present, as members participate in the cultural-change interventions, a feeling of advocacy, self-worth and commitment to the organization develops. The growing numbers of individuals who are aware of the realities of the "isms" in the organization and who have learned and practiced the skills of working effectively with people who are not "like" them are able to confront those co-workers who have not yet accepted the new values. The empowered individuals will support the leadership as it examines the policies, practices, goals, and norms of the organization to weed out habits and patterns that prevent full participation of the entire workforce. Top management will be able to move confidently to initiate changes that will carry the initiative forward.

The concept of the six stages—confrontation; dialogue; experiential learning; challenge, support, and coaching; action-taking; and organization and culture change—may be used either as a guide in planning a culture change program or as a diagnostic tool in assessing where individuals and groups within an organization are in their cycle of growth and empowerment. The manager or facilitator who is committed to creating more equitable work groups and organizations may also use the model to assess her or his personal emotional states and to equip himself or herself to be more effective in the next effort.

CHAPTER

Diversity Shock

Sylvia Liu

It is not "business as usual" when you are an Asian woman manager in an American corporation. I first became aware of this when I attended a "managing diversity" education and awareness workshop.

Two of the white men in upper management positions were having a conversation. One asked the other, "Suppose you had the choice of having either Sylvia or me as your boss; who would you choose?" The second man thought it over and answered, "Sylvia."

We were all shocked. He went on. "I know with 99 percent certainty that Sylvia will have a white boss. I can easily go around her—I can play golf with her boss and disregard her. But if I have a white man as my boss, I don't have a chance."

This incident opened my eyes. I grew up in Taiwan, in a highly educated and open-minded family. I've been on a fast track professionally and have always felt I could do anything I wanted. I have tried to fit into American culture and to learn the business rules and play by them. I have accomplished a lot and have generally accepted the status quo.

As a result of that first managing diversity workshop, I realized that I have been treated differentially, as a woman, all my life. As a child, I was taught that I would have to work twice as hard as a man to be equally recognized; I just accepted that. In my work life since I came to the United States, I have often been cut short when I speak in meetings. I would be in the middle of presenting a study or an experiment when a white man would finish my sentences for me. Before the workshop, I didn't think about it or allow myself to acknowledge my feelings. But after that experience, I began to recognize what was happening.

In that first workshop, I also learned some unpleasant things about my own attitudes. Throughout my career, I thought I had equal respect for good veterinarians, whatever their race. But in the workshop, I recognized that my feelings were different: Overall, as a group, I had treated blacks differently.

That realization shocked me. But as I thought back over my experiences, I recognized that when I was growing up in Taipei, my attitudes about black people were shaped by American cartoons and soap operas we watched on television. I was surrounded by American racist attitudes.

After that workshop, I did a lot of soul-searching. I thought about how racist and sexist attitudes affect all of us, whoever we are and wherever we come from. Since then, I have worked very hard at understanding these attitudes—in the culture and in myself. My perspective and my management approach have changed significantly since then. Effective management of diversity requires this kind of self-education and awareness.

The "awareness" aspect is particularly difficult because it requires us to get in touch with our feelings. Like the men I work with, I was taught to think logically and analytically—not to express my feelings in public. In one of the workshop sessions, a black woman asked the men, "If you don't feel, how can you understand?" Not acknowledging feelings—anger or resentment or excitement— keeps us from developing effective work teams. We may even avoid scientific debates because we are afraid someone will become angry or upset. We lose the benefits of that creativity and energy.

AWARENESS IN ACTION

We have to work on awareness, horizontally across the organization, all the time. But we also have to work vertically (at the system level) in order to move the process both up and down in the corporation.

At Ethicon, we've started several groups for this purpose, both at the corporate and division level. In the research and development division, for example, we have a System Core Leadership Group—an alumni group for people who attended the initial workshop—and a Diversity Action Team, as well as other departmental groups and committees that provide support to the managing diversity process.

Each group has a different function. The **R & D System Core Leadership Group,** for example, plans to assess results through system audits, to establish clear targets and measurement criteria for the diversity process.

The **Diversity Action Team** defines its mission in this way: *to facilitate change in the ETHICON R & D culture to allow all people to thrive, and to nurture our differences in gender, race, and culture.* This team is mixed by race, gender, and level. All of its members must be alumni of the managing diversity education and awareness workshop. The tools of change will include the following:

- Communication, education, initiation of dialogue.
- Data analysis and interpretation.
- Policy and practices.
- Action.
- Celebrating successes.
- Modeling the process.
- Encouraging, supporting, confronting, affirming.

The corporate level **People of Color group** includes people from many backgrounds: African Americans, Asian Americans, people from the Caribbean, Latin America, and more. We learned to look at our own attitudes about race, and how we sometimes collude in the racist attitudes of our society. A "People of Color" workshop—one of the first ever held in the United States—was conducted for Ethicon Associates in April of 1992. At this workshop, we learned to look at our own attitudes about race and gender and how we sometimes collude in negative attitudes of our society.

There are racist and sexist behaviors in many cultures. One Asian Indian told us that when a child is born in his society only two things are valued: that the child be a boy and that it be fair rather than dark. Those of us in the People of Color group realized that we have brought these attitudes with us to the American culture, and they have become entangled with the racist and sexist attitudes here. Managing diversity won't work unless we all examine our own "filters" and try to understand the filters that other people use in their daily lives.

NEW LEADERSHIP STYLES

Another workshop called "Management Skills for Managing Diversity" gave me some additional diagnostic skills and tools to observe and track behaviors. After that workshop, I understood better that managing diversity effectively not only requires changes in personal attitudes and in intergroup interaction, but also in leadership style. It requires an approach to management that is more open, more flexible, more participative. If we take the culture change seriously, we will not merely tolerate or accept differences, we will value them.

Sometimes I hear criticism that management is not really supportive of the managing diversity process. People often expect management to tell them how to "do diversity" just as they have instructed them how to accomplish other business tasks. But none of us has had experience in this kind of leadership. All of us have to take ownership, to learn new patterns, both of managing and being managed.

People still tend to look to the traditional leaders—white men—for guidance; they don't think to look to those who have experience in this area, those who know more about how the new culture should look and feel; that is, white women and people of color.

The top management team indeed does have to be very visible in supporting the new culture, including finding ways to encourage people to look to different people for guidance. For example, we have to learn to observe what happens in meetings: Do people automatically turn first to the white men in the group for direction, even if other people have more experience and more information? We have to monitor the mix of any group, small or large, to be sure we include people of different talents and backgrounds, both genders, and different races.

Day-to-day application of the diversity process requires education, awareness, lots of practice, and consistent support from everybody. And it takes time. I find that I have to take work home at night in order to spend some time every day on diversity. I'm glad to do this because I feel that the effort spent on working on diversity pays off in real benefits to me, my department, and the corporation.

CHANGING POLICIES AND PRACTICES

All the work of changing the culture will not pay off if we keep doing "business as usual." We have to put our ideas to work and change both our policies and our practices. Some of the policy changes at Ethicon are symbolic: taking away the reserved parking spots, for example. But others are central to the way we do business. The most important change is our work and family policy. We realize that we are protecting our investment in hiring and training good people when we honor their family values.

For example, one of my associates was out of work for a long time because of family illness. When she was ready to come back, I had no position for her. But our policy required that we find a place for her, equal to the position she left. With the assistance of the research and development vice president, we found a creative solution: a floating position where she can work until something opens up in her own specialization. I consider this a real implementation of the managing diversity philosophy.

PERSONAL AND PROFESSIONAL BENEFITS

While new efforts such as the work and family policy are quite visible, other changes are more subtle. For example, with my managing diversity experience to draw on, I no longer allow white men to finish my sentences. When someone tries to do this now, I call him on it; or even better, another white man will point out that behavior.

Most important, learning to manage diversity more competently has made me a better manager overall. Of all the professional and management courses I have attended since joining Ethicon, the managing diversity ones have helped me learn the most. They have helped me put myself in other people's situations and better understand where they are coming from. Personally and professionally, I am blessed because now I can choose the best of both Eastern and Western cultures. As I learn more about people of other races and cultures, and their ideas and experiences, I think I will have even more options. This will help me reach my life goal of achieving success and fulfillment in my personal life and in my career—while still just being myself.

CHAPTER

The Diversity Assessment Survey

Joseph Potts

Some years ago, the management committee of a Fortune 500 company was struggling to understand why it had such a poor track record in retaining "minority" employees. The CEO complained in great frustration, "It seems to me that if everybody in this organization treated everyone else with genuine respect, our diversity problems would go away."

The consultants had heard this many times. It *does* seem that people would get along just fine if we all simply followed the Golden Rule and treated each other respectfully.

But as management committees all over the country are learning, it isn't that simple. Even *if* we were all "nice enough" to treat others kindly, our differences wouldn't disappear. The battle of the sexes is not just an old joke, and conflicts across racial and ethnic lines seem to be part of the human condition.

But American business believes that we can no longer afford to let these conflicts contaminate our business environment. Therefore, we must understand why individual change is not enough. We must be able to demonstrate to senior management *where* the problems lie in each organization and to point out what remedies are effective for those particular problems in that particular company.

The diversity assessment survey we have developed is one tool for the task. In this article, I describe the survey in brief and give an overview of some of the comparative findings between two organizations: a major division of a manufacturing organization in the Midwest, which we call "JKLCorp," and a financial services organization on the West Coast, "InvestCo."

THEORIES OF CHANGE

The theoretical underpinnings for the diversity assessment process lie in the field of systems theory, which states that changes at any level of a complex system will impact and be impacted by other levels of the system.[1] As Kate Kirkham has shown, the management of diversity involves at least three levels of system: individual, group, and organization. She further suggests that several types or "layers" of perception—ideas, behaviors, attitudes, beliefs, feelings and values—are required in order to decide what actions are appropriate.[2] Kirkham proposes that to understand the dynamics of race and racism, gender and sexism, or other forms of oppression in organizations, all three levels of system must be analyzed, and all layers of perception must be explored. Kirkham calls the levels of analysis "breadth of awareness" and the layers of perception "depth of insight."

Understanding at one level or even two levels is insufficient. Action taken without understanding all three levels and their interaction is likely to be misguided or inappropriate.

THE THEORY APPLIED TO MEASUREMENT

Most instruments that have been developed to measure diversity have taken a "multicultural approach" and have focused on the individual level of analysis. Since this approach does not acknowledge that the social *system* within which the individuals operate is itself biased and oppressive to those who are different from the norm, it does not assist the organization in identifying the systemic bases of difficulties. The multicultural approach also fails to acknowledge that there *is* a norm that is unstated. As Minow has shown, the unstated norm is actually part of the problem.[3]

A few surveys do look beyond the individual level, but the dimensions chosen for measurement tend to lack coherence and are not theoretically based; therefore, they are difficult for the client organization to interpret and use.[4]

A further limitation is that while many cultural audit or climate surveys include some questions about diversity, few allow analysis by race and gender; thus, the differences tend to get "washed out" in the averaging process. [5]

Focus group data collection has been the best available alternative for obtaining comprehensive information about diversity in an organization. Although the focus group is effective for this purpose, it requires skilled consultants who can conduct effective interviews that get at multiple system levels and many layers of perception. Further, the focus group method does not provide quantitative data; thus, accurate measurement of progress and comparison with other organizations are not possible.

The diversity survey that my colleagues and I have developed and that is the basis for this article enables organizations to examine the multiple levels of both system and perception and provides a basis for quantitative analysis. [6]

ADVANTAGES OF MULTILEVEL ANALYSIS

Analysis based on multilevel assessments provides a concrete basis for the development of appropriate change-oriented actions. The analysis also provides the methodological basis for measurement of progress.

Multilevel analysis helps top management understand that white men—themselves included—do not perceive the organization in the same way that white women and people of color do. The data collected in this way give concreteness and legitimacy to the perception of white women and people of color that race and gender affect interactions and consequently affect how they do their work. The data demonstrate that the unstated norm of being white and male is a legitimate issue to be dealt with—the norm itself is part of the problem to be solved.

The diversity survey also can show how the formal policies and procedures of the organization may provide advantages for white men or disadvantages for people of color and white women. The survey data begins the process of demonstrating how the culture—the informal ways of doing work—is impacted by race and gender identity.

To set the strategic direction for the organization, management must have information that is valid, reliable, and comprehensive. Armed with solid evidence, management may charge a task force—which should be diverse by race and gender—to develop tactics and action plans for management's review and authorization. The task force can also use the data to guide analyses and develop mechanisms to measure progress.

Although the survey we have developed is focused on race and gender, its multilevel analysis can be used for other issues. If the client organization is interested in sexual orientation, age, physical disabilities, or other differences, these can be added to the diversity survey. As few or as many levels and layers can be analyzed as desired or needed by the organization.

THE DIVERSITY SURVEY

For this article, I have chosen to discuss some of the findings of two of the organizations in which the instrument has been used, "JKLCorp" and "InvestCo." The number of respondents was more than 1,200 and more than 500, respectively. No group used in any of the comparisons had fewer than 40 people. The survey itself was tested for validity and reliability using various standard techniques.[7]

THE DIMENSIONS

The dimensions measured in the diversity survey are based on the theory outlined above. The individual, group, and organization levels are probed. Behaviors are distinguished from the more deeply held attitudes, beliefs, feelings, and values.

The behavior of supervisors and the attitudes of different levels of management are key elements in organization dynamics. These positions have historically been filled by white men. This is, however, no longer always the case. The survey provides analysis of the behavior and attitudes of people in these positions, whatever their race or gender. To gain a comprehensive understanding of organization dynamics the survey probes the organization's culture and the attitudes about managing diversity.

The diversity survey measures these dimensions:

1. **Individual behaviors.** Measures the individuals' involvement and satisfaction with their work.

2. **Individual beliefs, attitudes, feelings.** Measures beliefs, feelings, and attitudes that individuals have about the influence of race and gender on themselves and others.

3. **Supervisory behaviors.** Measures how known supervisors are perceived to deal with tough interpersonal issues and their behavior toward different race and gender groups.

4. **Management attitudes.** Measures the perception of change required by different levels of management to obtain the full utilization of all employees.

5. **Group behaviors.** Measures the perception of how membership in a race/gender identity group influences treatment in the organization.

6. **Group beliefs, attitudes, values.** Measures the attitudes and beliefs about the influence of race and gender on acceptance within the work environment.

7. **Organization behavior.** Measures the perception of the impact of organizational policies and procedures on race/gender identity groups.

8. **Managing diversity.** Measures the perceptions about the importance of and the commitment to managing diversity in the organization.

9. **Organization culture.** Measures the climate and norms of the organization regarding race and gender differences and the ability to talk openly about them.

THE RESULTS

Although each evaluated organization has shown a unique profile, some patterns have emerged. The two cases included in this article were chosen because they represent two different sectors of business and two different geographic areas.

All of the statistical comparisons discussed here are between white men and the other race/gender identity groups. Our earlier work showed us that white men generally are the largest group, the group the organizational norms were developed for, and the group that has the most positive view of the organization.[8] This leads to the conclusion that when organizations are able to create a climate that is as accepting of all race/gender identity groups as it currently is of white men, the problems related to race and gender will be resolved. There will still, no doubt, be management problems—but they will presumably affect all groups equally.

In this overview article, I discuss the findings on eight of the nine dimensions. One dimension, individual beliefs, did not show significant differences among the groups.

Individual Behavior

One of the questions we asked along this dimension dealt with perceptions of opportunities for advancement. When the answers were compared for the four groups (white men, white women, men of color, and women of color) there were notable differences between JKLCorp and InvestCo (see Figure 13–1 on page 150).

In JKLCorp, nearly one-third of *all* respondents were skeptical of their opportunities for advancement. In InvestCo, on the other hand, more than twice as many women (both white and women of color) felt they lacked opportunity than did the men (both white and of color).

This finding shows that both organizations have serious problems, but the nature of the problems is different. JKLCorp must review its promotion policies and practices *overall*. This action is especially important to this organization because it is a culture in which "hard work is rewarded" and managers are developed from within. If such a large number of people feel they have little chance to advance, the company may be squandering its investment in them.

At InvestCo, the problem resides in gender dynamics. Since only about 10 percent of the men feel they have few opportunities for advancement, and more than twice that many women, InvestCo must ferret out how it is providing such a discouraging atmosphere for its women employees. This finding is of serious concern because an increasing number of college recruits in financial management and financial services are women.

Supervisory Behaviors

Since supervisory behavior is a crucial element in the management of diversity, the survey explored 12 different items on this

FIGURE 13–1

Percentage Disagreeing That They Have Opportunities for Advancement

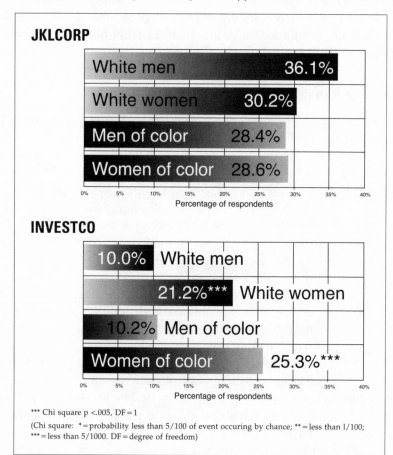

JKLCORP
- White men — 36.1%
- White women — 30.2%
- Men of color — 28.4%
- Women of color — 28.6%

Percentage of respondents

INVESTCO
- White men — 10.0%
- White women — 21.2%***
- Men of color — 10.2%
- Women of color — 25.3%***

Percentage of respondents

*** Chi square p <.005, DF = 1

(Chi square: * = probability less than 5/100 of event occuring by chance; ** = less than 1/100; *** = less than 5/1000. DF = degree of freedom)

dimension. While there were significant statistical differences on many items, two items—the practice of mentoring and the supervisors' encouragement of equality of treatment for all races— provided especially useful data (see Figures 13–2 and 13–3).

At JKLCorp, for example, responses to the questions about whether mentoring is available indicated that fully one-fourth of the white men and over one-half of the women of color feel that it is not. This dramatic finding plainly shows that JKLCorp must pay close attention to the need for *general* supervisory training in the area of mentoring and the need for *special* attention to the race and gender components of this training. InvestCo showed no differences among the race/gender identity groups, with all showing a 7 percent to 15 percent level of disagreement.

When participants at the two organizations were asked if their supervisors encouraged equality of treatment for all races, there were strong similarities in responses from one company to the other. In both, for example, most white men felt that supervisors did encourage such equality of treatment, while a significant percentage of men and women of color disagreed. The perceptions of white women at JKLCorp, however, were similar

F I G U R E 13–2

Percentage Disagreeing that Mentoring is Practiced in JKLCorp

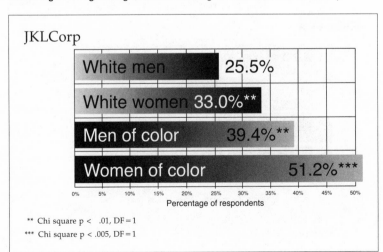

JKLCorp

White men — 25.5%
White women — 33.0%**
Men of color — 39.4%**
Women of color — 51.2%***

Percentage of respondents

** Chi square p < .01, DF = 1
*** Chi square p < .005, DF = 1

to those of white men; whereas, at InvestCo the white women tended to share the perceptions of the people of color.

The findings, when combined with similar data for gender, show that both organizations need to incorporate race and gender dynamics into their supervisory training programs. In addition, they should look at their reward system for supervisors and develop expectations for performance that include specific measures of equal treatment.

FIGURE 13–3

Percentage Disagreeing that Supervisors Encourage Equality of Treatment for All Races

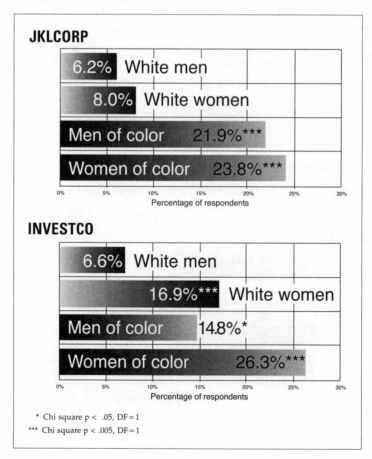

* Chi square p < .05, DF = 1
*** Chi square p < .005, DF = 1

Management Attitudes

A major factor in how well a diverse workforce functions is the attitude of senior management. When we asked how much change in senior management attitudes would be necessary to create a productive work environment for all employees, more than 25 percent of all respondents in both organizations responded that "much" to "enormous" change would be required (see Figure 13–4).

F I G U R E 13–4

Percentage Perceiving That Large Change in Attitudes of Senior Management Is Needed for Full Utilization of Employee Abilities

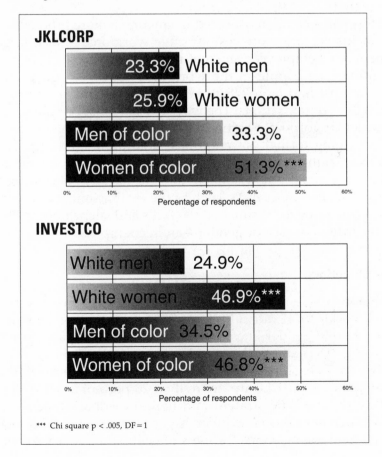

JKLCORP

23.3%	White men
25.9%	White women
Men of color	33.3%
Women of color	51.3%***

Percentage of respondents

INVESTCO

White men	24.9%
White women	46.9%***
Men of color	34.5%
Women of color	46.8%***

Percentage of respondents

*** Chi square p < .005, DF = 1

The breakdown of the answers by race and gender indicates that the "more than 25 percent" *average* does not accurately reflect the real situation. At JKLCorp, race seems to be a more important factor than gender. A far greater number of people of color (33 percent of men of color and *over 50 percent* of women of color) see a need for change in the attitudes of senior management. White women share the views of white men, but the fact that 25 percent of *all* whites perceive the need for change in senior management attitudes is notable.

At InvestCo, gender seems to be the more important factor. While the "baseline" of 25 percent of white men perceiving a need for change remains constant, at InvestCo almost 50 percent of *all* women have negative views of the attitudes of top management.

How can a company succeed in creating a more productive, more inclusive, and more cost-effective workforce if such large numbers of its employees feel that management must change to fully utilize the people in the workforce? Both JKL Corp and InvestCo must find more effective ways to present that commitment to their organizations. The ways chosen must be tailored to the particular corporate culture but might include senior management doing formal presentations, holding open group discussions, making presentations to community groups, writing articles for company newsletters, and the like. They must also sponsor *systems-level changes,* such as the establishment of diversity task forces, which assure that the skills and talents of employees—regardless of race or gender—are recognized.

Group Behaviors

A common problem in achieving successful relationships in a diverse workforce is difficulty in giving and receiving feedback across race and gender lines. Therefore, we queried participants concerning the feedback they receive (see Figure 13–5).

The answers showed that there are different patterns in the two companies. At JKLCorp, more than 20 percent of *white men* feel they receive little straight and honest feedback, and even more women have this view (over 40 percent of women of color). Since an item asking about "fairness of evaluation by managers"

F I G U R E 13–5

Percentage Perceiving They Get Little Straight and Honest Feedback

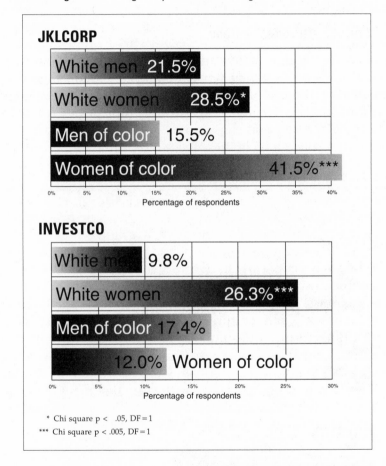

does not show similar race or gender dynamics, it is likely that the women's perceptions are influenced by the lack of feedback from peers and associates.

To address this problem, specific training may be required to enable men and women to feel more comfortable in their interactions with each other as peers and in soliciting and giving feedback across gender differences as colleagues.

At InvestCo, white women constitute the largest group that feels it does not receive adequate feedback; this does not seem to be true for women of color. More information—probably through focus groups—is required before a specific action plan is developed.

Group Beliefs, Attitudes, Values

Sexual harassment is a continuing fact of life in organizations, with estimates of the numbers of women being harassed ranging up to 50 percent.[9] Therefore, we asked respondents if they believed that sexual harassment was a significant problem in their organization (see Figure 13–6).

FIGURE 13–6

Percentage Agreeing That Sexual Harassment Is a Significant Problem

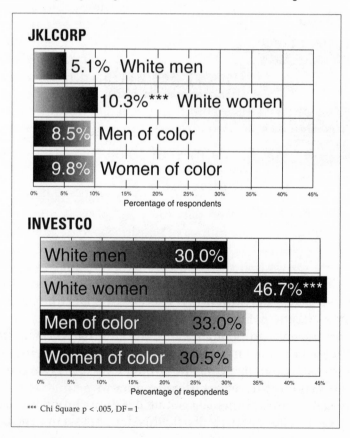

JKLCORP

5.1%	White men
10.3%***	White women
8.5%	Men of color
9.8%	Women of color

Percentage of respondents

INVESTCO

White men	30.0%
White women	46.7%***
Men of color	33.0%
Women of color	30.5%

Percentage of respondents

*** Chi Square p < .005, DF=1

In this analysis, in both JKLCorp and InvestCo, fewer white men perceived sexual harassment to be a problem than did the other race/gender identity groups. There was a statistically significant difference in both companies between white men and white women.

There is also an obvious difference between the two organizations. More than 30 percent of *all* the respondents in InvestCo agree that sexual harassment is a significant problem, while 5 to 10 percent of the respondents perceived that to be the case in JKLCorp.

To understand why the perceptions of men and women are so different, the companies must vigorously investigate what is going on. Is this a general problem, or is it isolated to a few individuals who are harassing? Why do white men perceive it to be less of a problem than others? The investigation could be pursued through focus groups, individual interviews, or perhaps a review of HR records.

In InvestCo, the fact that more than 30 percent of *all employees* regardless of race or gender identity group perceive sexual harassment to be a significant problem is the most immediate concern. A small task force could be formed to conduct interviews to determine the main causes of this widespread perception. The task force must also look at InvestCo's policies and practices and possibly its awareness training to determine where best to attack the problem.

Another item we looked at under the "group beliefs, attitudes, and values" dimension was the way the unwritten rules of organizations affect the abilities of employees to do their work effectively (see Figure 13–7).

This item shows that there were very significant differences in the perceptions of white men and the other groups—and startling similarities between InvestCo and JKLCorp: White men do not perceive that their race or gender affects their ability to make a full contribution, whereas *all* the other groups perceive that their race/gender makes it difficult for them to contribute fully.

Since approximately 40 percent of JKLCorp and 60 percent of InvestCo employees are white women and people of color, this perception reflects an enormous loss of contribution to both organizations.

Clearly, some of the norms of these organizations need to be changed. However, changing the unwritten rules, or norms, of an organization is a difficult task because "wholesale change" is not what is required. The organization must maintain its core values and precepts and yet eliminate those aspects that create inequities.[10] JKLCorp and InvestCo, like the many other companies whose data would reveal similar disparities, need to use a combination of task force and management effort, and possibly outside consulting help, to create appropriate change. For these efforts to be effective and credible, formal policies and procedures must also be addressed.

FIGURE 13-7

Percentage Agreeing That Unwritten Rules Make It Difficult for Respondent and Others of Respondent's Race and Gender to Make a Full Contribution

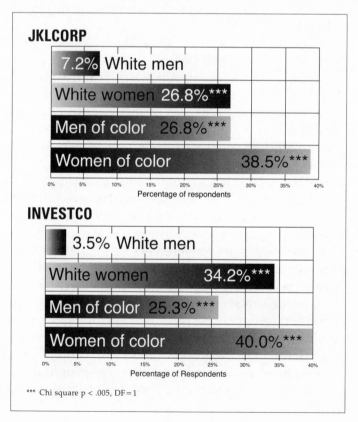

JKLCORP

- 7.2% White men
- White women 26.8%***
- Men of color 26.8%***
- Women of color 38.5%***

Percentage of respondents

INVESTCO

- 3.5% White men
- White women 34.2%***
- Men of color 25.3%***
- Women of color 40.0%***

Percentage of Respondents

*** Chi square $p < .005$, DF = 1

ORGANIZATION BEHAVIOR

The questions on the survey relating to organization behavior elicit information regarding the impact of organizational policies and procedures on such issues as hiring, retention, and promotion. In both organizations studied, all groups agreed that their organization did a good job in hiring, retaining, and promoting white men. But there were considerable differences when these same factors were explored as applied to the other race/gender identity groups (see Figure 13–8).

F I G U R E 13–8

Percentage Disagreeing That Organization Does a Good Job Retaining Women of Color, by Race/Gender Group

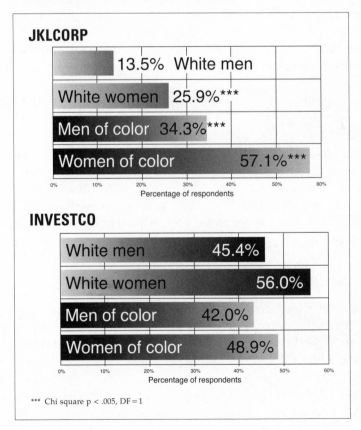

*** Chi square p < .005, DF = 1

For example, one item dealt with how well the organizations handled the responsibility of retaining women of color. At JKL-Corp, fewer than 15 percent of the white men perceive a problem in the retention of women of color. More than half of the women of color feel that the organization does not do a good job in supporting or encouraging them to stay with the company.

At InvestCo, on the other hand, nearly 50 percent of *all* groups perceive a problem in the retention of women of color.

These differences indicate that the two organizations will need to take different approaches to resolving the problems. In JKLCorp, a communication and education process concerning actual turnover rates must be implemented before white men are asked for a commitment to reverse the trend. Because InvestCo has a management objective of recruiting the best and the brightest, they will need to look at the impact of the perceived low retention rates on their ability to attract the best and brightest women of color. InvestCo may also need to evaluate why the practices that lead to the low retention rates continue to exist when so many employees—including management—are aware of the problem.

Both organizations will need to quantify the costs of turnover and include that information in the education process about the problem.

While it is important to learn about the specific issues impacting differential retention, the "fix" for this problem usually lies elsewhere. It is more effective, for example, to look at the mentoring and coaching practices, and the practices that affect an employee's sense of acceptance and opportunity in the organization, than merely to set higher numerical goals for retention.

MANAGING DIVERSITY

One important measure of the attitudes about managing diversity is the general perception of senior management's beliefs about and commitment to the process. We therefore included questions about management's views of managing diversity in the survey (see Figure 13–9).

Successful change efforts require leadership from top management. The widespread perception in InvestCo that senior

FIGURE 13–9

Percentage Disagreeing That Senior Management Believes That
Effectively Managing Diversity Adds to the Organization's Performance,
by Race/Gender Group

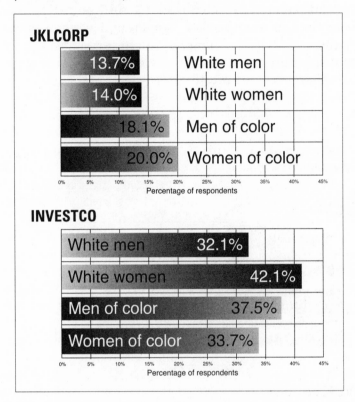

management does not see the value in managing diversity will
be troublesome for a successful change effort. Senior management
must find ways to communicate their interest in this topic. More
importantly, they must take actions that demonstrate their commitment. This might include the establishment of a "steering
committee" that has key senior managers as members.

ORGANIZATION CULTURE

The questions under the "organization culture" dimension of
the survey measure the climate and norms of the organization

regarding race and gender differences and the ability to talk openly about them. One of the questions we asked was about the perceptions of double standards for race and gender in the organizations; that is, how often people were aware of the existence of double standards (see Figure 13–10).

In both organizations, white women and women of color perceived the application of double standards for race and gender to occur significantly more than did white men. Men of color in JKLCorp also perceived a difference.

F I G U R E 13–10

Percentage Who Perceive that Double Standards for Race/Gender Occur Frequently in the Organization.

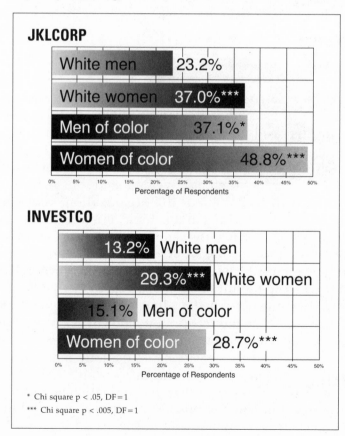

* Chi square p < .05, DF = 1

*** Chi square p < .005, DF = 1

The perception that there is a double standard for race and gender is especially important in JLKCorp because of the high percentages of all groups responding that it occurs frequently. Although many white men do not feel there is a double standard, nearly one in four white men do share the perception that a double standard occurs very frequently. In InvestCo, the percentages are smaller, and there seems to be a gender split.

Although this aspect of the organization's culture could be attacked directly by using focus groups or interviews, it is generally more effective to address more concrete issues first. As the more concrete actions are taken, the organization culture items such as double standards tend to diminish in magnitude and the differences between race/gender identity groups also decrease. If the improvement is not satisfactory following other actions, in-depth analysis of this area is essential.

IMPLICATIONS

The survey helps break up the complex topic of diversity into manageable chunks. Each organization can study the results to determine which areas need the most attention. When the priorities are set, actions can be taken, and progress can be monitored.

The information from the survey permits task forces and management to operate from objective data and thus reduce the impact of their own biases about the organization. Given the tremendous emotional loading on this topic, it is very important for other employees to see that the action-taking groups are working on the basis of solid evidence.

When management understands the data, it is possible to set concrete goals and identify measures of success. This permits management to be realistically accountable for bringing about change. The axiom of quality/continuous improvement is, "You can't manage what you can't measure." This is also true for diversity. The survey allows that measurement. It allows management to get away from the trap of measuring success only from financial data. It begins to make clear that discrimination has a "cost" to those who discriminate as well as to those who are discriminated against.[11]

The data from the survey helps reduce the resistance to change. It gets organizations out of the cycle of accusation, guilt, and resentment. This data and that from other organizations shows that many aspects of the problem are not known to white men or to managers. The data helps the organization understand that lack of awareness of the problem is actually part of the problem. Commitment to the change is increased, and resentment about the change is minimized. The fact-based revelation that management (mostly white men) is part of the problem discourages strategies that are only aimed at "fixing the victim."

Data collected through the diversity survey demonstrates the many facets of diversity. It leaves no doubt that any single approach to solve this complex problem is doomed to fail.

The survey is designed to provide multiple levels of analyses. This allows each organization to determine what areas are most important to them. In a sense, the survey data acknowledges the diversity among organizations as well as people.

The survey also permits comparisons to be drawn not only among various organizations, but also among entities within one organization. The analysis of data that we provide does not specifically identify organizations or entities, but we do provide a description of the type of organization ("manufacturing company," for example) or geographic location ("Midwest"). This helps to answer the nagging question of whether "x percent" is "high" or "to be expected."

In the final analysis, the acceptability of a number must be determined within the organization or the entity itself; but the opportunity to make comparisons, anonymously, is helpful.

Success in learning to manage an increasingly diverse workforce depends on management's skill at leading the change process. For the skills to be effectively used, the diagnosis of the system must be accurate. The diversity survey is, we propose, a very useful instrument in the diagnostic process.

END NOTES

1. For an in-depth analysis of systems theory concepts, see Ludwig von Bertalanffy, *General Systems Theory* (New York: George Braziller, 1968).

2. See Kate Kirkham, "Managing a Diverse Workforce: From incident to 'ism." *The Diversity Factor* 1, no. 3 (Spring, 1993), pp. 22–26. A discussion of the framework for breadth of awareness and depth of insight is found in Kate Kirkham, "Dimensions of Diversity," a paper presented at the Institute for Women and Organizations Conference, 1988, Long Beach, California.

3. Martha Minow, *Making All the Difference* (Ithaca: Cornell University Press, 1990).

4. Seven surveys designed to obtain race and gender dynamics were reviewed. None of them were comprehensive in the sense of understanding more than two levels of system, and none of them differentiated behavior from attitude. Information from the pilot testing of the Diversity Assessment Survey and our experience in consulting with organizations on race and gender dynamics show both of these to be important areas to understand.

5. For an example of this phenomenon, see Margaret Blackburn White, "Leadership for Workforce 2000: The CoreStates Experience," *The Diversity Factor* 1, no. 4 (Summer, 1993), pp. 26–31.

6. For a general introduction to the survey, see Joseph Potts and Carol Brantley, "On Measuring Diversity: Race and Gender Dimensions," *The Diversity Factor* 2, no. 4 (Summer, 1994), pp. 20–26.

7. See Pamela Alreck and Robert Settle, *The Survey Research Handbook* (Homewood, IL: Irwin, 1985) for a discussion of techniques used.

8. See Potts and Brantley, "On Measuring Diversity: Race and Gender Dimensions" and Minow, *Making All the Difference*.

9. See Andrea Zintz, "All in the Family: Confronting Sexual Harassment in the New Culture," *The Diversity Factor* 2, no. 3 (Spring, 1994), pp. 25–31.

10. See Peter Senge, *The Fifth Discipline* (New York: Doubleday, 1990) for a helpful discussion of this topic.

11. See Barbara Blumenthal and Philippe Haspeslagh, "Toward a Definition of Corporate Transformation," *Sloan Management Review,* Spring 1994, for a review of why measuring success only on the basis of financial data is counterproductive; and Gary Becker, *The Economics of Discrimination,* 2nd ed., (Chicago: University of Chicago Press, 1970) on the costs of discriminating.

Validity and Reliability of the Survey

VALIDITY

The validity of the survey (does it measure what and only what it is supposed to measure) was evaluated in three ways:

1. The original pool of items that were selected to be tested came from workshops designed to look at race and gender dynamics in the workplace. Most of the original questions were ones that were asked of individuals before the workshop and were then discussed in the workshop. Those items that were verified in the workshop discussions were the ones selected to be pilot tested.

2. Focus group data confirmed the survey results in three different organizations where the survey was administered, and race/gender identity focus groups were also conducted. The focus groups were facilitated according to a protocol designed to examine systemic as well as individual and group level issues in the organization. The one problem with this level of validation was that the focus groups did not all respond to the protocol in an identical way. Some groups tended to spend more time in particular areas, and the level of detail varied. This problem aside, the data from the two processes provided very similar information. Of course, the focus group data was more personal and allowed for specific examples to be given as well as general observations. The examples were consistent with the survey information, and the general observations from the focus groups verified the survey results.

3. Factor analysis was run on more than 2,000 respondents to assess the construct validity of the diversity assessment survey. The analyses were conducted on all respondents together as well as the four race/gender identity groups (e.g., white men, white women, men of color, and women of color). The results demonstrated that there are nine dimensions, with three of the dimensions being further divided into subscales for a total of 14 scales.

- Organization behavior is broken down into four subscales; (1) policies and procedures; (2) hiring, retention, and promotion of white men; (3) hiring, retention, and promotion of white women, men of color, and women of color; (4) discrimination.

- Managing diversity is composed of two subscales. The first is the individual's perception of the value of diversity. The second is the perception of how much other groups value diversity.
- Organization culture is made up of two subscales. One deals with the acceptability of discussing race and gender differences in the organization. The other deals with the climate and norms of the organization regarding race and gender.

Overall, the subscales possess a high degree of construct validity. Their validity seems to hold for all of the race/gender identity groups though the factor patterns do change among the groups. The factor structure for white men was distinct and very similar to the overall pattern. Within the white women, men of color, and women of color groups, several of the scales tended to combine. Women of color showed the most merging while white women showed the least.

The merging of some of the scales for the groups that are perceived to be disadvantaged in the organization is expected. To the extent a group feels that bias and prejudice exist in the organization or the larger society, all work-related attitudes will be affected.[1, 2]

RELIABILITY

The reliability or ability to get the same data from several measurements has been examined for each of the scales with over 3,000 respondents. The internal consistency of each of the dimensions and their subscales has been analyzed using Cronbach's alpha α statistic. In effect, this statistic evaluates each of the items within a dimension for its consistency with all other items in that dimension or subscale. Only items with sufficiently high correlations were included in the dimension or subscale.

The overall internal consistency as measured by the α statistic ranges from high to very high on 10/14 sub-scales (Cronbach

α = .80 to .91). On four subscales (individual behaviors; individual beliefs; hiring, retention and promotion of white men; and managing diversity—individual perceptions) it ranges from passable to moderate (Cronbach α = .62 to .79). The reliability analysis is nearly identical to the overall analysis when applied to all of the race/gender identity groups individually. The single exception is that the α for white men in the group beliefs dimension drops to the passable level (Cronbach α = .60).

APPENDIX END NOTES

1. Gail McGuire and Barbara Reskin, "Authority Hierarchies at Work: The Impacts of Race and Sex," *Gender and Society* 7, no. 4 (December, 1993).
2. Joe Feagin and Melvin Sikes, *Living with Racism: The Black Middle-Class Experience* (Boston: Beacon Press, 1994).

CHAPTER

Racetalk

Thinking and Talking about Racism

Mark A. Chesler

As a white man, I know how hard it is for white people to talk about diversity and racism in this society—especially with people of other races, classes, genders, and statuses. But we must learn to talk about race openly and effectively, in order to collaborate in actions and change programs that will make our increasingly multicultural society productive and vibrant.

There is hot debate over how to do this. There are ill-conceived "diversity training" programs that seem to be targeted at whites—particularly white men. Some programs glorify coercive reeducation, appear to foster rage and guilt, engage in "white male bashing," and drive meaningful exploration underground. Others "celebrate differences" but fail to deal with underlying issues of power and privilege.

Such programs do a serious disservice to the organizations that present them and to the effort of creating a diverse and productive enterprise.

The best diversity training, however, addresses "racetalk"— the need for whites to learn how to understand, explore, and deal with personal and institutional racism and to collaborate with people of color in the effort to build effective organizations

169

that support and utilize differences and reduce discrimination. Such talk and action help create a sense of community amidst difference.

In this article I, too, am exploring how to talk about race with others—primarily with other white men. The traditional analysis of racism examines its meaning and impact for people of color, for those oppressed and disadvantaged by its operation; this must be complemented by an analysis of its meaning and impact for white people, for those beneficiaries of its workings. I do not claim to have "solved" these concerns. I am still learning. What follows is, however, not an exercise in confession. It is a tale of the experience of white men—myself and others—as both the subject and object of analysis. My history and my reality are, in large part, the history of all of us—and vice versa.

DEFINING TERMS

What is racism? There is no agreement on the meaning of this commonplace term. We once thought of it as describing overt and raw negative expressions about and actions toward people of color. It was viewed as a mostly lower-class phenomenon and as being synonymous with the prejudices and discriminatory actions of individuals.

Today, scholars talk about multiple forms of racism: old and new, overt and covert, white and black, forward and reverse, individual and institutional, passive and active, material and symbolic, cultural and instrumental. We realize that racism is relatively universal among white people and pervasive and powerful in our institutions. We also recognize that much of the resistance to change in our organizations arises from racism—unexamined, unacknowledged, and therefore unreachable.

I use the term *racism* to indicate that we **live in a society that contains, maintains, and reproduces major differences in life opportunities for people of different racial and ethnic groups.** I differentiate racism from "prejudice" and "discrimination," reserving the term *racism* for attitudes and behaviors that are generated by people and organizations with **superior power and privilege towards others with less power and**

privilege. Racism in this institutionalized form, then, is part of a system of domination.

Prejudice and bigotry practiced by people of color, though noxious, are not usually linked to power or codified in institutional norms and cultures. People of color may hurt and offend whites—but seldom dominate us. Thus, in my view, it is not sensible to speak of "reverse racism" nor to speak of a person of color as "racist."

This has nothing to do with romanticizing people of color as a group or with perceiving that they are "better than" white people. It is a factual recognition of the way power is distributed; it is necessary to face these facts if we are to learn how to change them.

Our culture and our institutions are dominated by white people; they oppress and demean people of color. They create and pass on privilege for whites. And in the process they create a great deal of racial conflict—some open and acknowledged, in other cases, muted and underground.

This process of institutional racism is deeply rooted in our history as a nation and operates still. It often seems to have a life of its own—even when individuals, groups and whole organizations commit themselves to operating in accord with nonracist principles, the specter of racism creeps in and spoils the effort.

The legacy of racism coexists with our legacy of commitment to the ideals of equality and pluralism. Our religious and educational institutions, the media, and many covert family and peer group teachings present us with a racial/ethnic ranking system—while simultaneously telling us about the inherent worth of every human being. The split is built into our Constitution—which determined that a black person was only a percentage of a human being—and has been passed down through many permutations to every generation.

Many white people try to act on the ideals of equality and pluralism and to respect others, including those who are different from us by race. But in times of stress or in periods of ignorance and laziness, I and others often—unintentionally, and even unknowingly—act out messages of racial superiority and inferiority. And the thin veneer of civility that masks the underlying reality of racism of our society cracks.

Racism is real. We can't get over it, under it, or around it. We have to look at it, understand it, acknowledge it, and then try to dismantle it. That's why, I propose, we have to learn to do racetalk.

TALKING ABOUT RACE

Racetalk, as I use the term here, is not the same as a monologue. It is not persuasion, debate, or contest. By racetalk, I mean the process of engaging hearts and minds in honest discourse and dialogue about race and racism. And I mean the kind of racetalk that hastens rather than delays action for change.

The power of racism is well reflected in how difficult it is to have open discourse or dialogue about it. It is not only hard for us to talk about race and racism, it is hard for us to listen as well—either because we don't want to or don't know how. The results usually are shouts and yells or whispers and grumbles. Attempts at mutual conversation quickly produce general discomfort, interactions rapidly become heated, and patterns of attack and defense are created that lead to debates or fights rather than dialogue.

Most of us white people do not experience ourselves as "racialized persons." I am seldom defined or identified by my skin color. But as long as having "white" skin or black skin or brown or other color skin is relevant to the way power, privileges, and resources are distributed, we whites must learn to see ourselves as racial beings among other racial beings. This requires a novel set of self-conscious and deliberate acts.

"Whiteness," is, after all, more than skin color and a personal racial identity; it is a social construct based upon power relations, in which white people dominate people of color. It denotes a status of racialized privilege, long ratified by U.S. law and codified by social custom.

UNDERSTANDING THE DIFFICULTIES

Part of the reason racetalk is hard is because race and racism affect our lives deeply—even in ways I do not fully understand. The privileges and the costs associated with attitudes about skin color (and gender and class, to be sure) account for a lot of who I am, what I do, the position I hold in society, and how I am seen and treated by others. Confronting my/our lack of clarity about this reality often leads to confusion and pain about my identity and my true worth.

Learning to talk about race forces us to look at ourselves— our hidden or forgotten prejudices and privileges, the things we have done that we wish we hadn't and vice versa—and the racially oppressive cultures and structures of the society in which we live. We cannot learn to talk honestly with people of other races without dealing with our history of slavery, seizure of the lands of others, internment or concentration camps, forced relocation, selective immigration, impoverishment, and other forms of oppression.

Further, we all have different kinds and levels of information about race and racism. When we try to talk about race, we often are afraid of exposing our ignorance and of committing embarrassing social blunders. I, and many other white people, often fear being criticized and trashed by others' reactions to our ideas and actions about race. This fear is increased when we are not fully aware of the meaning and impact of our ideas on people of color— or even of our own intentions. Attempting racetalk thus may create emotional caution, intellectual tentativeness, overreactive arrogance, or strong emotional reactions—all in the interest of self-protection. Even though racetalk provides opportunities to learn from and about difference and domination, and thus enables us to begin dismantling the barriers erected by racist systems, it also carries the scent of danger.

Our emotional reactions to the subject of race arise from our earliest experiences. I was born into an East Coast, Jewish, middle-class, liberal family. I was taught values of racial tolerance—and also the belief that I was different from (better than) whites who were not liberal and tolerant. Nonetheless, I absorbed many of the racist attitudes of my white community—I, too, counted off singing "eeny meeny miny mo, catch a nigger by the toe." I played cowboys and Indians with my buddies. And in the face of ball-game cheating I could shout (or murmur) "chinky shows" just as well as my peers.

As I grew, I "knew" that Beethoven was superior to the Beatles or James Brown, that Rembrandt's and Van Gogh's work were far more valuable than New York subway graffiti or the work of Diego Rivera, that Castilian Spanish was better than Puerto Rican Spanish. And that Shakespeare was superior to . . . anyone.

I also learned that the possibilities of interracial friendships ended short of courtship and marriage.

And I learned what I was supposed to say, or not say—about whom, to whom, when, and how—and still be accepted in my corner of polite society.

My understanding of race and of my position as a white person was thus formed by the ostensibly liberal messages of my family, held in uneasy alliance with the messages of my white peer group—a group that I wished and needed to be accepted and respected by. These contradictory messages still hold power in my life.

Nonetheless, I know that I am not just a member of a relatively privileged class; I am also a unique person. My views and my position in life are not due solely to my race or my family or my social world. I am a member of multiple "identity groups" and communities, and my gender, class, religion, ethnicity, age, sexual orientation all interact with my race to create my unique social experience and responses—my social nature.

Nor are all of us white men alike. We don't all have equal privileges or access to "the white male club." We don't all think the same or act the same on racial, religious, or political matters; we don't all have the same sexual orientation. Yet we are all members of a social category that has greater privileges than do most members of the "category" of people of color—and we share a history of oppression with regard to them.

We are *both* individuals and members of a social group. Thus, while we must avoid stereotyping white men (or anyone else), it is also essential to recognize that in this society *race matters* in one's access to life opportunities, health and wealth, pain and privilege, and so on. Whites and people of color have different life experiences—reflecting their different statuses in our stratified social structure. We cannot deny these social and experiential differences, but neither can we equate them with biologic or essentialist distinctions.

THE BENEFITS OF BEING WHITE

No matter what I and other white people do, we continue to benefit from the advantage of being white. For instance, a senior colleague recently conferred with me on a raise being offered to a junior faculty member of color, because the raise was larger than my own. I accepted the call as a courtesy—but later realized that I would not have been called if the junior faculty member in question had been white. An act aimed at advancing equity was thus interwoven with special deference to me as a member of the white male club.

Such instances make me more aware of my privileges as a white person in this society. There are many such privileges: whites generally have greater life expectancy, more money, more education, better housing conditions, more social freedom in general, and better standing before the law.

Other privileges are less obvious: Partly because of my gender as well as my race, I can walk into a room of academics and know that no one thinks I am there as a token; partly because of my class as well as my race, I can expect police to treat me fairly if I am stopped for a traffic violation. I never have to worry about being trailed by store detectives; I can easily purchase "flesh-colored" bandages; I can anticipate being shown to a desirable table in a restaurant; and I can expect that my opinions will be responded to on their individual merit, rather than on the basis of my race.[1]

These advantages thrust me, and other whites, into a variety of roles. We may be **active oppressors,** as I was when attacking an African-American administrator who I felt had been unfair; my attack took a form that I do not think I would have employed with a senior white colleague or supervisor. We may be **passive observers or implementors** of racism, as I was when I failed to challenge racist policies and programs in my organizational unit, when I did not challenge racial slights, or even when I benefited disproportionately from racially biased SAT and GRE exams that gave me an edge in college admissions and financial aid opportunities.

On the other hand, we may be **intervenors**, as I have been when I challenged racist jokes or have helped organize protests against racist policies and practices.

My conscious antiracism and my unconscious (or at least unintended) racism may exist side by side. And while my unconscious racism may be neither deliberate nor intentional, it privileges me and demeans and harms others nevertheless.

FACING THE MYTH OF MERITOCRACY

Recognition of my privileges forces me to recognize that my achievement is not based solely on my own efforts. The "meritocracy" does not actually present us with a fully competitive arena; since white men begin with a leg up, as it were, we are not usually forced to compete with people of color or white women, who are often not even admitted to the contest.

Acknowledgement of privilege often makes us white men feel guilty or angry and creates feelings of insecurity and pressure. After all, our privileges are in reality determined by other white men with greater power and resources and could just as easily be withdrawn by them. Now our privileges are not only being closely held by more powerful white men and contested for by other white men, they are being challenged by white women and people of color with less power and resources.

Thus even within what seems to be a privileged existence, there is no safe place. We consequently long to close our eyes to the reality of our privileges, to wall ourselves off from our vulnerabilities and the oppression of our neighbors, and to ignore the simmering racial conflict all around us.

Being forced to recognize our racialized advantages often feels like stereotyping, like an assault on our individuality and uniqueness. Being "named" or "placed" as "white" feels strange and uncomfortable; such naming may create feelings of powerlessness, anger, betrayal, or victimization and may generate hostile counterattacks.

For those of us who are liberal, who may have been involved in the civil rights movement, such identification may feel like betrayal of our hopes and contributions. For those of us who are conservative, such identification may be the last straw and shreds the last bit of our patience with what are seen as inappropriate complaints, demands, or attacks.

But most of us whites can escape the challenge altogether. We don't usually have to interact with people of color, nor does being named "white" usually create material deprivation, emotional pain or humiliation, or institutional exclusion or degradation—as does being identified as a person of color. Being labeled "white" may be uncomfortable, but it is a new experience, not one vested in social history, and it touches only relatively small and situationally limited portions of our lives for relatively short time periods.

When we do meet the challenge of examining and discussing our whiteness, however, we may find a strange new world, a world for which we have no chart or compass. As I have struggled to articulate my own racetalk, I have perceived many barriers:

▪ The possibility of losing the privileges we had seen as our social birthright often leads to blaming those who have never had such privileges for threatening our own. This blame can be as specific as charging a person or organization with "reverse racism," or it can be as subtle as complaints about the ways in which real or imagined gains by people of color threaten our "rights" to career mobility, freedom of choice, freedom of speech, safety from verbal criticism, safety from abuse, or control over our own futures.

▪ Awareness of our potential racism coupled with lack of knowledge about how to deal with it may lead to a paralysis of thought and action, for fear we may offend a racial etiquette that we do not understand. We find it difficult to give honest feedback to people of color, with the result that issues such as the perceived performance of African-American employees, co-workers, students, or colleagues; the difficulties of financing social services for Latino or Asian immigrants; the extent of crime committed by black men; or the existence of poverty and illiteracy in the white population are not discussed and analyzed. Instead of honest and searching exploration and confrontation of "minority problems," and how they are rooted in the flaws of American society, we quickly blame the victims of oppression or deprivation. Or—out of guilt and paralysis—we try to ignore or apologize for the situation.

▪ Taking a position that articulates a recognition of white skin privilege may result in resounding attacks by white peers. I have been called a "self-hating Jew" for challenging policies and actions of the state of Israel. I have been called a "knee-jerk liberal" for advocating affirmative action criteria in the hiring of university faculty. I have been accused of "pandering" when I have advocated for African-American or Latina students embroiled in controversies with white faculty and staff. And I know I have not always had the courage to speak up in such situations.

■ Speaking out may also generate charges of promoting "political correctness." There certainly are increased examples of people of color (and white women and men) challenging whites' demeaning racial rhetoric and behavior, and some of those whites who are challenged now claim that they are the "new victims" of political correctness. But in my experience the real political orthodoxy still is for whites to exclude and oppress—personally or institutionally, consciously or unconsciously—people of any race and gender who champion antiracism. What is most "politically correct" in U.S. corporations and universities still is racism, sexism, and classism, often now practiced "most correctly" in relatively covert fashion.

Thus, this currently fashionable term is a smoke screen. Its aim, and effect, is to distract attention from the continuing realities of racism, sexism, and other forms of discrimination. But it carries weight in some quarters—no one wants to wear that label.

■ It is not always possible for me, or any white man, to walk the talk. For example, my family holds a variety of investments in U.S. corporations whose personnel policies and practices I know to be discriminatory. My failure to confront this and other such issues head-on troubles me. It also leads me to fear that such gaps between my beliefs and my actions may be exposed, that I may be seen as a hypocrite by those whose goodwill I cherish.

■ Speaking out and acting against institutional or personal racism threatens my standing in the "white male fraternity" and leads me to feel marginalized. I then must decide how to respond. Do I just accept being "on the margin," a place of pain and powerlessness? Or do I use it as a place of strength and leverage—a platform for action?

■ Speaking out may lead to being excessively or even compulsively critical of the speech or behavior of other whites. Indeed, there is a certain seductive appeal to being "innocent" or "blame-less," or at least "less blameful" than other white people, and this quest sometimes requires finding other whites to blame, or inap-propriately attacking other white people at every opportunity for using language we consider racist—or even for making minor faux pas against what we perceive as proper racial etiquette. This can take the form of "showing off" by trying to be the "most antiracist" white person around. I have been part of many racial conversations where I and other white men have slid into "one-upping" each other in competition for use of the latest language, the most advanced analyses, or the preferred political turf.

THE BENEFITS OF RACETALK

I reiterate that race*talk* alone is not the answer to racism. Talk can be cheap, talk does not necessarily lead to action, talk can delay action—while people continue to be oppressed and suffer. Race-talk must lead to action, to well-conceived, well-designed, and well-implemented programs and strategies that address the sys-temic manifestations of racism.

But the process of planning, change, improving the bottom line, and seeking social justice requires a new consciousness and new information and skills among whites. Racetalk can help, and learning this sort of racetalk is a way to begin. There are numer-ous benefits to be derived:

▪ Learning racetalk can help reduce some of the confusion about one's racial identity and can help me, and other whites, clar-ify who I really am—my value as a human being apart from the privileges and myths I receive as a member of the white race.

▪ Racetalk may help me understand that I and other whites pay a high price for our privileged racial position. The material costs of institutional racism are evident in the taxes we pay for prisons and police, as well as for social services for those denied the opportunity to compete on an equal basis. Psychic costs include confusion about our racial identities and history, fear of random or organized attack by people of color, and alienation from our neighbors. Intellectual costs include unrealistic views of "meri-tocracy," the use of whiteness as a social norm, and our costly ignorance of other cultures. The moral costs are far-reaching, including vague senses of illegitimate gain and—when we allow ourselves to look around us—distress at the suffering we see in the lives of many people of color.

White children—myself as a child included—do not think of themselves as white. Race defines "other people." Racetalk can help us progress through stages of racial consciousness—passive acceptance of racism, "color blindness," understanding "the problem" but not seeing ourselves as part of it—to a coherent understanding of institutional and personal racism and to a commitment to change ourselves and our society.[2]

Racetalk can also help us be more aware of the gender, class, and ethnic variations in "whiteness" as well as more aware of the racial diversity among groups of people of color.

▪ Racetalk can reduce the gaps between our walk and our talk. Information, awareness, skill, and will (or courage) can help reduce fear and guilt about racial interaction, especially the fear that arises when I or other whites are not in positions of superior power.

▪ Learning to communicate effectively around race also gives me a competitive advantage in the new world of increasing power and presence of people of color. Developing effective relationships in a highly diverse world requires genuine understanding of others, not role-playing or "psyching out" the other.

▪ This personal authenticity can also help white men have more genuine relationships with other white men. We can be who we are—rather than maintaining relationships based on illusory "macho bonds," fear of others, or defense of privilege.

Without this authenticity, we tend to seek out other white men to "whine and complain" about fantasies such as "women are emasculating men," "all the openings are going to people of color," "there is a loss of standards," "blacks now have it better than whites," "they're going to rise and kill us all," and so forth. We sometimes falsely portray ourselves as "the new victims."

We know these are fantasies; white men are still in charge almost everywhere in our society. We "whine and complain" because we are afraid of losing our power and our privileges, and the fantasies must be examined in this light. And we white men must learn to do this examination for ourselves and with each other.

This is not easy. We are trained to be competitive and not supportive with one another, and we tend to look to the "experts" on race—that is, to people of color—to both nurture and educate us. But it is inappropriate to expect them to continue to "teach us" about these realities that have, after all, been around us for many years. Moreover, it is unrealistic to expect white women and people of color, the primary victims of racial and gender oppression, to listen to much of the—even quite real and justifiable—pain and confusion experienced by members of the dominant group.

■ Racetalk can help us see that all the "isms" are connected. As I work on improving my racial awareness, I realize I sometimes ignore my role in maintaining gender and class discrimination.

PITFALLS

There are some potential dangers in racetalk among white men. Our history of interaction is characterized by secret jokes and stories at the expense of women and people of color. We tend to tease and harass other white men who do not "fit in"—and we often have gotten together to design, defend, and implement programs and policies that exclude and oppress people of color.

Breaking these patterns is difficult. It is a challenge to use racetalk opportunities for real growth, greater intellectual and emotional openness, expansion of our racial consciousness, and for change.

HOW TO LEARN TO DO RACETALK

One way of learning is through **self-examination**. It is very hard to do this alone, however, since such work calls for new ways of understanding ourselves and dealing with information and often creates internal conflict that may be difficult to handle without encouragement and support from other committed learners and a trained educator or facilitator.

A second learning path is to **read the works of other white people** who have wrestled with these issues, as well as whites who feel themselves victimized by attempts to redress racial wrongs. While it may seem counterproductive to study the thoughts of those who wish to defend their privileged status, we will find, if we look, parts of ourselves in them, and of them in us. We can learn about ourselves and perhaps about our own sources of pain, anger, powerlessness, resistance, and feelings of victimization by reading others' stories.

It is also helpful to **learn about the factual state of oppression,** especially racial oppression, in this society. Although white people often complain of being tired of "hearing about slavery and racism all the time," few of us are actually aware of the facts of slavery, forced or limited immigration, land conquest, incarceration, and their aftermaths. Even fewer have attended carefully to the ways in which institutional racism works in contemporary society—although there is a large and important literature that provides this information.

In this effort, it is helpful to read not only historical accounts of oppression but also personal accounts of the experiences of people of color. Many of us relate more immediately to the life stories of individuals than to more abstract and analytic accounts.

In this study, we must not see black–white relations as the sole concern. Racism has so warped our life together as to have affected the relations of whites with all people of color—and of groups of people of color with one another. Seeing and challenging racism beyond a limited black-and-white frame frustrates the ways in which powerful white groups set various peoples of color against one another—a "divide and conquer" strategy.

Broadening our views of racism could also help us learn about the shape of racism in other societies—information that is increasingly important in an era of global diversity.

A fourth learning path involves **engaging in open discussion of racism with other white people.** As noted above, it is hard to learn about race, racism, or racetalk alone. We need to get feedback for learning to be effective; we need to bounce our hopes and fears, insights and reflections, anxieties and vulnerabilities off others whom we trust. It is crucial that our partners be "others whom we trust"; we cannot learn about racism if we fear being demeaned, treated as ignorant or unsophisticated, laughed at, pitied, seen as wimpy, labeled as "reverse racists," or treated as traitors to the "club."

One approach to group learning about racism is called "racial awareness training," or racial consciousness-raising. Experiential education techniques used in such training provide opportunities to learn about ourselves and the issues directly; this cannot occur solely in a stand-up lecture format. It is important that the leaders or facilitators of such groups and activities be mixed-race teams or have considerable experience working in such teams, so they can act as models of interracial teamwork. It also is important that such educators or leaders have done extensive work on exploring their own racial attitudes and that they have exceptional skills in managing group and organizational dynamics. These explorations must go beyond an intrapersonal or interpersonal focus to include institutional racism and oppression. And they must go beyond discussions of difference to unpack privilege and domination.

An effective though difficult learning path involves **joining dialogue groups with people of color,** either for common inquiry or in preparation for change efforts. Here, too, a trusting environment must be created, and skilled leadership or facilitation—by leaders of different races—is crucial. Despite the potential advantages of this learning path, critics have pointed out that mixed-race dialogue carries the dangers of assuaging white guilt, of "cooling out" protests generated by people of color, and of focusing on attitudes and interpersonal relationships when structures of privilege and domination are the real issues. This is why acting together is at least as important as talking together.

Mixed-race dialogue groups help overcome some of the problems of race-separate explorations and may permit all participants to directly explore, experience, understand, and act together in the struggle against racism. However, we must not assign to the people of color alone the task of educating white members about ourselves. We whites are responsible for our own learning, and the task of changing the oppressive system is primarily ours—not that of those who are members of the oppressed groups. I do not argue that people of color cannot teach us about ourselves (indeed, members of oppressed groups often see our society's racial situation more clearly than we do) but that placing the sole or primary responsibility for our enlightenment on them reinforces white passivity and distance.

A final opportunity to learn about racism is **engaging in the struggle to overcome it.** Whether in the corporate setting, the university, the community, or elsewhere, working with others to design and implement strategies to confront systemic racism contextualizes our learning and permits us to test our new consciousness in reality. Further, as we confront the white male hierarchy and the challenges of our white peers, we are forced to continue exploring our own attitudes and behaviors, our personal residue of white elitism and privilege, and the benefits and costs to us of our commitment.

These proposals for racetalk do not imply that talk is enough. Nor is attitude change sufficient. We must walk the talk, and we must create new organizational and institutional paths as well as personal ones.

White men are an important part of any change effort in this society. We cannot and should not exclude ourselves from such work (racework), nor should we be excluded. But we will have to learn new behaviors and roles in order to work with others effectively in diversity and social justice pursuits.

When we work together with people of color in social and organizational change efforts, that collaboration itself is a learning ground. In such settings, we may learn how to behave steadfastly and powerfully but in ways that do not continue oppressive patterns of domination by whites. We can learn to be partners and to create coalitions for antiracist and pro-multicultural work.

We all have a lot to learn about our racism. It is often hard to overcome our privileged defensiveness and ignorance and engage fully in this learning. It is often hard to find the words and thoughts to converse with each other meaningfully about these issues. But if we do not do racetalk, if we do not converse with one another, if we do not learn and explore, and if we do not act to alter the patterns of racism in which we and our institutions are engaged, we contribute to the maintenance of racism and to the production of increased inequality and injustice.

In writing this article, I have been helped enormously by the critical feedback and comradeship received from André Modigliani, James Crowfoot, Diana DeVries, Howard Gadlin, David Schoem, Amy Schulz, Todd Sevig, Warren Whatley, Margaret Blackburn White, and Mayer Zald. Thank you.

END NOTES

1. The nature of unacknowledged white privilege has been addressed most clearly by Peggy MacIntosh, "White privileges: Unpacking the invisible knapsack," *Peace and Freedom,* July 1979, pp. 10–12.

2. For theories about the different types or stages of racial identity development see W. Cross, *Shades of Black: Diversity in Afro-American identity* (Philadelphia: Temple University Press, 1991); J. Helms, *Black and white racial identity* (Westport, CT: Greenwood Press, 1990); R. Hardiman and B. Jackson, "Racial Identity Development: Understanding Racial Dynamics in College Classrooms and on Campus," *New Directions in Teaching and Learning* 52 (Winter 1992), pp. 21–37; B. Jackson and R. Hardiman, "Racial Identity Development: Implications for Managing the Multi-Racial Workforce," in *The NTL Managers' Handbook,* eds. R. Ritvo and A. Sargent (Arlington, VA: NTL Institute, 1983), pp. 107–119.

CHAPTER

Power Tools for Managing Diversity

Michael Burkart

Consider this scenario: The management of CDE Corp has decided to go metric. Key managers are told in one-on-one meetings with their superiors that this change is the top priority of the company and that their careers depend on how well they lead their subordinates in making the shift. Coalitions are quickly formed to design the strategies to put the decision into action. Goals and timelines are established and published throughout the company. A "GO METRIC" day is announced, and eye-catching posters are plastered on bulletin boards throughout the company. The CEO issues a series of communications urging prompt compliance and laying out the financial consequences of delays.

Where training is needed to let employees know how to do what is expected of them, it is specifically designed and carefully focused to achieve the goal. Top management participates in the training to be sure their own skills are on target and to demonstrate the commitment of the organization to the change.

Managers who accomplish the shift smoothly and efficiently are rewarded with promotions, better assignments, and bonuses. Those who are not so successful are reminded of their weaknesses,

and counseled or challenged to improve. Any who refuse to support the change are "counseled out."

Compare this scenario with the typical company's approach
to "managing diversity." In many companies, the decision to
engage in a "diversity initiative" is based on the assumption that
what is required is education: If enough individuals learn to be
more interpersonally competent, the theory goes, then the organizational culture will change, and the goals of having a more productive *and* more diverse workforce will somehow be met.

Attempting to change a corporate culture around diversity
through education and awareness alone is no more sensible than
trying to change a technical process through personal persuasion. Any attempt to achieve a major organizational shift—one
that requires people to examine old attitudes, learn new skills,
exhibit new behaviors, and develop new organizational structures—that does not address the core of the organization—the
power structure—is unrealistic.

A POWER STRATEGY FOR CULTURE CHANGE

The power structure of every major American company is still
inhabited by white men—white men who, to some degree, understand how to manage change. The literature is replete with stories of companies—Motorola, Xerox, Harley Davidson, to name
a few—that have been brought back from the brink by such managers. Diversity efforts need to use strategies that allow these
competent white men, operating from the seats of power that
they hold, to use what they know.

The following outlines major elements in an approach to
diversity that openly acknowledges the power dimension and
allows white men to use their power to bring about culture
change. It is based on the belief that it is in the *self-interest* of the
dominant group—whites and men—to amend the power distribution in organizations to enhance the participation of white
women and people of color. Although *individual* white men may
feel that such redistribution of power threatens their preferential access to power, as a *group* white men benefit from the
increased earning potential and creativity of an expanded pool
of workers.

■ **Step One.** The CEO announces the organization's commitment to a diversity initiative and chooses a team of key managers who are charged with implementing it. All members of this team acknowledge that their performance on this project will have a major impact on their immediate and long-term career prospects. Consultants are called in to assist with the development of the team and to help plan strategies.

■ **Step Two.** The team, including the CEO, participates in an intensive program of awareness training—at minimum, three days. If the team is not mixed by race and gender, men and women of color and white women are "imported" from various segments of the company.

■ **Step Three.** As a follow-up to the initial training, the team participates in a two-day session for strategy formation and team building. In this session, the team applies learnings from the awareness workshop to diagnose how to begin changing the company culture. The prime strategy is coalition building with managers who will be held accountable for modeling and implementing a management style that values diversity.

■ **Step Four.** The consultants continue to meet regularly with the CEO and the change team. The team sets goals for desired behaviors and creates a system of appraisal that assesses whether the goals are being met. The team also develops the new norms and behaviors they commit themselves to and that they will propose as norms and behaviors for the entire company.

■ **Step Five.** Each manager, aided by a consultant, selects a key group of subordinates and initiates a series of meetings aimed at achieving the culture change. The strategy is to identify managers and workers who will become "allies" of the effort—who will support and model norms that embody diversity. Together, this group of allies develops an operational plan that does the following:

- Institutionalizes the new norms.
- Identifies rewards (for example, promotions, assignments, and so forth) that will be used to reinforce the new norms.
- Identifies a mechanism to monitor how well people adhere to the new norms—a mechanism that becomes part of the MIS systems.

- Rewards people who support the new norms and imposes sanctions (for example, negative feedback, demotions, undesirable assignments) on those who will not or cannot support the change effort.

- **Step Six.** Awareness training is provided as needed and is facilitated by key managers. Consultants provide "train-the-trainer" workshops for key managers to assist them in leading introductory awareness workshops. These workshops prepare managers to work with subordinates in nonpunitive ways that encourage reflection and self-awareness. The training emphasizes the company's expectation that people will learn to cooperate in new ways and reinforces the career development benefits of success in this effort. The workshop provides a safe environment in which people of different races, both genders, and different sexual orientations can share their experiences, beliefs, and feelings.

- **Step Seven.** The team of key managers continues to work with the consultants to develop specific strategies to support and institutionalize the commitment to diversity. Strategies will reflect both the culture of the organization and the nature of the desired change. Ongoing training will be closely targeted to the needs of the organization and management's perception of where pockets of resistance remain.

A THEORETICAL FRAMEWORK

This strategy is based on Richard Beckhard's classic formula for change:

$$C = a \times b \times d > X \text{, in which}$$

$$
\begin{aligned}
C &= \text{the change} \\
a &= \text{dissatisfaction with the status quo} \\
b &= \text{a clear statement of the desired end state} \\
d &= \text{concrete first steps toward that goal, and} \\
X &= \text{the cost of the change.[1]}
\end{aligned}
$$

In the formula, **dissatisfaction with the status quo** is the pivotal element.

Diversity initiatives often fail because the dominant group members (whites, men, heterosexuals) are satisfied with the status quo. Because they do not see that there are any benefits for them—either as individuals or as a group—in change they seek to define the status quo as both fair and efficient.

The reeducation strategy that underlies a training approach to the management of diversity assumes that dominant group members will adopt new behaviors and develop strategies that change the balance of power if they "see the light." That is, the belief is that if whites and men understand that they are members of a group that holds the reins of power and that other groups do not have equal access to that power, they will change the policies and practices that maintain that power balance.

This assumption is highly questionable. In cultures built on a power orientation, where power is seen as a scarce commodity, those who have acquired a "piece of the action" would be irrational to simply give it away. Who would give up benefits—whether earned or not—so that others can acquire them at one's own expense?

How, then, do we create strategies that meet what corporations are defining as "the business necessity" for broadening the power base and utilizing the resources, skills, access to markets, and creative talents of our increasingly diverse population? How does management (a) generate among the dominant group members a sense of dissatisfaction with the status quo, (b) create a clear vision of the desired new culture, and (c) lay out concrete first steps?

I propose that an effective approach is through a combination of coalition building, application of rewards, and behavior modeling. Taken together, these approaches constitute a **power strategy** of force sufficient to overcome the cost of change. The power that is already inherent in the organization must be brought to bear if change is to occur. Those who hold the power must utilize their influence to support the change effort. Linkages must be built between those at the top of the organization and allies of the effort at each level in the hierarchy. Those who visibly demonstrate support for the diversity change effort must receive visible and immediate rewards and recognition.

POWER TOOLS

One of the classic tools for solidifying power is **reorganization**. In this model, management uses reorganization to place supporters in key positions and to isolate those who resist the change. In companies where "managing diversity" has been instituted as a public relations ploy or as a way to subvert affirmative action programs, reorganization has often served to displace a diversity program that has begun to unsettle the balance of power.

If a company is, however, serious about its diversity initiative, reorganization can be used as a strategy to help managers create the necessary coalitions for creating change. A restructuring that rewards those who support the new culture will demonstrate that people at all levels must take the change effort seriously if they want their careers to be successful. It will put people on notice that, even if they do not agree with the new norms, failure to abide by them will have negative consequences. A clear indication that the strategy is working is a chorus of complaints about an atmosphere of "political correctness." Those who sing in this choir are clearly indicating that they recognize there are now tangible consequences for those who refuse to support the change effort.

To accomplish the desired effects, supportive managers will need to learn to use other "power tools." First, they must have the opportunity to continue to develop their own awareness through education and awareness workshops—as participants and, later, as facilitators in partnership with trainers and consultants.

Skill building for competence in managing in the new culture is provided through a combination of workshops and pairings with subordinate group members who provide ongoing feedback. An elaborate system of **performance evaluation** is also necessary. Those who want to support the change effort must know they have to demonstrate that they can not only hear feedback on the competence, they can incorporate the feedback and make the necessary changes in their behavior.

This approach also assumes that white men who support the change effort will form **coalitions** with other managers and employees who are members of subordinate groups (white women, people of color, etc.). The new "players" in the company will be those who support the change—whatever their race or gender. Those men/whites/heterosexuals—or anyone else—who lack the self-esteem, ability, or will to thrive in the new culture will have to "act as if." It is not required that everyone be able to fully support the norms emotionally, at least at the outset; all they need to do is behave according to the new norms. Over time, the new norms will become the new cultural climate, and those who are still "acting as if" will either get in line or move on.

The **role of consultants** in this power strategy is to support the change, not lead it. If key whites and men perceive that there are tangible rewards for them—and for the company as a whole—in the diversity initiative, they will use their power to promote the effort. The consultant will then be called on to advise the "chain of command"—where real business is taken care of—on how to accomplish the goals that the leaders have established for themselves.

One of the traps that diversity initiatives often fall into is that the change effort is relegated to a "parallel structure" or a temporary system. Parallel systems—set up outside the power structure and lacking direct access to it—are perceived as part of "flavor of the month" projects and aren't taken seriously. Consultants who try to "lead" a diversity initiative from a parallel system end up becoming the "extra pair of hands" of which Peter Block speaks.[2]

Training as a power tool should be offered solely as a means for people to learn something they feel is essential to their careers. Training makes sense only at the point where the workforce believes that management is committed to a diversity change effort and top managers are modeling the new norms. Then employees will want to get the training so they can compete in the new culture. Organizations that have been successful in institutionalizing a diversity strategy report that they have waiting lists for their diversity education and awareness, skill building, management development and other training activities.

In addition, managers who firmly believe that both their own self-interest and the future of their organization depends on the success of the change effort will realize that they need to learn how to facilitate diversity workshops so that they can assist their subordinates in learning what they need to know. While few managers are skilled trainers, they certainly have more clout and credibility among their employees than any internal or external trainers ever will. By publicly training and coaching their subordinates in the new skills, managers demonstrate that they indeed have the expertise to help "their people" be successful in the new culture.

While employees may fear being punished if they speak honestly in the presence of their supervisors, that risk is more than offset by the impact of having managers assume visible responsibility for diversity initiatives.

If diversity efforts are to have the clout they need to bring about meaningful change in corporate culture, they must be seen and experienced by employees as "nonnegotiable." This means that the effort must have a strong **public relations** component. The traditional media for communications within the company— the company newsletter, E-mail, posters, or whatever—must be utilized to get the message out and to emphasize that management is not only committed to the effort philosophically but is also committed to putting in place a new set of norms and practices for conducting business based on that philosophical belief.

If this message is conveyed and believed, the great middle who are waiting to see which way the company is going will climb on board and support the new direction. The diehards will still resist—but they will no longer be in a position of power.

Anything less than this adaptation of the strategies of corporate power toward the end of creating the desired change dooms diversity efforts. As long as "managing diversity" is relegated to some variant of "make nice"—that is, to "celebrating diversity by recognizing that we are all different"—it can and will be undermined as illegitimate, unnecessary, or impotent.

END NOTES

1. Richard Beckhard and Reuben T. Harris, *Organizational Transitions: Managing Complex Change* (Reading, MA: Addison-Wesley, 1977), p. 25.
2. Peter Block, *Flawless Consulting: A Guide to Getting Your Expertise Used* (Austin, TX: Learning Concepts, 1981), p. 20.

FOUR

WORKPLACE INITIATIVES

Theory is one thing; practice is another.

Mature diversity efforts have many common characteristics, beginning with a clear and continuing commitment from top management. That commitment must be built into the full range of policies and practices, including holding all employees responsible through the performance appraisal and reward system.

Such mature efforts also demonstrate that a culture-change program must be carefully tailored to the particular characteristics of the specific organization. No off-the-shelf, one-size-fits-all approach will serve.

In this section, leaders and managers in four organizations review specific components of their diversity programs. "Leadership for Workforce 2000" describes the commitment that CoreStates Financial Corp CEO and Chair Terrence A. Larsen made to helping his organization become one in which all employees are valued and given equal access to opportunity.

With the aid of experienced diversity consultants and trainers, CoreStates has launched a far-reaching, systemic culture-change effort which provides a useful model for other start-up efforts.

Keith Woods' article provides a thoughtful—and painful—review of what the editorial and reporting staff of New Orleans' *Times-Picayune* newspaper discovered when they set out to do a series of articles on race. How could they clarify race issues for their readers when they were unable to find effective and comfortable ways to communicate with each other? Every organization that is serious about diversity will find the same challenge.

IBM's Ted Childs, in an interview with *The Diversity Factor*, candidly shares his own experience growing up black in the United States, and draws on those experiences to discuss the components of IBM's diversity initiative. Childs points out that, at IBM, learning to work and manage effectively in a diverse workplace is not only a moral imperative—it is a business necessity.

In "Diversity at DuPont," Bernard Scales, manager of diversity, and Mike Emery, senior vice-president, operations, review DuPont's diversity programs and processes. With the firm support of CEO Edgar S. Woolard, DuPont offers a full range of education and training opportunities on diversity issues, beginning with the intensive five-day, off-site "Multicultural Awareness Workshop." Training opportunities are offered to wage-level and contract workers as well as managers.

As a white man and a senior-level manager, Emery offers a unique perspective on the diversity effort. As one of the chairs of the Valuing People committee, Emery became more aware that competence comes in "all kinds of colors and from many different backgrounds." He shows how white men can capitalize on their positions in organizations to move the diversity initiative forward—to the benefit of everyone.

The central theme to this section is "Authenticity Counts." What is needed to develop a cost-effective and lasting diversity culture-change program is respect for others, the self-confidence to examine one's own attitudes, a willingness to admit to imperfect knowledge, and a genuine desire to learn about other people and other cultures. With this solid foundation, organizations can move ahead to build structures that are large enough to allow all of us to live and work together harmoniously.

16

CHAPTER

Leadership for Workforce 2000

The CoreStates Experience

Margaret Blackburn White

In his 1992 address to the officers of CoreStates Financial
Corp, Chairman Terrence A. Larsen reported bluntly:

It has been painfully obvious this year that our nation has significant areas of utter failure in interpersonal relationships. There is
profound inequity, lack of respect, and even deep hatred among
different groups of Americans. We cannot be satisfied with allowing CoreStates to mirror society in these vital relationships. We
must do better than that . . . We can be a leader. Over the last couple of years, with your help and participation, we have moved
toward that . . . leadership.[1]

What is the kind of leadership that Larsen envisions and that
CoreStates is moving towards? What were the motivating factors
that led the organization down this road? What are the lessons
that other organizations facing similar dilemmas can learn from
this experiment?

THE SETTING

CoreStates Financial Corp operates several banks and other
financial services in Pennsylvania and New Jersey. Its 14,000

employees run eight "core businesses." Over the last decade, like the rest of the banking industry, CoreStates has faced pressures ranging from the loss of regulatory protection to the fallout from the S&L debacle. Many banks were unable to adapt to the changing times and began to fall by the wayside in the 1980s. In his address to the annual officers meeting in December 1990, Larsen said CoreStates would not be one of those left in the dust. In addition to providing a clear five-year projection for the direction of the core businesses, he described his commitment to the theme, "People are at the core of CoreStates":

> For me it means a sense of *family*, where we care about each other as a family. . . . It means *mutual trusting* . . . It means *teamwork* and a *team spirit* . . . And it means *appreciation* and *respect* for each individual and what that individual brings to the family.
>
> In the CoreStates I envision, everyone will be treated with *respect* and *courtesy* and *caring*—whether they work at one of our banks or at the holding company, man or woman, black or white, whether staff or line—everyone will be well-treated.[2]

Larsen admitted that the CoreStates he envisioned was not the CoreStates he saw every day. The organization, as perceived by its employees, was very different.

The process leading to this statement and the sequence of events since that time are instructive for those who are confronting similar issues. In retrospect, events seem to fall into three phases: discovery, taking the lead, and moving forward.

PHASE ONE: DISCOVERY

In 1987, CoreStates hired Frances Stancill as its first full-time director of affirmative action and equal opportunity. Stancill, who is presently director of human resources for one of the CoreStates banks, recalls that one of her first tasks was to hold a series of focus groups with professional-level women and professional-level people of color. "The objective," she says, "was to have them identify what they perceived to be issues and concerns pertaining to recruitment, retention, advancement—all the issues in the employment arena."

These initial focus groups led to ongoing networking meetings among the senior women and senior people of color. In both groups, there was initial fear and reluctance to participate. People wondered: Will I be seen as a troublemaker—or a "feminist"? Will I jeopardize my opportunities for advancement? What are the appropriate parameters of concern and action?

These senior people felt they had a lot to lose. They were successful in the organization and had worked hard for that success. Each individual felt that she or he had been accepted as "one of the guys"; they might be risking that acceptance by banding together with others of the same race or gender.

Nonetheless, the common concerns that began to surface in their meetings outweighed the anxiety. They met with Chairman Larsen several times, and he invited them to summarize these concerns in a report and recommend how the organization should respond.

Their report was straightforward and clear. There are problems around race and gender at CoreStates, it said, and these problems are not being addressed. It recommended that Larsen appoint a high-level manager, reporting directly to him, to investigate the problems and begin to formulate action plans.

PHASE TWO: TAKING THE LEAD

Larsen responded to the recommendation by making two key appointments—both white men at the highest levels of the organization, reporting to him. Bob Murray was designated assistant to the chairman, charged specifically with responding to the problems defined in the report and creating structures for addressing them. Les Butler was appointed chief human resources officer and challenged to make important changes in what had been a problematic division.

The appointment of two white men in these key positions sent an unmistakable message. Anyone who may have imagined that the organization intended to give only lip service to the challenge of addressing the problems was put on notice that this was a serious effort. Those who might have expected that an old boys' club atmosphere would continue undisturbed were forced to rethink that idea.

The People Task Force

Murray and Butler, working with representatives from the women's and people of color groups, began by creating a People Task Force, populated by a select group of senior executives from all functional areas of the company. The level of its members demonstrated the importance of the task force and its authority to initiate change. While there was some mix of race and gender, the decision to include only senior executives limited this somewhat, since there were only three senior vice presidents who were people of color and similarly few women.

The task force settled in to do its homework, studying what other corporations facing the same challenges had done and developing a statement of "CoreValues":

CoreValues

We Value People

We will treat all people with respect and courtesy and create an environment that supports the attainment of their personal and professional aspirations.

We Value Performance

Exceptional contributions by individuals and by teams are critical to CoreStates' successful performance. Such contributions at all levels of the organization will be appreciated and recognized.

We Value Diversity

We will actively promote an atmosphere of mutual respect for each other's differences, recognizing that our diversity creates a breadth of perspectives, which strengthens our organization.

We Value Teamwork

Teamwork is critical to our success. Trust and mutual respect for each other's responsibilities, functions, skills, and experience are essential ingredients of teamwork.

We Value Communication

Open, candid communication flow in all directions will be the norm. We emphasize that listening is a crucial component of the communication process.

We Value Integrity

We will strive to be recognized as an organization of the highest ethical standards and unquestioned integrity.

PHASE THREE: MOVING FORWARD

Over the next few months, the People Task Force developed three specific initiatives to move the work forward: a major employee recognition event called the Corey Awards, based on the CoreValues; the design and implementation of a benchmarking employee opinion survey; and the development of a diversity subcommittee of the People Task Force.

The Corey Awards

The Corey Awards gave visibility and reality to the efforts of the People Task Force. Criteria for nomination reflected CoreStates' core values:

- Does his or her job and does it well.
- Is supportive of his or her co-workers/customers.
- Is always ready to help, even when it isn't "part of the job."
- Trusts his or her co-workers and inspires the trust of others.
- Works well with others.
- Treats co-workers/customers with courtesy, respect, and caring.
- Accepts responsibility.
- Consistently delivers a high level of customer service.
- Consistently performs at a high level.
- Is active in civic or volunteer organizations in his or her community.

More than 700 CoreStates employees were nominated for the awards the first year; from that number, the People Task Force selected 30 winners. First-place winners received $1,000 each, and runner-ups took home $500. All of them received a crystal Corey Award. The event itself involved considerable ceremony and was held at a major Philadelphia hotel.

Employee Opinion Survey

The second initiative was the employee opinion survey. Conducted by an outside research firm and tailored to the CoreStates environment, the survey attempted to determine how people felt about working at CoreStates. Questionnaires were given to all employees; more than 64 percent responded.

The initial analysis, in which the total responses were averaged, seemed to indicate that things were pretty good in the organization. But subsequent, more detailed, scrutiny indicated that the averaged scores obscured patterns of serious concern. The researchers and the People Task Force decided to take another look, this time focusing on race and gender issues.

The new analysis showed very different results. About 80 percent of the African-Americans, for example, indicated they felt race was a block to their progress. Many white women and people of color indicated they were concerned about opportunities for advancement, the ability to transfer to another job and attain career objectives, and the availability of role models.

The People Task Force, still under Murray's leadership, took the findings straight to the chairman. He found the information disturbing:

> It's clear that all of our people count, and if we have elements of our population who are dissatisfied or unhappy, who are not able to function at their maximum, it is just unacceptable for the whole organization. Some of those results would be troubling no matter what your view about people or the value of people. The intensity of the feelings that were expressed . . . magnified the issue for me. To see these emotions, and recognize the intensity of what we are dealing with not just at CoreStates but in all of society, is staggering. It makes one wonder how we are going to manage that at CoreStates when the rest of the world isn't trying as hard to manage it.[3]

The Diversity Subcommittee

At this point, the People Task Force, with Larsen's concurrence, realized that the issues of race and gender that had surfaced from the survey required attention and action. In addition to bringing in a consulting firm that specializes in race and gender issues, the Task Force established a diversity subcommittee to address these concerns.

The organization turned to Senior Vice President Donn Scott to lead the new subcommittee. Scott was one of two black senior vice presidents who had been appointed to the People Task Force at the outset. He had made a major commitment to the effort and had direct access to both Murray and Larsen. His responsibility for new business development and account maintenance for the national middle market placed him firmly on the business side of the company. In short, his leadership could not be discounted, and his appointment further emphasized the commitment of top management to the diversity effort.

Scott and the diversity subcommittee, along with the consultants, designed a strategy for conveying information about the race and gender issues to the organization and for developing action plans to begin addressing the concerns identified in the employee survey. They decided that the best way to present this explosive information was to use it as the basis of a series of education and awareness workshops for top managers. Faced with documentation, it would be difficult for top management to deny that the problems existed or to claim the consultants, the white women, or the people of color were "exaggerating" the problems.

Larsen acknowledged that he had not been fully aware of how the firm's policies and practices were providing a disparate experience for people of color and white women. "I looked at individual cases that I saw, of things happening, or people feeling that life was unfair in one fashion or another," he said, "and it was easy to overlook or rationalize what was taking place. I could say, 'That's not so bad,' or 'If this is the worst thing that happens, then that's acceptable,' or 'That isn't necessarily discrimination because it happens to white males, too'." He added, "I think what changed for me was seeing the magnitude of what's happened to elements of our workforce, learning that these things occur over and over again a dozen times a day, and seeing the cost to people who have managed to succeed despite all these influences."[4]

The workshops were followed by a "crash course" for 108 people in middle management and below to share the employee survey data and prepare them to discuss and interpret it within their organizations. Several initiatives were launched to reshape the culture of the organization and bring it in line with the vision statement. For example, a videotaped conversation between Larsen and the consultant was distributed widely throughout the company, emphasizing that the CEO had heard the problems and was on record saying they would be addressed. Business unit heads were advised they must work on race and gender issues—using any approach they wished to gather information— and share their findings with the diversity subcommittee, the People Task Force, the consultants, and management.

The issues that came back from the business units were clear: recruitment, retention, the relationship of the diversity effort to other management initiatives, communication throughout the organization, salary equity, and promotions.

The diversity subcommittee was charged with translating this information into an action plan focusing on five broad areas:

- Representation of women and people of color at all levels of the CoreStates organization.
- Feedback and mentoring across race and gender lines.
- Support for all groups during the period in which the organization is changing.
- Management accountability on diversity issues.
- Significant prioritization for diversity in the overall vision for CoreStates' future.

Soon, the diversity subcommittee discovered it could not meet the demands for leadership in regularly scheduled monthly sessions. The committee found itself gathering at least twice a month, with smaller groups meeting weekly or in some cases, even daily. Planning sessions focused on the development of strategies for 1993, identification of roles the committee would play, and the assignment of "coaches" for the various roles to ensure their successful implementation. Timetables for completion of specific tasks by different units and divisions were established and communicated.

The diversity subcommittee recognized that timely and effective communication of its activities and concerns is a key target issue. Facts about what is and is not really happening must be constantly and forcefully relayed to the organization, in part to confront the inevitable charges of "reverse discrimination" from white men. Scott says that the organization recognizes that whatever position they take relative to the promotion of people, a segment of the population is going to react negatively, and a segment will react positively.

This has always been true, in his view; what is different is that there will now be more white men who are feeling left out, and more white women and people of color who feel included. The key, Scott suggests, is to be as fair as possible in making decisions, to make certain that the people who are being promoted have a right to be promoted, and that no position is filled with an unqualified individual.

LOOKING TO THE FUTURE

In the spring of 1993, the managing diversity intervention at CoreStates was still in the toddler, if not infancy, stage. Some significant changes were made in the leadership of the effort: Murray moved on to planned retirement, and Larsen himself assumed responsibility for chairing the People Task Force. A corporate office of diversity now reports directly to Larsen through Donn Scott, chair of the diversity subcommittee. An experienced black woman, Yvette Hyater-Adams, has been named vice president and director of diversity, to provide day-to-day guidance for implementing the diversity work.

One thing that has not changed is the organization's commitment to its CoreValues. Larsen summed up that commitment in his 1992 address to the CoreStates officers:

> We are committed to making the cultural and interpersonal gains that are possible, and we will refuse to accept behavior that is opposite to that of our CoreValues. We will not tolerate bigotry. We will not tolerate sexism. And we will not tolerate "bully" managers. Beginning next year, we are all going to have numerous opportunities to learn how to manage our relationships even better. And be prepared! Those who do not want to, or over time are unable to build good relationships, will be managed out of the organization so that the rest will have a chance to succeed.[5]

E N D   N O T E S

1. Larsen, "Reinventing CoreStates: Value by Value," Special Insert, Annual Address to Officers, December 15, 1992.

2. Larsen, "Vision of CoreStates," A speech delivered at the CoreStates Financial Corp Annual Officers Meeting, December 18, 1990.
3. Larsen, Interview with Elsie Y. Cross, Videotape, Fall 1992.
4. Larsen, Interview with Elsie Y. Cross, Videotape, Fall 1992.
5. Larsen, "Reinventing CoreStates: Value by Value."

CHAPTER

Covering Race, Covering Ourselves

Keith Woods

Former Ku Klux Klan Grand Wizard David Duke's 1991 Louisiana gubernatorial campaign set the stage for *The Times-Picayune's* race project.

His shocking second-place primary showing, his 665,409 runoff votes—55 percent of the state's white electorate—and the explosive collision of values that happened whenever his platform brought white and black people together was ample evidence that there was important journalistic work to be done on the subject of race relations.

Still, it would take several meetings, several months, and a major racial conflict on the city council before the idea of a race project could gain enough momentum to merit a project director—then-suburban editor Kristin Gilger—and a 20-plus team of reporters, editors, a photographer, and a graphic artist.

It wasn't that race was an untouchable subject. Long before the specter of a sheet-wearing governor loomed over Louisiana, we had begun the endless work known in societal shorthand as "diversity training." Hatched from the discontent of African-American and white female reporters, the drive to open eyes and

The Times-Picayune series is organized into six main sections. Their covers are reproduced together on a reprint of the series (left). The first section (center and right) introduces many themes, often by juxtaposing personal images.

doors at the newspaper began in 1990 and had reached most of the newsroom managers by the fall of 1991.

Its most immediate benefit in the newsroom was that it opened a channel of communication across races that simply didn't exist before and may have helped us see clearer how to cover Duke, then a state legislator who had run a closer-than-expected race for the U.S. Senate just two years earlier.

Many of us could hear him better, armed with a new race decoder that sent up flares every time *welfare* or *inner city* or *poor* or, often, *New Orleans*, was used as a euphemism for *black*; every time *Western Christian values* or *middle class* or *law-abiding* was encoded to mean *white*. We raised red flags every time logic and fairness were twisted to align with the simple prejudices of his supporters.

It informed our story planning and improved our stories.

But when a small group of editors gathered on a sunny November 1991, afternoon, two days after Duke had been sent down the path to obscurity by populist Democrat Edwin Edwards, we were a fatigued group, tired of the tension, the conflict, the phone calls from white people complaining that we were pandering to black people by condemning Duke.

It was a momentum-killing weariness that has plopped itself down in the middle of the road to success often since then—strengthening some who climb over it, enlightening some who negotiate a way around it, defeating the rest who see no way past it.

As a story, race relations can be ignored. The media, no less uncomfortable with the subject than anyone else, often will write about crime fears or education spending inequities or a New York borough's attempt to secede from the city as though those stories were not joined at birth to racial prejudices.

In many cases, it's better that way. The media's typical treatment of the subject tends to be insultingly superficial and little more than a study of black pathos; a mixture of intellectually deficient anthropology and pop sociology, each seeking to unearth the "black experience," to expose black pain, as though those are noble ends unto themselves.

Maybe they were once, when it was considered the vanguard of enlightened journalism to step outside of the middle-class white world of the newsroom for a breast-beating look at the lives of people who otherwise seldom made the news unless they were criminals or corpses. That kind of inquiry, alive and thriving in some newsrooms today, serves little purpose now but to salve white guilt and offer a one-way look into how those other people think.

CONFRONTING DYSFUNCTION

That's what many of the black staff feared when we gathered for the first meeting of the race project group in April 1992. Black and white, male and female, veterans and virtual newcomers were called together just days before Los Angeles exploded in racial violence following the acquittal of five white police officers accused of brutalizing black motorist Rodney King.

Our first meeting was a study in dysfunction, a microcosm of American race relations.

The group was charged with the simple task of brainstorming an outline. That, after all, is how newspaper projects get done: Conceive the project; sketch out an outline; master the subject; write the stories.

Conflicts over approach, scope, length of stories, those are common. But when most newspaper projects are launched, the

The second part (left) covers the history of race relations using local details and event timelines; the third (center) explores New Orleans's particular perspective on what race is; and the fourth (right) examines childhood experiences.

team typically agrees on something as basic as the definition of the problem being studied.

Not so for the race project. The dissonance surfaced almost immediately when a white reporter questioned the working definitions of *racism* and *prejudice*. A black reporter said the discussion, like the project, should begin with a look at American slavery.

Silence and sighs greeted both. Planning yielded to posturing, and the polarized distrust that had sat unseen, the distrust that belies the cordiality of countless conversations between black and white people, surfaced in the conference room and brought the meeting to a dispirited end, an end that, in retrospect, was nothing if not predictable.

The fears and biases that accounted for the distrust had to be extracted from the questions because nobody came right out and said what they were afraid of. Some white team members feared the series would end up doing little more than blaming white people for the woes of black Americans. Some black members feared the series would be just another *National Geographic*-style probe into the ghetto: a study of the black "condition" that speaks only of victims, never of perpetrators.

Both sides had good reason to worry.

In an effort to keep the project together, the group stopped the journalistic process, and we retreated to a downtown office building for two more days of diversity training. It was, for me, the most balanced and intellectually challenging session of the four I had attended.

The group was, first of all, more racially balanced: 13 white people, 5 black. In the first three diversity workshops I attended, the ratio was typically 22 to 4. More importantly, in this session, the black participants were all bold, outspoken and thoughtful, offering a concentration of qualities seldom seen in the arbitrary selection of participants that characterized the previous groups.

FINDING COMMON GROUND

What resulted was two days of frank, often tearful discussions that sought out the origins of our fears. Unsatisfied with the amount of work done in those two days, the project team went on without facilitators for several more three-hour sessions, including a painful, friendship-wrecking attempt to get white team members to admit to racial prejudices.

Throughout, the work toward a common goal and a common vocabulary was taking place in unusual places—in the cafeteria, at a desk, at our homes—anywhere two or more people from the team got together. It would be more than two months before the outline we were dispatched to write in the first chaotic meeting would be completed. Far from the traditional week-long series treatment most subjects get, we committed to a story that would take 18 months and 104 newspaper pages to tell.

But the problems didn't disappear when we emerged from the exhausting preliminaries. Team members fought constant battles to see to it that the true ideals of diversity—mutual respect, shared power, valued difference—were being honored. It was not an easy balance to negotiate in an organization pushed by ceaseless deadlines, hostile to all delays, and entrenched in a hierarchy dominated by white managers.

We tried to institutionalize input, requiring that all stories for the project—and ideas as well—get passed through the hands of at least one black team member. When it worked, black and

The fifth installment (left) delves into cultural differences. The last presentation (center) looks at the current social situation and possible trends. Over 6,000 people called on recorded phone lines; 50 pages of comment were printed (right).

white team members acknowledged their skewed lenses, learned from the exchange of perspectives, and walked away happy that what resulted was the best we could achieve.

When it didn't work, and it often didn't, frustration reigned. Stories were sometimes conceived, assigned, written, and edited with little or no black participation, an oft-repeated backslide to the view that white people can choose when black people are necessary and when they can be bypassed.

It was difficult—impossible for some—to remain engaged in such a volatile project when we knew that, on a whim, we could be excluded. The simmering anxiety of knowing that I and some of my colleagues might have to go uninvited into a meeting or force our opinion upon an idea or story was a heavy, tiring burden.

ABIDING BY TRUTH

The project we produced reflected those disparate experiences: extraordinary stories that challenged convention in ways few newspapers have dared; mediocre stories that skimmed the surface the way newspapers have for years.

Evidence that we are a better newspaper as a result of the experience exists but not where most people hope to find it. Some broken friendships remain broken, and the tension that the project revealed, tension that emerges whenever race is discussed in such raw form, lingers in the newsroom. No organizational catharsis. No holding hands to sing "We are the World."

Our success lies largely in the potential to do important, honest, constructive work on race relations, potential realized in the project's truly great stories. When we are willing to endure the anger, bitterness, misunderstanding, or confusion that doggedly follow such undertakings, when we are willing to abide by the truths most of us can now at least recognize, we are a better newspaper.

The work we've done in the past four years has provided us with that still-rare insight. But no amount of diversity training or journalistic inquiry into race will give us courage to do something with it. That, we'll each have to find on our own.

C H A P T E R

Managing Diversity: The IBM Experience

Ted Childs

The Diversity Factor: *Ted, I think everyone is aware that IBM has always taken a leadership role in hiring people of color, white women, and people with disabilities. With that kind of history, why did the company decide it needed a specific diversity program?*

Ted Childs: It's an evolutionary process. If we look at diversity as a family of issues, we can still see it as a half-empty, half-full glass. Half-full: We have made significant progress. Half-empty: The task is not completed. What we have is a foundation. We continue to improve our representation, and our availability system—the system by which we measure our progress—continues to improve each year in terms of representation of women and minorities and their movement into the senior positions. But we're not there yet.

TDF: *Why not? What is it that keeps us from being there?*

TC: Attitudes and people. We have to respond to the attitudes of people who are not accustomed to dealing with people who are different from them. We have a white male population, many of whom may not have had peer relationships professionally with women or with people of color. We are still dealing with removing the problems that occur from not being exposed to people who are different from you.

We feel we have moved from the moral imperative that motivated the civil rights movements to a strategic imperative. We're a company that used to sell big computers but now has a major piece of its business devoted to PCs—a product that we want everyone to take home. We view every citizen in every country as a potential customer. We must be able to communicate with a very diverse consumer population.

To do that, we want consumers to look in at the IBM company and see people like them and be comfortable knowing that people like them are working here and prospering as a result of their contributions. We believe that if our consumers believe that people like them are respected here, they will view us as a place worthy of spending their hard-earned dollars.

TDF: *What about the situation of white men?*

TC: First, I think we need to emphasize that this is a great company and a great country and, whatever the historical circumstances, it was white males who made it that way. Yes, they had the whole pie, and the issue is today that they have to share some of that. But the fact is that they brought us to where we are, and we will not continue to be great if they leave. Diversity includes white men; it's not diversity *and* them—diversity means everybody.

By the same token, if white men constitute about 60 percent of the work force but hold more than 80–90 percent of the executive jobs, that's an inequitable distribution of power and responsibility.

We also must recalibrate our expectations about success. We must have, for everyone's benefit, meaningful discussions about what failure is not. It is not failure if you do not become an executive. There are few positions at the top, and the competition for those positions is fierce—as it should be. We do all people a disservice when we give them the message, "You've failed if you haven't made it to the top." Reality is that most white men don't make it to the top—yet we don't perceive them as failures.

We are dealing with people and their professional lives and their sense of dignity and self-respect. People have varying abilities and ambitions. Whatever one's gender or color, some people's highest achievement is the first floor, and other people reach the top. But for most of us—it's somewhere in between.

TDF: *How do you help white men buy in to the idea that diversity includes them?*

TC: I think we have to continue to discuss it. We have to keep it in front of everybody. We have to continue to provide people the opportunity to work with people who are different from them so that we can dispel any myths that exist.

For example, over a period of years, our college hiring has attracted students who have a grade-point average of between 3.3 and 3.5—and our minority college hires fit that profile as well. When we point that out, it helps dispel myths and stereotypes.

When we began this journey in the 1960s at IBM, we understood that it was a journey that would not conclude overnight. We understood that hiring people is not the answer; you are not going to satisfy any thirst simply by giving people a job. People we hire will expect that other people—like them—will migrate upward in the firm, and, sooner or later, they are going to be knocking on the boardroom door.

In the 1960s, we dealt with entry-level hiring and filling first-line management positions. In the 1970s, we dealt with middle managers; in the 80s, with senior managers; and in the 90s, we're dealing with executives. But, at every stage we were building the foundation, filling the pipeline with candidates who could then move on to the next level.

Throughout this process, it has always been important that we strive to ensure that people have an environment in which they can reach their maximum level of performance. We're finding that white women and people of color and people with disabilities are just moving on through and making it to the top of this business—we want to be sure this continues. They must be able to reach their maximum level with dignity.

And of course, as I stated earlier, we have to have fair definitions of failure and success. Once again, everyone will not get to the top, and we can neither expect all of our women, minority, and disabled candidates to get to the top nor conclude that racism or sexism is automatically the reason they do not.

FROM MORAL SUASION TO BUSINESS NECESSITY

TDF: *How do you define workforce diversity at IBM?*

TC: At this point in our nation's history, diversity in the workforce means that a growing proportion of the employee population is other than white, Anglo-Saxon, heterosexual, married men whose wives are full-time homemakers. That "other than" includes not only white women and people of color but anyone whose lifestyle doesn't quite mirror the traditional family reflected in "Leave it to Beaver." Today, the term *diverse* can be applied to most people in the U.S.

At IBM, we have what we like to describe as our diversity "house." The house has three pillars: equal opportunity, affirmative action, and work and personal life balance programs.

The concept of equal opportunity means an equal opportunity to be employed and to work in a harassment-free environment. Affirmative action represents those actions that we take to help individuals compete—not to give anyone an advantage, but to eliminate disadvantage. Our work and personal life balance programs are intended to eliminate attitudinal, policy, and practice barriers that impact on employee productivity and inhibit an individual's ability to balance work and personal life.

All three pillars support the common goal of our "diversity house": providing "access to the workplace."

TDF: *In your video and literature, there is a lot of talk about a "perception" of a glass ceiling. Why are you so careful to use the word* perception, *and is there a glass ceiling in your diversity house?*

TC: I don't believe there is a glass ceiling at IBM. But we have not satisfied everyone's aspirations. Our senior management would like for us to have made more progress than we have; there is room for more progress and we will achieve it.

Let me put it another way: prior to meaningful penetration of a given level, one might say there is a glass ceiling. But if we have fueled the pipeline well enough, and people have moved through into that level, we believe that dispels the idea that there is a glass ceiling *at that level*. Now, that doesn't mean that we still do not have a couple of levels where we haven't had that meaningful penetration, so there is still room for that perception. But we have the efforts underway to shatter it, and we have a CEO and senior executive team who are focused on accomplishing that.

THE LESSONS OF EXPERIENCE

TDF: *Ted, you talk about these issues as both questions of morality and questions of business. When I listen to you, I am aware that we are not just talking about your job. What in your personal life brought you to this point?*

TC: It's true that several experiences from my childhood had a profound influence on me in terms of where I am today.

I grew up in Springfield, Massachusetts, and attended integrated schools. When I was a kid, I had two primary occupations: I was either reading or playing ball. The summer I was 12, the basketball hoop at the school where we played kept falling down. They would put it up, and it would fall down again. One day, I went home and called the mayor's office to ask for help. They could tell I was a kid, so they told me he was home for lunch, but they gave me his phone number. I took a few minutes and made a list of what I wanted to say, and called.

I told him we were a group of guys, black and white, and our mothers always knew where we were because we'd be down at the schoolyard playing ball. So we needed a decent hoop.

While I was talking to the mayor, my dad walked into the bedroom and heard this conversation. He thought I was crazy—calling up the mayor of Springfield.

So I said to my dad, "You told me I could talk to anybody I wanted to as long as I respected them." He had to agree.

A few days later, we got a new hoop, and I had learned an important lesson about dealing with people—especially executives: Be direct and be honest, with yourself and with them.

I also learned a lot, as a child, from our family trips to North Carolina, my mom's home, though some of the lessons didn't take hold until much later. For example, once or twice my mother and I took the train from Springfield to Durham. Until we got to Washington, we sat anywhere we chose; after that—although I didn't notice when I was a child—we sat in a car reserved for black people. When we reached Durham, the cab drivers who took us to my grandmother's house were always black; somehow, the significance of that escaped my young mind.

Similarly, I didn't think about why my mother always packed a large basket of food when the family traveled by car to North Carolina. To me, that was just part of family vacation—a traveling picnic. It was much later that I realized that was a survival basket—we were not allowed to eat in the roadside restaurants.

One incident, though, did make an immediate and powerful impact. We had been driving a long time and came to a motel with a vacancy sign prominently displayed. We went expectantly to the desk, and my father requested a room for the night. The clerk said, "Sorry, no vacancies tonight." "But the sign . . .," my father said. "No vacancies," the clerk insisted.

A woman called out from the back. "It's OK, I just cleaned a room. Let 'em have that one."

The man was flustered. Just then, the woman came around the corner and saw who was looking for a room. "Oh, I made a mistake," she said. "There's no rooms available tonight."

There was no way I could avoid getting that message.

One summer, I went to North Carolina alone to visit my grandmother. Now we weren't a rich family, but my dad knew I had a lot more than most of the kids I would be playing with there. So he said, "Don't take your stuff with you. Just figure out how to have fun the way they have fun, but think for yourself and don't join them if they're doing something stupid." But he didn't warn me about racial issues.

My grandmother sent me to the store to get some snuff. The counter divided the store and there were two doors, one on either side of the counter. All the blacks used one door and all the whites the other, but I didn't even notice. I just walked in the nearest door, which happened to be the white door.

A kid who lived across the street from my grandmother looked in and saw what I had done and that the white people hanging out near their door were about to hurt me. So he opened the door and yelled in, "That's Miss Emma's grandson. He doesn't know. He's from Massachusetts." So they let me go.

My folks made me come home; they decided it was too risky to have me stay there. You have to remember that was just a couple of years after Emmet Till's murder.* So I went home. But I never forgot it.

---

* In 1955, 14-year-old Emmet Till was lynched while visiting his family in Mississippi. His alleged offense was that he whistled at a white woman.

TDF: *That's not something you could forget! What about your college years?*

TC: I went to West Virginia State College, one of the historically black colleges that became mostly white following the Brown decision. The on-campus population, however, remained about 90 percent black—the white students commuted.

I was president of the sophomore class, but when I ran again, in my senior year, I lost the election to a fellow black student, who became a superb class president. A white student, however, won the election for president of the student body. He asked me to be his social committee chairman, and I accepted, if we would agree that our key goal would be to integrate our college at our 1966 homecoming, the college's 75th anniversary. Prior to that, from 1954 when integration started, there had never been more than six white couples attending our homecoming dance. We put together a joint strategy to appeal to black and white students—and that year 600 white couples attended!

I had another memorable experience that year. I had a white professor who had never given a black student an A. The first day of class, he stood right in front of me and announced—knowing I sometimes skipped class—that if you missed more than three sessions you'd fail the course. (The profs knew me because I waited tables in the faculty dining room and was the dormitory resident for a floor in the freshman men's dorm.) So I went to class.

The second semester, however, I missed more than three sessions because I was going on job interviews. This professor had worked for General Motors, and when he saw how I used our Human Resources in Business classroom material to respond to the interview questions, and that I was hired by IBM, a company with leading HR policies, he passed me anyway; in fact, I received an A that semester.

That year focused me on what I wanted to do professionally. The two experiences together anchored me on a precise point about myself. I loved being at the core of dealing with issues that exist because of people's differences and being a catalyst for causing people to talk to, not about, one another—as well as to respect and value those differences instead of viewing them as incompatible with their business or personal objectives.

I was a psych major, and I knew I wanted to deal with people in business and business-related problems.

TDF: *So you've been with IBM ever since?*

TC: Yes. I started off in a training program in Kingston, New York. The training was designed as four six-month assignments. Shortly after I arrived, I expressed a concern to my manager about how IBM recruited on black campuses. He suggested I look into it, and I wrote a paper on how I thought we ought to recruit on minority campuses. They liked it so much they offered me a permanent job there as a recruiter instead of completing my rotation. I thought it over carefully but finally accepted it.

My manager and the personnel manager and I sat down and established a goal: For that year, 1968, we'd be successful if we recruited 19 black employees out of the 300 people we planned to hire in Kingston. By the end of June, we had 53 accepts from black college students around the country!

I learned something valuable out of that experience. Kingston was not ready for 53 young black professionals— nor was IBM. And the 53 black students weren't ready for IBM or Kingston either. We were faced with a situation where the white people had had limited interaction with blacks, and the black people—most of whom had grown up in the south and gone to black schools and black college—had had limited interaction with whites as well.

A key example of the significance of limited interaction was the issue of rental housing. Because there was a shortage of rentals, IBM maintained a housing office to assist employees. Landlords could register a listing by phone but had to indicate that the space would be rented to anyone, regardless of race, gender, etcetera. Prior to 1968, the odds were that there would be no minority applicants, so everyone automatically made the "yes" declaration. Well, we changed those odds! And placed some very constructive stress in the housing resource system—good for progress, but painful for those who lived through it.

I don't think there was a lot of hostility—certainly there was some. I think there was a lot of puzzlement because people were coming face-to-face with myths. It reminded me of going fishing in Vermont with my dad and a buddy when I was about 11 or 12. We were meeting white kids who had never seen any black people except on television. And they wanted to touch us because they thought the black would rub off, or they wanted to run their hands through our hair. You just couldn't get angry—they weren't calling us "nigger" or anything, they were just enormously curious.

That experience helped me when I got to Kingston. I think that concept of curiosity is still a factor today, in terms of people having to deal with things on a personal basis—face-to-face—that they've only read about before.

Last year I was speaking to a group of military people and I read them a newspaper article; I read all the key phrases—"our soldiers won't live in barracks with them"; "it will destroy the morale of our fighting men"; "it is not the Army's role to implement national social policy"—but I didn't say who or what the article was about.

Then I asked them, "What subject am I reading about?" And they said, "This gay thing in the Army." I said, "No, I'm reading a story from 1948 in *The New York Times* about Harry Truman's executive order allowing blacks into the military. Isn't it interesting how little has changed?"

TDF: *Your personal experience certainly illustrates one aspect of the civil rights struggles in this country. In your view, how have we moved through these struggles to where we are today?*

TC: Let's take a walk through our nation's history. First, our nation was born from a set of principles—a key one being freedom from religious persecution. From that point

on, a common thread in our national history is a series of
civil rights struggles: The Boston Tea Party was a form of
civil rights rebellion. From then to the present, there have
been the debate about slavery, which led to a war; the
fight for respect and dignity by Italian, Irish, and other
immigrants; the women's suffrage struggle and victory,
followed by the debate over equal pay and, recently,
family leave; the treatment of our early Chinese workers
in the settling of the West; our abuse of our Japanese
citizens following Pearl Harbor; the black civil rights
struggle against lynching and discrimination in sports,
schools, and public access; the continuing battle for
respect and dignity by our disabled citizens—a battle that
has often centered around a fair and responsible definition
of the word "disability"; the current active and visible
search for fairness and dignity for our gay and lesbian
citizens; and if freedom from religious persecution was an
early goal, the prevalence of antisemitism says we have
not achieved it.

In each of these struggles, people have died for their
beliefs. Frederick Douglass said, "Without pain there is no
progress." No matter who you are, if you are involved in
any of these issues today, then you are standing on the
shoulders of someone before you—particularly in the
world of business.

TDF: *Given that national history, do you have a civil
rights hero?*

TC: Absolutely: Jackie Robinson. We are a literate
country anchored in the fundamental principle that every
citizen will have access to a public school education—a
principle that was intended to ensure that our citizens
would be able to read and write, interpret their readings,
and make informed decisions, particularly in the privacy
of a voting booth. And yet we integrated our national
pastime—baseball—five or six years before we integrated
our classrooms, the source of that literacy. Baseball
preceding schools made Jackie Robinson's task all the
more difficult, all the more significant, and I believe gives
insight into how we establish priorities in the United

States. If valuing diversity is the process by which people who are different get to know one another and dispel myths, then sports may be the greatest process we have created—not to dispel myths, perhaps, but to help people get to know one another.

TDF: *In your view, then, our history demonstrates that we have moved from a moral imperative to a strategic one?*

TC: That seems quite clear to me. The people who worked on these issues 30 years ago had to preach. We had social disruption, we had riots. I don't think the boardrooms of America had a clear vision that the numbers of minorities, women, or the disabled were going to grow and become critical parts of their workforce and their marketplace. I think they felt that they were buying peace. They thought it was enough to pat you on the head— if you were a woman or a person of color—and say, "Now we solved the problem. We gave you a job." That's a kind of moral imperative.

We still have riots. But the boardrooms of America know it is no longer possible to solve problems by patting people on the head or offering them token jobs. The American business community understands that success— in the present and the future—lies in enabling a diverse workforce to serve a diverse marketplace.

This is a strategic imperative that says, "How I interact with you is directly linked to the survival of my business, and I'm going to respect you because disrespecting you is going to lead to my company's difficulty in surviving." These are not parallel processes; they are two very different ways of thinking and doing business. One says that you can be my partner in growing and maintaining this business; the other says in my free time I will give you some attention.

TDF: *How do you know IBM's investment in diversity is paying off?*

TC: Well, we clearly track our progress in terms of representation. Even though we have experienced approximately a 50 percent reduction in our population since 1986, we have been able to sustain a good deal of our progress in retaining women, people of color, and people with disabilities. We have had some losses: From 1991 to 1994, the representation of women has declined from 29 percent to 28 percent; our minority population, half of which is black, is 18 percent; and we have seen a modest decline there. But in the senior management population, we have sustained our progress in retaining people of color and women. Our senior management keeps a very close eye on this so that we do not in fact wreak havoc on the investment in people that we have made over the last 30 years on the subject of equal opportunity.

THE WORKPLACE DIVERSITY PROGRAM

TDF: *Could you describe some specific aspects of your diversity training program?*

TC: All our managers are now attending a two-day diversity imperative seminar, an experiential learning opportunity which culminates with the development of a diversity skills action plan by all individuals. The action plan enables participants to map their own progress on acquiring and honing this set of behavioral skills.

We have initiated a number of other training opportunities as well: an "overview" of diversity awareness for any employee with a minimum knowledge of workforce diversity issues; "The Diversity Imperative" for senior managers; a strategic planning session on diversity for diversity councils or task forces or champion teams; and a course called "Workforce Diversity: Your Competitive Edge" for external customers.

Our human resources function in the United States has been restructured so that we now have a diversity service center, similar to our benefits center; the customers for this center will be line managers and human resource staff across the United States responsible for developing staffing, AA compliance, and diversity plans.

Finally, we have developed a video on diversity which is used in the two-day management workshop and then is available for managers to use in departmental meetings with their employees. We have also provided a 45-item Q & A document to assist managers in leading discussions of the video. Every manager in IBM is required to have at least one meeting a year devoted to the subject of workforce diversity—an expectation that has existed for about 20 years.

CONFLICTING VALUES

TDF: *Sometimes a commitment to diversity may come into conflict with other kinds of cultural values. For example, I recently visited a Midwest corporation which is struggling with heterosexism and homophobia; they want to create a viable working environment for their gay and lesbian employees, but the surrounding culture does not support the effort. What do you think a corporation's obligation is if its commitment to diversity comes in conflict with the religious or cultural values of its particular work location, community, or workforce?*

TC: I don't believe that you can make a commitment to diversity and have a "but" at the end of the sentence. Valuing diversity must be all-inclusive and involve respecting all people. I do hear the debates surrounding the subject of religion as it relates to the gay and lesbian community. I'm puzzled by that, quite honestly. In my lifetime, I've seen very high elected officials in this country stand in school doors and say that God did not intend for black children and white children to go to school together—but we integrated our schools. I've seen the prime minister of South Africa say that God did not intend for people who are of different colors to live together—and now—think of this!— we have President Mandela and Mr. De Klerk in one government! In both cases, hatred and bigotry were at some time compatible with someone's religious beliefs.

I am not talking about endorsing lifestyles or behavior that may generate debate and that many may find distasteful. I am talking about respecting all people for their ability to contribute to our common work objectives. As I said earlier, we must view every citizen in every country as potential customers. To do that, we must create a workplace where everyone can do two things: come to work and come to shop. Any group that feels that their group can't come here to work—and be respected and valued—won't come here to shop either. A key element in that strategy is to have people leave their biases at the door if they are disruptive of the workplace. If we are not doing what is necessary to help people want to come here to shop, then we are not focused on our primary business objective: beating the competition.

It's a little like being in battle. If you are in a foxhole, your concerns are whether the people who share that foxhole can do the job. You don't worry about how they live their personal lives; those concerns remain outside the foxhole. Such concerns should also stay outside the workplace. Our day-to-day business competition must be viewed as a kind of economic war; what matters is who can help us win the war.

It's a question of attitude versus behavior. If you can come in here and work with your co-workers towards the best objectives of the IBM company, then we can get along here. You must demonstrate behavior that reflects the expectations that flow from our IBM principles. If your biases are disruptive, then we won't get along here, and someone's going to have to leave. We just can't have war in the workplace. And we're not going to start asking people on their applications for employment if they are gay or lesbian, or even if they are bigots. We make our expectations of how we treat each other pretty clear from the day we hire you. So if you step outside those expectations and treat other people abusively—no matter what you think of them or their sexual orientation—you know there will be consequences.

TDF: *And you would still argue that is a strategic imperative more than a moral imperative?*

TC: Emphatically. I'm not saying the moral imperative doesn't exist. But in terms of the global economy and our need to be competitive and profitable, we don't have time to preach today. We don't have time to walk around and say, "You know, you really ought to be nice to that person." The only factor should be: Can he or she help you meet your objectives and beat your competition? If that can happen, why are you worried about it? If you find out that person is gay or lesbian, does that make them less qualified?

THE GLOBAL CONTEXT

TDF: *You spoke of competition in the global economy. We've been thinking about how what we construe as a strategic imperative around diversity might be seen in other places as another kind of American cultural imperialism.*

TC: We do business in more than 130 countries, so this is a real issue. We have developed an approach with our international constituencies that asks each country IBM management team to tell us what their workforce diversity subjects are. Our corporate policy essentially says we don't discriminate against anyone; the individual country team then implements that general viewpoint in a manner most appropriate to the customs, practices, and laws within that country. We propose that no matter what country one is in, there are people who are disadvantaged. We ask our general managers to identify those who are disadvantaged in their country and to find an appropriate response to them.

Let's put this in a framework. You're in a discussion where you're reviewing progress, and you see in a particular country that women aren't doing well, or they don't have women employees. It's a reasonable question to ask, "How do women fare here? Do they attend the colleges and universities? What women do we have in some of the key skill areas?"

TDF: *And if their answer is, "We don't believe women should be in the workforce?"*

TC: Then I think we can have a meaningful discussion about that. I don't consider having a discussion to be a dictatorial relationship. I think it's a process that says, "Let me share with you what's going on in other places in terms of the labor force and the marketplace and the contribution women are making, and I really hope that we are not losing an opportunity here to maximize skills that exist that are available to us."

We recently sent a letter to all our international human resource teams that stated that we want to work with them to develop a worldwide workforce diversity strategy and that we want our diversity focus to reflect the vision and promise of the marketplace. That's important. And to do that, we need to have some goals. A critical goal is to make sure that we respect people from all of the various constituencies that make up the IBM company, their intellectual value and their ability to contribute. And we must keep talking about that because we're going to be working in different places and with different people, and it's important that everyone feel respected and valued.

RESPECT AND RACISM

TDF: *I notice that you talk a lot about respect and strategic imperatives and diversity philosophy, but I don't hear much about systemic racism or sexism or discrimination. Why not?*

TC: I don't think it is necessary to use those terms in the context of the IBM corporation.

TDF: *Well, IBM lives in the world with the rest of us, and racism and sexism are systemic in our society, as well as in other societies.*

TC: In our society, we have deep-seated racial problems, and gender problems, and problems with homophobia and bias against older people, and problems with the disabled being treated in a fair and respectful manner. Our goal at IBM is not to deny that they exist. Our goal is to keep them from influencing our workplace, our productivity, or our competitive edge. We're committed to seeing that wherever discrimination is lurking, we'll track it down, and whenever disrespect occurs, we'll take steps to change that situation.

TDF: *Thank you very much for your time. One final question— an article last year in* The Wall Street Journal *said that the whole diversity industry is just a sign of "political correctness." What do you think your CEO would say about that?*

TC: He doesn't have to say anything about it; he's made his commitment clear in our video and in his writing and speaking. He's committed to what we're doing in diversity as a strategic imperative, as I've said.

Mr. Gerstner has given us eight principles to guide us in the management of our business. Four of those principles address the role the marketplace should play in all our actions, the concept of productivity, the importance of teamwork, and supporting our employees in their communities. The subject of workforce diversity blends quite comfortably with each of these four principles.

In addition, Mr. Gerstner has asked us to commit "to winning in the marketplace" and "to each other." He did not say "winning in those marketplaces that you like or are represented by your friends"; he did not define "each other" as people you like, play ball with, drink with, or go to church with.

The point is that we must all come together as a team if we are to beat the competition. And the only reason we are here is to beat the competition. That's reality.

CHAPTER

Diversity at DuPont

The Strategic Diversity Plan

Bernard Scales and Mike Emery

Two years ago, according to Bernard Scales, manager of diversity, DuPont took a hard look at the diversity effort and came away with a five-year "Strategic Diversity Plan." The plan is now the corporate blueprint for valuing people.

There are four significant initiatives in the plan: leadership involvement and development; education and training, organizational development, and cost-effectiveness.

LEADERSHIP INVOLVEMENT AND DEVELOPMENT

The shift in this initiative was from "telling" to "doing." Previously, according to Scales, leadership tended to set up programs and expect others to participate. Now, top management is expected to be involved at all levels, including personal participation in interactive educational events, adopting a "learn-and-teach" approach, and participating and leading network activities.

Senior managers are charged with not only talking about diversity values but also with modeling by their behavior how those values are to be put into action. They are expected to develop processes by which accountability for diversity progress is measured—and then to carry out the measurement and act on the results.

The CEO, Edgar S. Woolard, participates personally in the diversity task force, which reviews and responds to information from focus groups of managers of mixed and same ethnic and gender groups, from senior managers who are champions and advocates, and from other kinds of multicultural teams.

Scales points out that there has been a strong grassroots initiative at DuPont as far back as the 1970s. The current effort aims to capitalize on that grassroots commitment by structuring mentoring programs, recognitions and rewards, and networks in ways that connect these processes with leadership in a new and more powerful way.

EDUCATION AND TRAINING

"We had a bunch of consultants running around with OD hats on," Scales observes, "and then they put on the diversity hat." As a result, there was a proliferation of consultation, curriculum, and processes with no overall plan.

As part of the development of the Strategic Diversity Plan, DuPont reviewed its diversity offerings and came up with a "best in class" list of curricula. With list in hand, they structured a survey and focus group process to identify those consultants whose expertise could support the workshops that had been identified as key to the overall diversity initiative. Consultants must have a strong OD background and, for most courses, special competence in facilitating interactive workshops around race, gender, and other areas of discrimination.

Presently, the education and training function provides a core curriculum for all employees, with the goal of maximizing the direct impact of the workshops on the work environment. Further, the corporate values around diversity are integrated into *all* training programs, not just those identified as "diversity workshops." Finally, education and training is charged to find and implement the most cost-effective approaches.

ORGANIZATIONAL DEVELOPMENT

DuPont has identified key areas of organizational change that relate to the diversity initiative. Career development must be reviewed and upgraded to reflect the needs of the increasingly heterogeneous population. Diversity must be integrated into work processes. Communication of both strategy and results is key to success. A core mentoring program has been established, and "champions" of diversity are now to be included as part of the Valuing People Excellence Awards recognition.

COST-EFFECTIVENESS

According to Scales, DuPont had been spending about $20 million a year on education and training—about $5–$6 million of it on diversity. It was decided that cost was a negative factor in getting buy-in throughout the organization. So the strategic plan set out to use "leveraging" to reduce costs—utilizing existing resources in a different, more efficient way, to approach the same goals.

For example, Scales and his staff—all of whom have a technical not a human resources background—work with key trainers and developers in 20 strategic business units. Most of the SBU trainers have generic training and development duties in addition to their diversity assignments. Some are chemists or engineers—people whose technical or line experience lends credibility to their commitment to the diversity effort. These "leveraged" personnel participate in "train-the-trainer" workshops to prepare them for this work. All deliver "user-friendly" workshops that do not require a high level of OD skills—the initial half-day or full-day orientation or introduction sessions. They do not attempt to deliver the more intensive workshops that require skilled OD facilitation and assistance.

Other efforts at cost reduction include central coordination of diversity training programs and centralized administration of corporate contracts to assure that consultant per diem rates and cost of delivery of programs are the same across the corporation.

THE CORE CURRICULUM

DuPont offers a wide range of courses and workshops, some selected from earlier curricula and others recently designed. The best known are the introductory workshops, "A Matter of Respect" and "Personal Safety Program." Dealing with gender discrimination, sexual harassment, and rape, these programs grew out of DuPont's core value of safety: the belief that people should be able to come to work and go home the same way—uninjured and safe.

The two programs developed out of a monthly safety program for women, which gradually evolved into a standard training program marketed both internally and externally. The programs are delivered by internal personnel who participate in facilitators' workshops targeted to delivery of this material. Facilitators with no previous training experience receive an additional full day of training, including individual videotaped practice sessions and feedback.

The goals of the two programs are to create a respectful work environment free from sex discrimination or sexual harassment and to provide information and perspective on the violent crime of rape. In addition, an eight-hour workshop for women is offered to increase women's confidence in their ability to prevent rape and to cope with the aftermath if it occurs. Finally, a 24-hour hot line staffed by volunteers—allies, champions, former victims—is available to women wherever they are to report incidents and get assistance if necessary.

Other workshops provide introductory experiences. "A Workplace of Difference" program aims at helping employees of diverse cultures work together more effectively, utilizes simple awareness and skill-building exercises and videos, and is delivered by mixed race and gender training teams. A one-day "Welcoming Diversity" course focuses on helping individuals and groups examine deep issues of identity, unfreeze prejudicial attitudes, act on the basis of shared values, and know what to do when values are in conflict.

The flagship of DuPont's diversity program is the **"Multicultural Awareness Workshop."** This five-day, off-site, consultant-delivered workshop focuses on race and gender, "the fundamental social justice issues in our society," according to Scales. It is structured to explore the dimensions of diversity and its relationship to a business environment and utilizes individual experiences and group norms as the focal point of self-development around diversity issues and management skills for effecting change. Participants—who are balanced 50–50 by race and gender—are nominated by coordinators in the strategic business units. There is a waiting list of up to a year for participation in this dynamic experience. While the focus in the past has been on leadership and exempt levels, DuPont is now opening participation to wage-level and contract workers.

DuPont's curriculum includes many other options:

- **Women and Men: Working as Colleagues.** Enhances participants' awareness of and effectiveness in dealing with co-workers of the opposite sex.
- **Efficacy Seminar for Corporate Minority Professionals.** A carryover from the previous curriculum, this course was originally offered as an "empowerment" workshop for black employees and was a huge success. A similar program has been piloted for Asians and Asian-American employees, in response to a request from the DuPont Asian Network. Seminars for other groups will be developed in response to expressed need.
- **Corporate and Individual Realities for Women.** Provides a forum where women can learn from one another's experiences and manage gender-related issues in the workplace.
- **The Men's Forum.** A recently developed three-day, off-site course that helps white men and men of color understand and support the values of diversity.
- **Training Certification.** An intensive training program for internal personnel. Participants are employees who have been identified as change agents, diversity leaders, champions, and so on; they are trained by outside consultants to deliver introductory workshops.
- **Skill Building.** Two levels: one for managers and professionals, and one for senior leadership. Provides

requisite skills and abilities for leaders to manage in a
changing environment.

- **Sexual Orientation.** In development.

MONITORING PROGRESS

DuPont utilizes a full range of data-collection techniques—surveys, focus groups, developmental questionnaires, organizational
assessment instruments—to follow progress on the Strategic Diversity Plan. The CEO has challenged the organization to analyze
results by SBU, function, race, gender and other cuts, and tailor
initiatives to what the data shows. "Histograms" developed in
1994 demonstrated that while people of color and whites shared
similar views of some categories—such as compliance with AA
and EEO requirements—there were significant differences on others, such as the perception of the organization as "exclusionary"
or genuinely "multicultural."

Scales says, "We have just recently gotten to a place where
diversity is seen as a positive." In his view, there is still a residue
of skepticism, which is expressed as challenges to the business
value of the initiative. But the Strategic Diversity Plan provides,
for the first time, a definitive paradigm that demonstrates the
organization's belief in the realities of changing demographics
and its commitment to moving into the new era with strategies,
policies, and processes that will keep it competitive.

DIVERSITY AT DUPONT

VALUING PEOPLE: A WIN/WIN PROPOSITION

The Diversity Factor: *Why did you agree to be one of the
chairs of the Valuing People Committee?*
Mike Emery: I didn't really "agree"—nobody asked me to
do it. I just felt that there was value in having a committee
like that, and I knew other senior leaders who shared that
view. We got together and began to function as a network.
At first, we just concentrated on our own development;

then we began to explore how we could work to help other leaders see the advantages in "valuing people."

TDF: *Racism, sexism, and other forms of discrimination have been around in our country a long time. We've had the civil rights struggle, affirmative action, equal opportunity efforts, and all the rest. Why is it that "managing diversity" and "valuing people" are getting the attention of U.S. business at this point?*

ME: There are probably a lot of reasons. I know that from DuPont's standpoint, we are looking at the competition, and we know we can't afford to waste any of our resources. We're not interested in just having people on our rolls to meet a quota or to improve our image or meet the letter of the law—we can't afford to have nonproductive people!

We have to start thinking differently about the whole equation of civil rights and affirmative action and valuing people. We have to look at facts: We are a diverse culture. We need a productive workforce, so we must be able to utilize the best resources from that diverse culture. And every person we bring in must be able to achieve his or her full potential if we're going to have a chance to compete in the global world.

I'm not saying it's not difficult—it's terribly difficult. But the fact that it is so hard means that the company that can do it better—since, theoretically at least, everyone is trying to do it—should have a competitive advantage. The companies that really succeed in "valuing people" will be getting more value from their resources than those who don't.

TDF: *How did you arrive at this conclusion?*

ME: Let me tell you a little about my personal journey. I'm 56 years old. I grew up in a segregated community in the south, went to segregated schools from first grade through college. I had virtually no contact with people who didn't look like me, think like me, act like me, and share my values. I laughed at the same jokes, told the same stories, and had all the usual stereotypes of other races.

Then I went into the service. My first boss was a black man. He was an excellent supervisor. I figured this was just an exception—"He's just not like the rest of 'em." Then I met more and more black people, and they all seemed to be pretty competent. In fact, it began to seem that the black people I met who *weren't* competent were the exceptions!

Later, I had a business tour of duty in Asia, and I became very interested in this entirely new culture. This was exciting—new values, new ways of looking at things, new perspectives. I learned a lot, about my own limited experience and the stereotypes I had grown up with and taken for granted.

When I realized that competence comes in all kinds of colors and from many different backgrounds, I recognized that valuing people is not just a question of doing the right thing—it's also my responsibility as a senior leader, for the good of the company. I wanted other people to have the same kind of opportunity for new experiences that I had had. I moved from a position where I think "sensitivity" to these issues is most important to one where I see the value in capitalizing on our differences.

TDF: *What do you mean by "capitalizing" on differences?*

ME: Here's an example. I'm a big believer in the value of collaborative teams—from my own experience. We've moved from an era in which people believe the boss has all the answers to a recognition that lots of people have good ideas. I don't mean that the boss doesn't still have ideas; management still throws out decisions, and people have to follow some of them.

But many of the ideas we use at DuPont these days are the result of a manager saying, "We have this problem; here's what I think about it. What do you folks think about it?"

Now, if the team is made up of people just like the manager—usually white men, since that is still the predominant population of management in the U.S.— you're going to get ideas a lot like those the manager had to begin with. And that's limited; when I look at my own experience, at least half the time when I think I have the best answer, I find I don't.

In our competitive world, we have to get good results—we're measured in the company by our results. So I'm thankful for good ideas and for ideas that are different enough from mine to make up for that half the time that my answers aren't the best ones. I get more good, *different*, ideas from people whose life experience is not the same as mine: These may be people of color or white women or people with disabilities or white men from different backgrounds from mine.

So I deliberately create teams that are as diverse as possible. And it works great! Many managers at DuPont are doing this, and I think they would all agree that they get terrific results.

TDF: *What advice would you give to other people who want to develop collaborative teams of diverse people?*

ME: First, I would say just try it. And don't forget that diversity includes function and level as well as race, gender, disability and other kinds of difference. And second, I would remind people that it doesn't help just to put people together and act in the same old ways. We have to learn to *listen* to those new ideas; we have to get our listening antennae tuned to new broadcast channels.

TDF: *What are some other ways you feel DuPont is capitalizing on "valuing people?"*

ME: A key area is promotion. When I have the opportunity to help a person of color or a white woman move into the higher position he or she is qualified for—but would not achieve if we just did "business as usual"—I can provide an opportunity for other people to see that competent women or competent people of color or competent disabled people *are not exceptions.* But we have to be proactive about it. We have to rethink what we're looking for and what we really need.

Here's an example. If I have the opportunity to bring someone in to work closely with me, I can look for someone very much like me—same training, same background, same race and gender. Or I can look for someone who complements me, in different ways. I have had many such opportunities. One person I brought into a management track had no engineering experience but excellent people skills. I got a lot of flak at first, but when people saw her performance they recognized that what we needed was precisely those people skills, that she helped other people achieve their very best. This was another opportunity for all of us to learn that competence is not limited to one race or one gender or one ability.

TDF: *That's all very well. But isn't it true that there were equally qualified white men who didn't get that opportunity, because she did?*

ME: That's not really the question. For every big job, there are plenty of people who think they can do it—and only one person gets it. So there are many white men who don't receive specific promotions, no matter whether the one person who gets it is white, black, female, male or whatever.

TDF: *Why do we keep hearing about "white male backlash" then?*

ME: I know there are white men who resent what's happening. I think it's a question of where we are on our personal journeys. I've come to believe—and I know a lot of other white men who believe this too—that it's not a win/lose situation. If you and I are in the same boat and we have to get from one place to another under fire, I don't care if you're a man or a woman or a person of color or white. What I care about is whether we get safely to the other side. You can steer or I can steer—I don't care. I just want to get there—preferably ahead of the other boats!

I don't believe that if a woman gets promoted, a man loses. Or if a person of color advances, a white person has lost the opportunity. If one person wins, we both win; it's not a loss for me. We can be more competitive and have more security when there are more opportunities. It's a continuum of team development.

TDF: *But how do you get that message across?*

ME: We just get the facts out. Our Valuing People team deliberately decided to expose the metrics on what's really happening. We publish the stats in 10 different areas.

One of those is promotions. So if white men say that women and minorities are getting all the promotions, all we have to do is show that the stats indicate that 65 percent of all promotions *still*—in spite of all our efforts— go to white men!

Another area is raises. A common myth is that white women and people of color get bigger raises. We have what we call "targets." We took all the statistics about white men's "targets" in terms of raises and compared them to those of people of color and white women. There is virtually no difference in the average target of these two groups.

Of course this shows that we're still a long way from actually leveling things out—but it says to the white men, far from favoring others over you, we're still not even giving the others *enough* opportunity!

The way to counter backlash is simple: Provide the facts, be sure everyone, including white men, does have equal opportunity, and select people who can do the job. There are lots of people out there waiting in the wings who are capable of moving up, and we have to make sure they get a chance. We have to provide the coaching they need, the promotions they need, and the opportunities to succeed. Our statistics show us that all the competent people of color and white women in our organization are still not getting all the opportunities they could use—and that this limits our competitive edge.

We can say to our white male colleagues, "Look, we all benefit when we're more productive, and the stats show that you're still getting a bigger piece of the pie than anyone else anyway." That should give all of us time to adjust and recognize that "valuing people" is a win/win situation for everybody.

PART FIVE

RESOURCES
A DIVERSITY BOOKSHELF

Resources
A Diversity Bookshelf

GENDER AND SEXUAL ORIENTATION

Helen S. Astin and Carole Leland, *Women of Influence, Women of Vision.* Jossey-Bass, 350 Sansome St., San Francisco, CA 94104. 1991. $26.95.

During the past three decades, according to Astin and Leland, women have taken a leadership role in redefining fundamental aspects of our lives: work, family, sexuality, equality, and justice. They have influenced how we define reality, conceive of knowledge, and exercise leadership. Despite these accomplishments, there have been few studies of women leaders who made this happen and how they did so. This study undertakes to remedy that situation.

Astin and Leland go beyond conventional views of leadership by looking not so much at the official positions of leaders but rather at what the women did and how they did it. They are interested more in defining leadership by its actions than in identifying a uniquely feminine style of leadership. What they found was that empowering cooperative approaches seemed most effective, and they believe this approach serves as a leadership model for the 21st century.

Sandra Lipsitz Bem, *The Lenses of Gender: Transforming the Debate on Sexual Inequality.* Yale University Press, 302 Temple St., New Haven, CT 06501. 1993. $30.00.

Bem argues that we must reframe the cultural debate on sexual inequality to focus not on female–male difference but on how difference has been used to rationalize discriminatory patterns and practices against women.

Teresa Odendahl and Michael O'Neill, eds., *Women & Power in the Non-Profit Sector.* Jossey-Bass, 350 Sansome St., San Francisco, CA 94104. 1994. $29.95.

The 11 authors in this book explore the nature and extent of the power women have and do not have in the voluntary sector. Among the subjects focused on are how women in nonprofits use power and who really holds the reins of power in the nonprofit sector.

Participants in the 1992 invitational conference, "Women, Power and Status in the Non-profit Sector," which provided the genesis of the book, agreed that special attention must be paid to the different experiences of women of color and white women, recognizing that the women's movement has too often been narrowly focused on the interests of white women.

Carol Pierce and Bill Page, *A Male/Female Continuum: Paths to Colleagueship,* 2nd ed. New Dynamics Publications, 21 Shore Drive, Laconia, NH 03246. 1994. $12.95.

This small book (48 pages) clearly describes what happens when relations between men and women begin to change from dominance and subordination towards equality and colleagueship, and how the process may be made more successful.

E. Anthony Rotundo. *American Manhood: Transformations in Masculinity from the Revolution to the Modern Era.* Basic Books, 10 E. 53rd St., New York, NY 10022. 1993. $25.00.

Rotundo reviews three phases in the development of American ideas about what constitutes a "real man" and demonstrates how concepts in each phase are based on underlying sexism; that is, the ability of men to maintain control over the access to power. His recommendation is that men not be expected to relinquish power to women, but to share it.

Vickie Seitchik, *Queer Son: Family Journeys to Understanding and Love.* Forty-eight minute video produced and distributed by Vickie Seitchik, 19 Jackson St., Cape May, NJ 08204. 1994. $20.

An important documentary by the mother of a gay son. The filmmaker interviews a group of families from diverse racial, ethnic, and social backgrounds in an effort to debunk stereotypes about gays and lesbians. We see the parents move from doubt and fear to understanding and activism. Personal and moving.

Leslie Kanes Weisman, *Discrimination by Design: A Feminist Critique of the Man-Made Environment.* University of Illinois Press, 54 East Gregory Drive, Champaign, IL 61820. 1992. $24.95.

"As a society, we fail to notice how the design and utilization of buildings maintains social inequality. Until we all notice, no change will occur."

James D. Woods with Jay Lucas, *The Corporate Closet: The Professional Lives of Gay Men in America.* The Free Press, a division of Macmillan Publishing Co., 100 Front St.,

Box 500 Riverside, NJ 08075-7500. 1993. $22.95.

An important introduction to issues involving attitudes about sexual orientation and how negative attitudes limit the productivity of gay employees.

RACE AND ETHNICITY

"An American Dilemma Revisited," *Daedalus,* Journal Of The American Academy Of Arts And Sciences, Winter, 1995. $7.95.

This issue of *Daedalus* commemorates the 50th anniversary of the publication of Gunnar Myrdal's groundbreaking study of race relations in America, *An American Dilemma.* The essays by 11 authors focus on different aspects of Myrdal's book and review developments over the half-century.

In his preface, *Daedalus* editor Stephen R. Graubard points out that no issues in American life are more crucial in 1995 than are relations between the races, and that few matters of such moment are being discussed less candidly and openly. "Race has become America's forbidden theme, with 'Bell curves' and other such nonsense substituting for serious discussion of real national and international problems."

An important reference for those who are responsible for making "diversity" work in American institutions today.

Luca Cavalli-Sforza, Paolo Menozzi, and Alberto Piazza, *The History and Geography of Human Genes.* Princeton University Press, Princeton, NJ 08540. 1993. $150.00.

The result of 16 years of painstaking research, this hefty volume (1,000 pages) measures how closely the world's current populations are related. The conclusion: Once genes for surface traits such as coloration and stature are discounted, the human "races" are remarkably alike. The variation among individuals within a "race" is so much greater than the differences among groups that the whole concept of "race" becomes meaningless at the genetic level. The authors— Stanford professor Cavalli-Sforza and his colleagues—say that the scientific evidence disputes theories that tout the genetic superiority of any one population over another.

The group's next research effort, the Human Genome Diversity Project, is to carry out a new survey, this time using DNA instead of blood groups. The study's ultimate aim, according to Cavalli-Sforza, is to put to rest conventional notions of race that cause discrimination.

The Color of Fear. A film by Lee Mun Wah from Stir-Fry Productions, 1904 Virginia St., Berkeley, CA 94709. 1994. Call 510-548-9695 for price.

A powerful presentation of the conversations of eight North American men of different races and ethnicities about the pain and anguish that racism has caused in their lives. Out of their confrontations and struggles to understand and trust each other emerges an emotional and insightful portrayal of the type of dialogue we need to engage in to confront our fears and develop effective relationships.

Ellis Cose, *The Rage of a Privileged Class: Why Do Prosperous Blacks Still Have the Blues?* Harper Collins. 10 East 53rd St., New York, NY 10022- 5299. 1994. $20.00.

Newsweek essayist Cose explores why successful blacks in corporate America are angry— and why white America understands so little about their feelings of pain and outrage.

"The racial gap can only be closed by recognizing it, and by recognizing why it exists."

Leonard Dinnerstein, *A History of American Anti-Semitism.* Oxford University Press, Inc., 200 Madison Ave., New York, NY 10016. 1994. $25.00.

This well-written, thoroughly researched history of attitudes towards Jews in the United States by a University of Arizona professor of history tackles a difficult and emotional topic with clarity and objectivity. Although Dinnerstein provides a wealth of documentation that supports his contention that prejudice towards Jews among both blacks and whites flowed from the same stream of Southern evangelical Christianity, he also points out that "in no Christian country has anti-Semitism been weaker than it has been in the United States."

In addressing the troubling topic of black anti-Semitism, Dinnerstein cites the view of sociologist Richard Simpson, who argues, "Contact between members of different groups, where one is subordinate to the other, is more likely to intensify any stereotypes and hostilities which exist." Since Jews have almost always been in superior

positions to blacks in this country—as shopkeepers, philanthropists, landlords, employers, and so on—this theory goes some way in explaining the problem. It does not, however, remove it.

Overall, however, Dinnerstein presents evidence that supports his belief that anti-Semitism is actually on the decline in the United States—though, as with all forms of bigotry, it will continue to lurk just below the surface and threaten to break out again without warning.

Gertrude Ezorsky, *Racism & Justice: The Case for Affirmative Action.* Cornell University Press, 124 Roberts Place, Ithaca, NY 14850. 1991. $25.00.

Ezorsky reviews the history of affirmative action, the ongoing patterns of both overt and institutional racism that continue to resist the resolution of the problems of racial discrimination, and the current arguments claiming that AA has failed or is no longer needed.

Ezorsky begins by examining the effectiveness of affirmative action as a remedy for institutional racism in the workplace. She analyzes the ways in which common practices—selection of employees based on personal connections, qualification, and seniority standards—perpetuate the injurious effect of past racial discrimination. She shows how the inability of whites to give appropriate feedback to people of color limits their opportunities for advancement, and also how "objective" but non-job-related testing has been (and still is) used as a device for screening out minorities. She indicates that major companies, using the AA mechanisms, had made significant advances in workplace integration—with no decline in productivity—by the early 1980s and demonstrates how those gains were undermined by the dramatic decline of enforcement in the later years of the decade.

She further forces us to recognize that for the first two-thirds of this century, racism was in many respects official public policy—compulsory segregation of schools; racially restrictive housing policies; discrimination in government practices such as public employment, voting registration procedures, manifest racial bias in the courts, and unchallenged police brutality towards people of color. Such pervasive and widely unquestioned policy and practice required strong measures.

Ezorsky examines the various arguments against affirmative action carefully and presents helpful counter-statements. Particularly evocative is her illustration of the fallacies of the "anti-preferences" challenge, using the example of veterans' preferences—to which no one objects. She points out that court-sanctioned veterans-preference policy has affected the employment of millions of workers, and in some states where veteran preference is practiced, nonveterans have practically no chance to obtain the best positions. "Veterans who enjoy hiring, promotion, and seniority preference are surely not the very same individuals who, absent their military service, would have qualified for the positions they gained by such preference" (p. 80). She further points out, in response to the argument that AA impinges on the self-respect of those aided by it, that other kinds of preference do not seem to have that effect: "Career counselors who advise job seekers to develop influential contacts exhibit no fear that their clients will think less well of themselves; indeed, job candidates who secure powerful connections count themselves *fortunate*" (p. 93).

The book concludes with useful case studies, including the history of equal employment opportunity in the Bell System.

Claire Gonzales, *The Empty Promise: The EEOC and Hispanics.* Policy Analysis Center, National Council of La Raza, 810 First Street, N.E., Suite 300, Washington, DC 20002 (March, 1994). $12.50.

American business faces a dilemma: the rapid growth in the Hispanic population offers exciting new marketing opportunities, but the current anti-immigrant and anti-minority climate limits both the buying ability of that market and corporate America's competence in reaching it.

Gonzales's well-researched text provides the facts needed to confront the dilemma. It shows that the rate of employment discrimination against Hispanic Americans is greater than for any other group and that Hispanics share with blacks and other minorities the brunt of ongoing prejudice and discrimination in U.S. society. The cost of this discrimination to the American economy is conservatively estimated at $11.7 billion in lost income annually—income that Hispanics could be using to pay taxes and to purchase products.

Full of facts, figures, charts, tables, graphs, and recommendations.

William P. O'Hare, "America's Minorities—The Demographics of Diversity." *Population Bulletin* 47, no. 4 (1992). Population Reference Bureau, Inc., Circulation Department, PO Box 96152, Washington, DC 20090-6152. 1-800-877-9881. $7.00 plus $1.00 postage and handling.

A statistical and evaluative analysis of the changing demographics of the United States Dispels myths and presents surprising new information. Essential reference material.

William P. O'Hare and Judy C. Felt, "Asian Americans: America's Fastest Growing Minority Group," *Population Trends and Public Policy* no. 19 (February, 1991). Population Reference Bureau, Inc., PO Box 96152, Washington, D.C. 20090-6152. 1-800-877-9881. $5.00 plus $1.00 postage and handling.

The numbers of Asians and Pacific Islanders in the United States grew by 80 percent between 1980 and 1989, increasing from 3.8 million to 6.9 million. Although there are still fewer Asians and Pacific

Islanders than either Hispanics or black populations, this segment of U.S. society is a highly diverse and increasingly influential part of American life. This report documents the changes experienced by America's Asian and Pacific-Islander population during the 1980s and assesses socio-economic trends in education, income, poverty, and labor-force participation. For example, while a large segment of this community has somewhat higher family income than non-Hispanic whites, poverty rates for Asians and Pacific Islanders are nearly twice those of non-Hispanic whites. Furthermore, among people at the same education level, Asians and Pacific Islanders have lower incomes than non-Hispanic whites, suggesting that this "model minority" may still face discrimination in the workplace.

This report is important for many reasons, including the fact that the analysis could not have been done without the categorization of Asians and Pacific Islanders as a separate group (begun in the 1989 Current Population Survey) and the ancillary fact that the data show that affirmative action is not just a concern for the African-American community.

Elizabeth Pathy Salett and Diane R. Koslow, eds., *Race, Ethnicity and Self: Identity in Multicultural Perspective.* National Multicultural Institute, 3000 Connecticut Avenue, NW, Suite 438, Washington, DC 20008. 1994. $19.95.

Nine articles explore the impact of race and ethnicity on identity development in the United States. Especially useful is the section that explores the impact of white racial dominance on identity development in U.S. society and a chapter by Rita Hardiman that further expands her theories of the five stages through which European Americans must move in order to reach a positive, antiracist identity in the context of a racist society.

Rafael Valdivieso and Cary Davis, "U.S. Hispanics: Challenging Issues for the 1990s," *Population Trends and Public Policy* no. 17 (December, 1988). Population Reference Bureau, Inc., PO Box 96152, Washington, DC 20090-6152. $5.00.

The 1990 census count showed our population to be about 190 million non-Hispanic white, 30 million African American, 24 million Hispanic, almost 8 million Asian/Pacific Islander, and about 1.5 million American Indian/Eskimo/Aleut.

The Hispanic community increased by 65 percent between 1980 and 1992. (The Asian/ Pacific Islander group increased by 123.5 percent.) These rapid increases have created confusion and fear in the majority population.

Valdivieso and Davis provide objective data that helps to understand the realities. They note that American businesses are realizing that Hispanics are constituting a growing proportion of U.S. workers and also a major consumer group.

This brief document provides a factual basis for developing diversity strategies that capitalize on the strengths of this growing population, minimize the systemic barriers that prevent their having ready access to success, and confront the "divide-and-conquer" strategies that too often set one minority group against another.

Cornel West, *Race Matters.* Beacon Press, 25 Beacon St., Boston, MA 02108-2892. 1993. $15.00.

"To engage in a serious discussion of race in America, we must begin not with the problems of black people but with the flaws of American society—flaws rooted in historic inequalities and longstanding cultural stereotypes." West's startling analysis shows how "corporate market institutions" contribute to the current climate of psychological depression, personal worthlessness, and social despair that young black people grow up in. Tough, realistic, and important.

C. Vann Woodward, *The Strange Career of Jim Crow,* 3rd revised edition. Oxford University Press, 200 Madison Avenue, New York, NY 10016. 1974. $8.95 paper.

This classic study of the history of segregation in the United States still has much to teach us, though it was originally written in 1955 and last updated in 1974. Woodward shows how the struggle for equality for African Americans has gone through repeated cycles.

In times of cultural confusion or economic, political, and social frustration, the common reaction is to find a scapegoat, and in the United States, the scapegoat closest at hand has been the black minority. At such time "permission to hate" issues from many sources: sometimes from the Supreme Court, sometimes from Congress, sometimes from the executive office, and right on down the line.

Nonetheless, as Woodward shows, the persistent American faith in equality of opportunity and equality of rights was never completely conquered. Through a combination of forces—the ongoing determination of blacks; the commercial, industrial, and financial interests of large groups; the force of ideology and idealism coupled with religious conviction; and the sometimes timely convergence of political expediency with the appearance of a competent leader—laws have been made and have been enforced that have created *more* equality of opportunity and *more* equality of rights than were present in the preceding era.

It would be helpful if Woodward could bring his study up-to-date. There would be few surprises: The patterns of progress and regression, of black rage countered by white screw-tightening, of political aspirants playing to the fears of threatened whites, all continue. The current affirmative action brouhaha embodies the full range of high emotions and low perception of reality that has characterized white attitudes towards blacks throughout our history.

ORGANIZATIONAL DEVELOPMENT AND CULTURE CHANGE

Nancy J. Adler and Susan Bartholomew, "Managing globally competent people." *Academy of Management Executive* 6, no. 3 (1992), pp. 52–65.

"Transnational firms need transnational human resource management systems." Based on a survey of 50 major North American firms, the authors show how today's human resource strategies are significantly less global than the firms' business strategies. To overcome this gap, they identify a series of illusions that prevent firms from creating human resource systems that are sufficiently global to support transnational business strategies.

Important for those concerned about "global diversity" and its challenges.

Taylor Cox, Jr., *Cultural Diversity in Organizations: Theory, Research and Practice.* Berrett-Kohler Publishers, Inc., 155 Montgomery St., San Francisco, CA 94104-4109. 1993. $19.95.

Provides a conceptual framework for understanding diversity and its effects on organizational behavior and performance, as well as a model to guide organizational change.

Elsie Y. Cross, Judith H. Katz, Frederick A. Miller, and Edith W. Seashore, The Promise of Diversity: Over 40 Voices Discuss Strategies for Eliminating Discrimination in Organizations. Irwin Professional Publishing, Burr Ridge, IL. Order through NTL Institute, 1240 N. Pitt Street, Suite 100, Alexandria, VA 22314. 1-800-777-5227. 1994. $50.00.

The Promise of Diversity is "about the struggle against oppression in organizations, and the promise of diversity." Like The Diversity Factor, The Promise of Diversity deals directly with the difficult, deep-seated, and tenacious ongoing effects of the legacy of oppression: slavery, genocide, indentured servitude, denial of basic human rights, disenfranchisement. Recognizing that it is premature to "celebrate diversity" when some groups are still excluded from full participation, The Promise of Diversity provides detailed information on how to achieve a society and a work environment in which celebration is appropriate.

A thoughtful and thought-provoking text for those who are serious about "managing diversity."

Charles Hampden-Turner, Charting the Corporate Mind: Graphic Solutions to Business Conflicts. The Free Press, 866 Third Ave., New York, NY 10022. 1990. $27.50. And Creating Corporate Culture: From Discovery to Harmony. Addison-Wesley Publishing Co., Rt. 128, Reading, MA 10867. 1992. $27.95.

These two important books provide a fresh way of understanding how the culture of organizations functions and take a hard look at the challenges of trying to make changes.

Edgar H. Schein, Organizational Culture and Leadership, 2nd edition. Jossey-Bass Publishers, 350 Sansome St., San Francisco, CA 94104. 1992. $25.95.

A diverse organization brings to a turbulent environment more coping resources than does a monocultural system. Schein's systematic and pragmatic approach makes liberal use of examples and case studies.

MISCELLANEOUS

Good For Business: Making Full Use of the Nation's Human Capital. A Fact-Finding Report of the Federal Glass Ceiling Commission, 1995. Order from the U.S. Government Printing Office, 202-783-3238, FAX 202-219-7368 or Internet via World Wide Web (http://www.ilr.cornell.educ) or GOPHER (128.253.61.155).

Originally targeted at the invisible barriers that were preventing women from entering the executive suite, the Glass Ceiling Act of 1991—introduced by Senator Robert Dole—quickly was extended to refer to obstacles hindering the advancement of minority men as well.

The current volume, the Environmental Scan, confirms that the "glass ceiling" metaphor is apt and enduring. "At the highest levels of business, there is indeed a barrier only rarely penetrated by women or persons of color." (p. iii.) The report reviews in meticulous detail the facts of continuing discrimination and the characteristics of successful programs that have been designed to create change:

- They have CEO support.
- They are specific to the organization.
- They are inclusive.
- They address preconceptions and stereotypes.
- They emphasize accountability.
- They track progress.
- They are comprehensive.

The overview of the report concludes, "It is against the best interests of business to exclude those Americans who constitute two-thirds of the total population, two-thirds of the consumer market, and more than half of the workforce (approximately 57 percent)" (p. 11).

Here are all the facts, figures, interpretations, and analyses any organization that still wonders if "there are really any problems" should ever need. A second report, including recommendations based on the findings, will be presented to the president and the Congress in the Summer of 1995. "The recommendations will speak to the imperative of dismantling artificial barriers to advancement . . . [and] will be designed to assure equitable opportunities for white men, minorities, and women" (p. 6).

Rosalie Maggio, *The Bias-Free Word Finder: a Dictionary of Nondiscriminatory Language.* Beacon Press, 25 Beacon St., Boston, MA 02108-2892. 1991. $15.00.

"Language both reflects and shapes society. . . . Culture shapes language and then language shapes culture." During this period of cultural transition, we need help in creating a common language. This matter-of-fact text is a useful tool.

INDEX

PUBLICATIONS AVAILABLE FROM ELSIE Y. CROSS ASSOCIATES, INC.

THE DIVERSITY FACTOR is a quarterly journal of ideas and practical help for executives and managers responsible for culture change in organizations. The LIBRARY JOURNAL said of THE DIVERSITY FACTOR, "Directed at corporations and organizations striving to build multicultural structures and teach tolerance, this journal supports one of the main personnel management trends of the 90s. Each issue offers both theoretical pieces and descriptions of programs in practice that can be adapted for use elsewhere. Though the human resources consultants and academics write in a surprisingly practical and jargon-free style, all articles carry appropriate citations, often useful as sources for further reading."

THE DIVERSITY FACTOR 1-year subscription, $195. SPECIAL DISCOUNT FOR PURCHASERS OF THE DIVERSITY FACTOR: CAPTURING THE COMPETITIVE ADVANTAGE OF A CHANGING WORKFORCE, $117. Call (201-833-0011) or FAX (201-833-4184) for special non-profit rates.

Some back issues are also available for special purchase. Reprints from out-of-print issues are available from: Reprint Management Services, 147 West Airport Road, Box 5363, Lancaster, PA 17606-5363. Call or FAX THE DIVERSITY FACTOR for a list of back issues and reprints.

ALSO AVAILABLE: Diversity Metrics

Elsie Y. Cross Associates, Inc., now offers five different ways of collecting and analyzing information about diversity

Data collection and feedback are an important part of any change effort. Most organizations have relied on focus groups or interviews for data but have been searching for more detailed and targetted techniques.

The "Diversity Assessment Survey" and four additional quantitative surveys were developed to meet the needs of specific organizations and are now being offered to the general public.

For more information, call THE DIVERSITY FACTOR.

THE DIVERSITY FACTOR is assisted by a distinguished Advisory Board:

> Eugene S. Andrews, General Electric
> David Barclay, Hughes Electronics Corporation
> Mary Belenky, co-author, Women's Ways of Knowing
> Sara Bullard, editor, Teaching Tolerance
> David L. Ford, Jr., University of Texas, Dallas
> Robert M. Garcia, City of Austin, TX
> Rosemarie B. Greco, CoreStates First Pennsylvania Bank
> La Donna Harris, Americans for Indian Opportunity
> Edwin A. Hill, Janssen Pharmaceutica
> Lennox E. Joseph, NTL Institute
> Iobal Paroo, Global Health Group
> Jerry Porras, Stanford University
> James B. Rose, Johnson & Johnson
> Derald Wing Sue, author, Counseling the Culturally Different: Theory and Practice
> Alejandro Valadez, Universidad de Monterrey
> Cornel West, Princeton University

THE DIVERSITY FACTOR, P.O. Box 3188, Teaneck, NJ 07666.

ELSIE Y CROSS ASSOCIATES, INC., is an organization development consulting firm which specializes in helping Fortune 100 companies and other organizations in managing diversity and removing barriers created by racism, sexism, heterosexism, ageism, and other discriminatory factors.

Other titles of interest to you from Irwin Professional Publishing . . .

THE PROMISE OF DIVERSITY
Over 40 Voices Discuss Strategies for Eliminating Discrimination in Organizations
Cross/Katz/Miller/Seashore
ISBN: 0-7863-0307-7   370 pages

DIVERSE TEAMS AT WORK
Capitalizing on the Power of Diversity
Lee Gardenswartz and Anita Rowe
ISBN: 0-786300425-1   175 pages

IMPLEMENTING DIVERSITY
Best Practices for Making Diversity Work in Your Organization
Marilyn Loden
ISBN: 0-7863-0460-X   200 pages